BELLA VISTA HIGH SCHOOL
8301 MADISON AVENUE
FAIR OAKS, CALIFORNIA 95628

German
today 1

German today 1

THIRD EDITION

Jack Moeller
Helmut Liedloff
Clifford J. Kent

BELLA VISTA HIGH SCHOOL
8301 MADISON AVENUE
FAIR OAKS, CALIFORNIA 95628

0106

HOUGHTON MIFFLIN COMPANY Boston

Atlanta   Dallas   Geneva, Illinois
Hopewell, New Jersey   Palo Alto   Toronto

About the Authors

Jack Moeller is the senior author of the series. Currently he is Chairperson of the Department of Modern Languages and Literatures at Oakland University in Rochester, Michigan. Professor Moeller has taught at both private and public high schools in the United States and Germany. He is a co-author of *Deutsch heute: Grundstufe, Blickpunkt Deutschland, Ohne Mühe!, Noch Dazu!* (Houghton Mifflin), and of several other texts.

Helmut Liedloff is Professor of German at Southern Illinois University in Carbondale, Illinois. Professor Liedloff is a native of Bremen, Germany, and has taught at the secondary school and university levels in Germany and at a number of colleges in the United States. He is a co-author of *Deutsch heute: Grundstufe* and *Ohne Mühe!* (Houghton Mifflin) and is a contributor to a number of professional journals.

Clifford J. Kent is Supervisor of Foreign Languages for the Beverly Public Schools in Beverly, Massachusetts, where he has helped develop an exchange program between Beverly High School and the Albert-Schweizer-Schule in Cologne, Germany. He has taught German at the junior high, high school, and college levels, as well as to adults, and he participated in an NDEA summer institute at Hofstra University.

LISTENING COMPREHENSION EXERCISES

Sonia Schweid Reizes is Assistant Program Administrator and teaches German, French, and Spanish in the Bedford Public Schools, Bedford, Massachusetts. She also teaches German at Middlesex Community College.

WORKBOOK

Sonia Schweid Reizes

CHAPTER TESTS

Constance E. Putnam taught German and Latin at John Marshall High School and at The Catlin Gabel School in Portland, Oregon. She also lived in Germany for several years and taught at the *Gymnasium* in Duderstadt and the *Pädagogische Hochschule* in Hildesheim.

Copyright © 1982 by Houghton Mifflin Company

All rights reserved. No part of this work may be reproduced or transmitted in any form or by any means, electronic or mechanical, including photocopying and recording, or by any information storage or retrieval system, without permission in writing from the publisher.

Printed in U.S.A.
Student's Edition ISBN: 0-395-29297-2
Teacher's Edition ISBN: 0-395-29512-2

Contents

German Around You viii
Atlas xii

Ich und du

KAPITEL 1
Tag. Wie geht's? 8
Wie heißt du? 9 • Wie geht's? 9
Bist du zufrieden? 11 • Warum ist Volker so sauer? 11
Wortschatzerweiterung 12 • Aussprache 15 • Übungen 16
Grammatische Übersicht 18 • Wiederholung 20 • Vokabeln 22

KAPITEL 2
Wie alt bist du? 23
Jung oder alt? 24 • Wann hast du Geburtstag? 25
Wortschatzerweiterung 26 • Aussprache 28 • Übungen 29
Grammatische Übersicht 32 • Wiederholung 34 • Vokabeln 35

KAPITEL 3
Heute nachmittag 36
Wo wohnst du? 37 • Marks Fotoalbum 38 • Was machst du? 39
Wortschatzerweiterung 40 • Aussprache 41 • Übungen 42
Grammatische Übersicht 47 • Wiederholung 50 • Vokabeln 51

KAPITEL 4
Ich und meine Familie 52
Der Brieffreund 53
Wortschatzerweiterung 55 • Aussprache 58 • Übungen 59
Grammatische Übersicht 64 • Wiederholung 67 • Vokabeln 69

Noch einmal 71

So leben wir

KAPITEL 5
Brauchst du neue Sachen? 80
Das ist zu teuer 81 • Toll! Für Mädchen und Jungen 81
Schick! Für Damen und Herren 82 • Welche Größe trägst du? 84
Wortschatzerweiterung 85 • Aussprache 86 • Übungen 87
Grammatische Übersicht 93 • Wiederholung 99
Kulturlesestück 102 • Vokabeln 103

v

So leben wir

KAPITEL 6
Der Schultag 105

Ingrids Stundenplan 106 • Im Klassenzimmer 107
In der Pause 108 • Wieviel Uhr ist es? 108
Wortschatzerweiterung 109 • Aussprache 111 • Übungen 112
Grammatische Übersicht 118 • Wiederholung 121
Kulturlesestück 124 • Vokabeln 125

KAPITEL 7
Willst du ins Konzert? 127

Poster 128 • Konzert im Jugendzentrum 129 • An der Kasse 131
Wortschatzerweiterung 132 • Aussprache 134 • Übungen 135
Grammatische Übersicht 144 • Wiederholung 149
Kulturlesestück 151 • Vokabeln 153

KAPITEL 8
Was hast du vor? 154

Ansichtskarten sind interessant 155
Thomas braucht ein Hobby 155
Was habt ihr heute vor? 157 • Komm doch mit! 158
Wortschatzerweiterung 160 • Aussprache 162 • Übungen 163
Grammatische Übersicht 169 • Wiederholung 174
Kulturlesestück 176 • Vokabeln 178

KAPITEL 9
Ich habe zu Hause geholfen 179

Ich habe mein Zimmer aufgeräumt 180 • Ich habe eine Torte
gebacken 181 • Arbeitsplan fürs Wochenende 182
Wortschatzerweiterung 183 • Aussprache 186 • Übungen 187
Grammatische Übersicht 192 • Wiederholung 194
Kulturlesestück 197 • Vokabeln 199

KAPITEL 10
Sport und Freizeit 200

Wer hat gewonnen? 201 • Ich lade dich ein 202
Wortschatzerweiterung 204 • Aussprache 207 • Übungen 208
Grammatische Übersicht 214 • Wiederholung 217
Kulturlesestück 219 • Vokabeln 221

Noch einmal 222

Zum Städtele hinaus

KAPITEL 11
Bäcker, Metzger, Supermarkt 232

Einkaufen in Deutschland 233 • Beim Metzger 235
Wortschatzerweiterung 236 • Aussprache 238 • Übungen 239
Grammatische Übersicht 246 • Wiederholung 248
Kulturlesestück 250 • Vokabeln 252

KAPITEL 12
Guten Appetit! 253

Essen bei Familie Wolf 254 • Im Restaurant 255
Wortschatzerweiterung 257 • Aussprache 259 • Übungen 260
Grammatische Übersicht 267 • Wiederholung 270
Kulturlesestück 272 • Vokabeln 274

KAPITEL 13
Über das Wetter kann man immer sprechen 275

Ein Quiz 276 • In Deutschland ist das Wetter anders 276
Wie ist das Wetter? 277
Wortschatzerweiterung 279 • Aussprache 281 • Übungen 282
Grammatische Übersicht 288 • Wiederholung 292
Kulturlesestück 294 • Vokabeln 295

KAPITEL 14
Christa macht den Führerschein 296

Aus Briefen an Jochen 297 • Dein Auto, dein Traum-Auto 299
Wortschatzerweiterung 300 • Aussprache 302 • Übungen 303
Grammatische Übersicht 310 • Wiederholung 311
Kulturlesestück 314 • Vokabeln 316

KAPITEL 15
Ein Stadtbesuch 317

Wohin gehen wir denn nun? 318
Wie kommen wir zum Western Club? 320
Wortschatzerweiterung 322 • Aussprache 325 • Übungen 326
Grammatische Übersicht 333 • Wiederholung 334
Kulturlesestück 337 • Vokabeln 339

Noch einmal 340

Appendixes 347
German-English Vocabulary 370
English-German Vocabulary 382
Index 389

German
around you

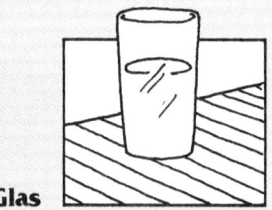
Glas

Hand

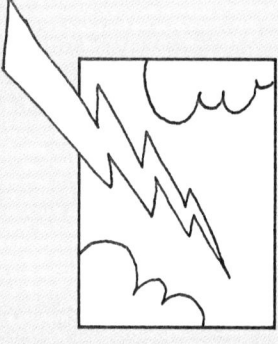
Blitz

As you begin to learn German, you will discover that you know more about the language than you think you do.

Maus

You can probably guess the meanings of the German words illustrated on this page, because they resemble English words. Words that are related in spelling and meaning and are derived from the same source language are called **cognates**. There are hundreds of German-English cognates.

Haus   **Gras**   **Bär**

Kaufmann

Koch

Schuhmacher

The German language and culture have been present in the United States since the colonial days. German settlers fought in the Revolutionary War, and they continued to play an important role as their adopted country grew and prospered. The names of many towns and cities reflect the German origin of their founders. Towns like Berlin, Hamburg, Bremen, and Vienna all have counterparts in one of the German-speaking countries. You probably know many families with German names. As in English, the name often refers to the occupation of the person's ancestors.

Kindergarten

Over the years, German immigrants have contributed to several areas of American life.

Rucksack

Oh Tannenbaum

Gesundheit!

Brezel

Harmonika

Make-up **Computer** **Fan**

The exchange in culture and language has gone the other way, too. Speakers of German have borrowed many English words that are now part of the German language.

Look around you and you'll find that cognates, borrowed words, and German names have given you a head start in learning German.

City

Atlas section

Ich und du

1

In der Schule. Classrooms everywhere look pretty much the same. From a crowded lecture hall at the university in Freiburg to individualized instruction in a school class in Munich, German students are expected to study hard. Education is considered very important, and even a bit of a privilege.

Was machst du? Walking home from school along the narrow streets in Dinkelsbühl is hardly typical of the many kinds of activities German young people enjoy — from a soccer game in Frankfurt to music making and life-sized board games in many towns.

Heute nachmittag. Quiet or even solitary pastimes are also popular: reading outdoors in Nuremberg or in a library, or just talking or going for long walks with a friend.

The 100 million speakers of German live in a number of countries, located mostly in central Europe. The **BRD (Bundesrepublik Deutschland,** or Federal Republic of Germany) is the largest of the German-speaking countries. It is about the size of Oregon and has a population of 60 million. Its capital is Bonn. The **DDR (Deutsche Demokratische Republik,** German Democratic Republic) is a little larger than Ohio and has a population of 17 million. Its capital is East Berlin. Both the **BRD** and the **DDR** are modern, industrialized countries, with a high level of production in agriculture as well.

Wie heißt du?

Ute Braun lives in Bonn. She meets a new girl at school and discovers they have something in common.

UTE BRAUN	Wie heißt du?
UTE SCHMIDT	Ute.
UTE BRAUN	Toll! Ich heiße auch Ute.

Du hast das Wort

A. Choose German names for yourselves from the list in the Appendix. Ask a classmate what her/his name is.

   Wie heißt du?   [Barbara.]

B. Guess a classmate's name. If you're wrong, your classmate will correct you.

   Heißt du [Mark]?   Ja°.
                                Nein°, ich heiße [Martin].

Wie geht's?

Ingrid runs into some friends and asks them how they are.

INGRID	Tag, Gisela. Wie geht's?
GISELA	Danke, gut.
INGRID	Tag, Dieter. Wie geht's?
DIETER	Schlecht.
INGRID	Was ist denn los?
DIETER	Ich bin müde.

Kapitel 1

▣ It is not uncommon for teen-agers in German-speaking countries to greet their friends with a handshake. The German handshake consists of a single movement downward rather than a series of up-and-down movements.

Du hast das Wort

A. A classmate asks how you are. How would you respond?

Wie geht's?	Prima°!
	Sehr° gut.
	Nicht° schlecht.
	Ganz° gut.
	Danke, es geht°.

B. A classmate asks what's wrong. How would you respond?

Was ist los?	Ich bin müde.
	Ich bin sehr müde.
	Ich bin kaputt°.
	Ich bin krank°.

▣ An important characteristic of German is the use of "flavoring" words like **denn** to express the speaker's attitude about an utterance. These flavoring words relate the utterance to something the speaker or the listener has already said or thought. Depending on the choice of the word and sometimes on the tone of voice, the speaker may express interest, surprise, impatience, and so on.

Denn, for example, is often used in questions. It gives a little extra emphasis to the question and implies that one is interested in the answer.

| Was ist los? | What's the matter? |
| Was ist **denn** los? | Well, what **is** the matter? |

The meaning of flavoring words varies, depending on the context. Frequently there are no exact English equivalents. With experience, you will gain a feeling for the meaning and use of these words in German.

Bist du zufrieden?

Monika and Volker are discussing the results of their last test.

VOLKER	So, Monika, bist du zufrieden?
MONIKA	Ja, sehr. Du auch?
VOLKER	Nein, ich bin wirklich sauer.
MONIKA	Das tut mir leid.

Du hast das Wort

Ask classmates whether they're satisfied with their work.

    Bist du zufrieden?   Ja, sehr zufrieden.
                                        Ja, ich bin glücklich°.
                                        Nein, ich bin sauer.
                                        Nein, gar° nicht.

Warum ist Volker so sauer?

Frank wants to know why Volker looks so gloomy.

FRANK	Wie geht's Volker?
MONIKA	Schlecht.
FRANK	Ist er wieder krank?
MONIKA	Unsinn! Er ist nur faul.

Du hast das Wort

How would you respond to a friend's question about a classmate?

    Ist [Dieter] faul?   Ja, er ist sehr faul.
                                          Nein, er ist krank.
                                          Nein, er ist müde.

    Ist [Gerda] zufrieden?   Ja, sie ist sehr zufrieden.
                                                Ja, sie ist wirklich glücklich.
                                              Nein, sie ist nicht zufrieden.

Wortschatzerweiterung

Greetings and farewells

Guten Morgen!
Guten Tag!
Guten Abend!

Auf Wiedersehen!
Tschüß!
Bis später.
Guten Abend!
Gute Nacht!

Guten Morgen is used to say hello in the morning.
Guten Tag is used to say hello at any time during the day.
  Tag is an informal version of **Guten Tag**.
Guten Abend is used to say both hello and good-by during the evening.
Gute Nacht is used as a farewell late in the evening and at bedtime.
Auf Wiedersehen is used at any time of the day or night as an expression of farewell.
Tschüß is an informal farewell and is equivalent to *so long*.
Bis später is equivalent to *see you later*.

A Respond appropriately to each of the following greetings and farewells.

■ Tag, [Ingrid]!   *Tag, [Frank]!*

1. Guten Morgen!
2. Auf Wiedersehen!
3. Tschüß!
4. Bis später!
5. Guten Abend!
6. Gute Nacht!

B How would you greet a person at the following times of the day or night?

1. 8:00 A.M.
2. 7:00 P.M.
3. 4:00 P.M.
4. 10:00 A.M.
5. 2:00 A.M.
6. 7:00 A.M.

Descriptive adjectives

Gerda ist **gesund.**

Paul ist **krank.**

Heike ist **sauer.**

Jürgen ist **fleißig.**

Georg ist **faul.**

Martin ist **müde.**

Tanja ist **glücklich.**

Petra ist **unglücklich.**

Isabel ist **zufrieden.**

C Ask a classmate whether he/she is tired, lazy, sad, etc.

■ Bist du . . . ?

D Ask a classmate how he/she is feeling. Then ask a second classmate to report what the first one said. Use the following conversation as a model.

YOU	Wie geht's?
CLASSMATE 1	[Schlecht]. Ich bin [krank].
YOU	[Stefan], wie geht's [Ingrid]?
CLASSMATE 2	[Sie] ist [krank].

▣ Greetings and farewells may vary in the different German-speaking countries and even within one country. For instance, in southern Germany or in Austria one might hear **Grüß Gott** or **Grüß dich**. **Servus** is another common greeting in Austria. In Switzerland one often hears **Grüetzi** or **Salut**.

Auf Wiedersehen can be shortened to simply **Wiedersehen**. In some areas **Auf Wiederschauen** or **Adieu** are also used to say goodby.

Aussprache

In the pronunciation sections of this text, special symbols in brackets are used to represent various German sounds. Each symbol represents only one sound. In written German, different letters or letter combinations may represent the same sound. Vowels are classified as long or short.

long vowel [i]   pr**i**ma, w**ie**
short vowel [I] b**i**n, n**i**cht, Uns**i**nn

A Practice vertically in columns and horizontally in pairs.

[i]	[I]
L**ie**d	l**i**tt
b**ie**ten	b**i**tten
Ihnen	**i**nnen
B**ie**nen	b**i**nnen
K**ie**pe	K**i**ppe

B Practice the sounds [i] and [I]. Read the sentences aloud.

1. Ingrid ist wieder krank.
2. Unsinn. Sie ist nur müde.
3. Wie geht's Ilse?

Stille Wasser sind tief.

kapitel 1

Übungen

The subject pronouns **ich, du, er,** and **sie**

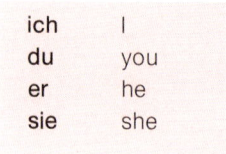

The subject pronouns **ich, du, er,** and **sie** are equivalent to the English pronouns *I, you, he,* and *she.*

A Give the subject pronouns you would use in the following situations.

■ You're talking about your mother.   *sie*

1. You're talking to a male friend.
2. You're talking about a female teacher.
3. You're talking about a male student.
4. You're talking about yourself.
5. You're talking to a female friend.

Present tense of **sein**: singular forms

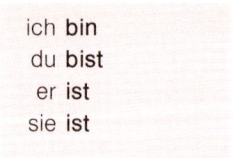

The forms of **sein** vary according to the subject used.

Hans! Bist **du** müde?   Hans, are *you* tired?
Ja, **ich** bin müde.   Yes, *I'm* tired.

B Your friends are trying to find out what's wrong with you. Answer their questions in the affirmative.

■ Bist du müde?   *Ja, ich bin sehr müde.*

1. Bist du sauer?   3. Bist du unglücklich?
2. Bist du faul?   4. Bist du kaputt?

C Your friends tell you how they're feeling. Ask them why they're feeling that way.

◾▪ Ich bin glücklich.   *Warum bist du denn glücklich?*

1. Ich bin kaputt.
2. Ich bin müde.
3. Ich bin sauer.
4. Ich bin unglücklich.
5. Ich bin zufrieden.

Sabine ist unglücklich. **Sie** ist krank.   *Sabine* is unhappy. *She*'s ill.

Robert ist unglücklich. **Er** ist krank.   *Robert* is unhappy. *He*'s ill.

D There's been a flu epidemic at school, but it's over now. When Christa asks about your friends, say they're well again.

◾▪ Wie geht's Stefan?   *Er ist wieder gesund.*

◾▪ Wie geht's Inge?   *Sie ist wieder gesund.*

1. Wie geht's Andrea?
2. Wie geht's Kurt?
3. Wie geht's Nicole?
4. Wie geht's Ilse?
5. Wie geht's Hans?
6. Wie geht's Georg?

E Form sentences, using the cued subject pronouns and adjectives.

◾▪ er / fleißig   *Er ist fleißig.*

1. du / müde
2. ich / unglücklich
3. er / sauer
4. sie / krank
5. ich / faul
6. du / unglücklich
7. er / gesund
8. sie / glücklich
9. ich / zufrieden

The negative word **nicht**

Ich bin **nicht** müde.   I'm *not* tired.
Ilse ist **nicht** faul.   Ilse isn*'t* lazy.

Nicht is equivalent to English *not*.

F   Tanja wants to know how your friends are feeling. Answer her questions in the negative.

> ▪ Wie geht's Udo? Ist er wieder müde?   *Nein, er ist nicht müde.*

1. Wie geht's Frank? Ist er wieder krank?
2. Wie geht's Inge? Ist sie wieder glücklich?
3. Wie geht's Barbara? Ist sie wieder sauer?
4. Wie geht's Walter? Ist er wieder müde?
5. Wie geht's Jens? Ist er wieder glücklich?
6. Wie geht's Heidi? Ist sie wieder sauer?
7. Wie geht's Ingrid? Ist sie wieder zufrieden?

Grammatische Übersicht

The letters in parentheses following grammatical headings refer to the corresponding exercises in the **Übungen**.

The subject pronouns **ich, du, er,** and **sie**   (A)

ich	I
du	you
er	he
sie	she

The pronouns **ich, du, er,** and **sie** are equivalent to the English pronouns *I, you, he,* and *she.* They are used as the subject of a sentence.

18   german today, one

Ist **Stefan** krank? Nein, **er** ist nur faul.
Ist **Ingrid** unglücklich? Nein, **sie** ist glücklich.

When talking about people, the pronoun **er** is used to refer to a male; the pronoun **sie** is used to refer to a female.

Present tense of **sein**: singular forms (B-E)

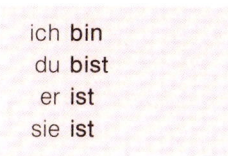
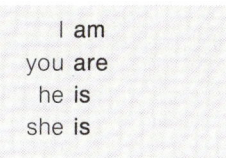

Subjects and their verb forms must agree. The German verb **sein**, like the English verb *to be*, has three different singular forms in the present tense.

The negative word **nicht** (F)

Ich bin **nicht** krank.
Christa ist **nicht** faul.

Nicht is equivalent to English *not*. The position of **nicht** in a sentence can vary. One common position is just before the element that is being negated.

Notes about written German

1. All nouns are capitalized: **Morgen, Tag, Abend.**

2. The pronoun **ich** is not capitalized, unlike its English equivalent, *I*.

3. An apostrophe indicates the omission of the letter **e**: **Wie geht's?** = **Wie geht es?**

4. The letter **ß** is called an **Ess-tset** and replaces **ss**:
   a. at the end of a word: **Tschüß**
   b. before a consonant: **du mußt** = you must
   c. after a long vowel: **fleißig**

5. In addition to **ß,** the German alphabet has three other letters that the English alphabet doesn't have: **ä, ö,** and **ü,** called **umlaut a, o,** and **u**. The symbol (¨) indicates that a vowel is umlauted.

Kapitel 1   **19**

Wiederholung

A Give a greeting appropriate to the time of day shown in each picture.

■ *Guten Morgen!*

B Complete each of the following sentences with the correct subject pronoun.

■ ____ bin müde.   *Ich*

1. ____ bin glücklich.
2. Bist ____ zufrieden?
3. Wie geht's Peter? Ist ____ krank?
4. Wie geht's Monika? Ist ____ wieder gesund?
5. Warum bist ____ sauer?

C Answer the questions after each dialogue.

INGRID   Wie geht's Frank?
DIETER   Er ist glücklich.
INGRID   Warum?
DIETER   Er ist wieder gesund.

1. Wie geht's Frank?
2. Warum ist er glücklich?

MONIKA	Wie geht's Gerda?
JÜRGEN	Ganz gut.
MONIKA	Ist sie nicht wieder krank?
JÜRGEN	Nein. Sie ist nur faul.

1. Wie geht's Gerda?
2. Ist sie krank?

D Express the following in German.

1. Hi, how are you?
   I'm exhausted.
2. What's the matter?
   Why are you unhappy?
3. I'm sick again.
   You're not sick, you're just lazy.
4. So long!
   See you later!

E Claudia meets Dieter at a party. Give the equivalent of their conversation in German.

CLAUDIA	Good evening, Dieter. How are you?
DIETER	Bad.
CLAUDIA	Really? What's the matter? Are you sick again?
DIETER	No, just very tired.

Vokabeln

Be sure you can recognize and use actively the following words and expressions before going on to Chapter 2.

VERBEN (VERBS)

sein   to be
  ich bin   I am
  du bist   you are
  er/sie ist   he/she is

ANDERE WÖRTER (OTHER WORDS)

auch   also, too
danke   thanks, thank you
denn   *flavoring word often used in questions*
du   you
er   he
faul   lazy
fleißig   industrious, diligent
ganz   quite; complete(ly)
gesund   healthy, well
glücklich   happy
gut   good
ich   I
ja   yes
kaputt   exhausted
krank   ill, sick
müde   tired
nein   no
nicht   not
nur   only, just
prima   excellent, fine, great
sauer   cross, annoyed; sour
schlecht   bad
sehr   very
sie   she
so   so
toll   great, fantastic
und   and
unglücklich   unhappy
warum   why
was   what
wie   how

ANDERE WÖRTER

wieder   again
wirklich   really
zufrieden   content

BESONDERE AUSDRÜCKE (SPECIAL EXPRESSIONS)

wie heißt du?   what's your name?
ich heiße ...   my name is ...
was ist (denn) los?   (well,) what's the matter?
wie geht's?   how are you (doing)?
es geht   OK, can't complain
ganz gut   OK, pretty well
das tut mir leid   I'm sorry
Unsinn!   nonsense!
gar nicht   not at all
guten Abend!   good evening!
guten Morgen!   good morning!
gute Nacht!   good night!
guten Tag!   hello!; **Tag!**   hi
auf Wiedersehen   good-by
tschüß!   so long!
bis später   till later, see you later

Kapitel 2
Wie alt bist du?

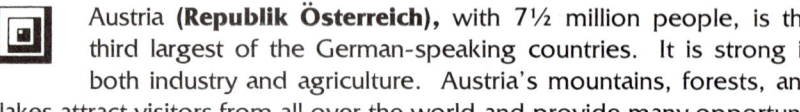 Austria **(Republik Österreich),** with 7½ million people, is the third largest of the German-speaking countries. It is strong in both industry and agriculture. Austria's mountains, forests, and lakes attract visitors from all over the world and provide many opportunities for outdoor recreation.

Vienna, the capital, is world-famous for its music and theater and its excellent food.

Jung oder alt?

Michael and his friends live in Vienna. Michael's birthday party prompts Heike and Dirk to compare ages.

HEIKE	Wie alt ist Michael?
DIRK	Sechzehn.
HEIKE	Und du?
DIRK	Auch sechzehn. Wir sind beide sechzehn.
HEIKE	Seid ihr *wirklich* sechzehn?
DIRK	Natürlich. Warum?
HEIKE	Ihr seid so jung.
DIRK	Wie alt bist *du* denn?
HEIKE	Schon siebzehn.
DIRK	Das ist aber sehr alt.

Fragen

1. Wie alt ist Michael?
2. Wie alt ist Dirk?
3. Sind Michael und Dirk jung oder alt?
4. Wer° ist siebzehn?
5. Ist Heike alt oder jung?

Du hast das Wort

A. A friend asks whether you're already fifteen. How would you answer her/his question?

Bist du schon fünfzehn?   Ja.
Ja, du auch, nicht°?
Nein.
Fünfzehn? Ich bin schon sechzehn.

B. Discuss the ages of various classmates with two friends.

Ihr seid beide sechzehn, nicht?

Ja.
Nein. Wir sind beide [fünfzehn].
Nein. [Petra] ist fünfzehn und ich bin sechzehn.
Ich bin sechzehn. [Petra] ist schon siebzehn.

Birthdays in German-speaking countries are usually celebrated either with family and relatives or with friends. There is apt to be a birthday cake with candles, often arranged in a circle around the edge, and some kind of display for birthday cards, flowers, and gifts. Frequently a group of friends will get together and sign a card to the **Geburtstagskind.** A common greeting on cards is **Herzlichen Glückwunsch zum Geburtstag.** Here are some other birthday greetings:

Alles Gute zum Geburtstag!	All the best on your birthday!
Alles Gute!	All the best!
Ich gratuliere dir auch.	I congratulate you, too.
Ich wünsche dir alles Gute.	I wish you all the best.

Wann hast du Geburtstag?

Petra finds she was mistaken about her friends' birthdays.

PETRA   Ich habe im März Geburtstag. Du auch, nicht?
DIRK   Nein.
PETRA   Wann hast du denn Geburtstag?
DIRK   Im April.
PETRA   Ach so. Hat Gerd nicht auch im April Geburtstag?
DIRK   Nein, erst im Mai.
PETRA   Ach ja, richtig.

Richtig oder falsch?
1. Petra hat im März Geburtstag.
2. Dirk hat auch im März Geburtstag.
3. Petra und Gerd haben im April Geburtstag.

Wortschatzerweiterung

Zahlen: 0–19

0	null	5	fünf	10	zehn	15	fünfzehn
1	eins	6	sechs	11	elf	16	sechzehn
2	zwei	7	sieben	12	zwölf	17	siebzehn
3	drei	8	acht	13	dreizehn	18	achtzehn
4	vier	9	neun	14	vierzehn	19	neunzehn

A Ask a classmate how old he/she is.

B Give your telephone number to a classmate.

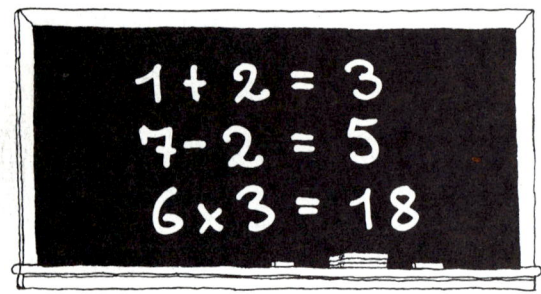

Wieviel ist eins und zwei?
Eins und zwei ist drei.

Wieviel ist sieben weniger zwei?
Sieben weniger zwei ist fünf.

Wieviel ist sechs mal drei?
Sechs mal drei ist achtzehn.

C Do the following arithmetic problems with a classmate.

■ 1 + 3 = ?   *Wieviel ist eins und drei?*
                 Eins und drei ist vier.

1. 3 + 7 = ?   3. 4 + 13 = ?
2. 2 + 9 = ?   4. 1 + 18 = ?

■ 10 − 7 = ?   *Wieviel ist zehn weniger sieben?*
                 Zehn weniger sieben ist drei.

5. 18 − 12 = ?   7. 17 − 13 = ?
6. 12 − 5 = ?   8. 18 − 1 = ?

■ 5 × 3 = ?   *Wieviel ist fünf mal drei?*
               Fünf mal drei ist fünfzehn.

9. 4 × 3 = ?   11. 6 × 3 = ?
10. 8 × 2 = ?   12. 5 × 2 = ?

Wieviel ist es denn?

Monate

Januar	April	Juli	Oktober
Februar	Mai	August	November
März	Juni	September	Dezember

D   Ask a classmate when her/his birthday is.

- Wann hast du Geburtstag?   Im [Mai].

E   Take a poll of your classmates to find out how many birthdays there are in each month. Write the total on the board.

- Wer hat im [Januar] Geburtstag?

Kapitel 2

Aussprache

long vowel [e] Eva, See, geht
short vowel [ɛ] es, denn, Männer

A Practice vertically in columns and horizontally in pairs.

[e]	[ɛ]
Beet	Bett
den	denn
wen	wenn
stehlen	stellen
fehlen	fällen

B Practice the following words horizontally in pairs.

[i]	[ɪ]	[e]	[ɛ]
bieten	bitten	beten	Betten
stiehlt	stillt	stehlt	stellt
Wiesen	Wissen	Wesen	wessen
vieler	Filter	fehle	Felle
wiegen	wickeln	Wege	wecken

C Practice the sounds [e] and [ɛ]. Read the sentences aloud.

1. Was ist denn los, Eva?
2. Petra hat im Dezember Geburtstag.
3. Detlev Keller ist sechzehn.

Reden ist Silber,
Schweigen ist Gold.

Übungen

The subject pronouns **wir, ihr,** and **sie**

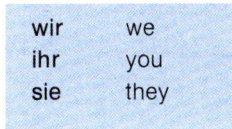

The subject pronouns **wir, ihr,** and **sie** are equivalent to the English pronouns *we*, *you* (plural), and *they*.

A Give the subject pronouns you would use in the following situations.

1. You're talking to two friends.
2. You're talking about your teachers.
3. You're talking about yourself and a friend.
4. You're talking about Erik and Ingrid.
5. You're talking to your parents.

Present tense of **sein:** plural forms

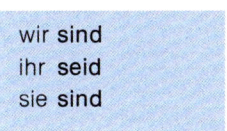

    Hans und Inge, seid **ihr** müde?   Hans and Inge, are *you* tired?
    Ja, **wir** sind sehr müde.   Yes, *we're* very tired.

B Beate expresses doubt about how you and your friend feel. Tell her it's true.

▪▪▪ Seid ihr wirklich glücklich?   *Ja, wir sind sehr glücklich.*

1. Seid ihr wirklich müde?   3. Seid ihr wirklich zufrieden?
2. Seid ihr wirklich kaputt?   4. Seid ihr wirklich sauer?

C Ask whether Dieter and Gisela really mean what they say.

▪▪▪ Wir sind müde.   *Seid ihr wirklich müde?*

1. Wir sind sauer.   3. Wir sind zufrieden.
2. Wir sind krank.   4. Wir sind kaputt.

      Alex und Tanja sind sauer.   *Alex and Tanja* are in a bad mood.
      Sie sind sehr müde.   *They're very tired.*

D   Jan always thinks people are a year older than they really are. Correct him, as in the model.

◾   Andrea und Erik sind siebzehn, nicht?   *Nein, sie sind erst sechzehn.*

1. Hans und Ursel sind vierzehn, nicht?
2. Eva und Monika sind sechzehn, nicht?
3. Helmut und Uwe sind achtzehn, nicht?
4. Silke und Lutz sind fünfzehn, nicht?

E   Form sentences, using the cued subjects and adjectives.

◾   sie *(pl.)* / müde   *Sie sind müde.*

1. wir / faul
2. Thomas und Ilse / sauer
3. sie *(pl.)* / fleißig
4. ihr / glücklich
5. ich / krank
6. du / jung
7. Frank / alt
8. wir / gesund

The pronouns **sie** (singular) and **sie** (plural)

      Ist **Birgit** müde?   Ja, **sie** ist sehr müde.
      Sind **Eva und Jan** glücklich?   Ja, **sie** sind sehr glücklich.

F   You and Gabi are discussing mutual acquaintances. Confirm what Gabi asks. Use either **sie** *(sg.)* or **sie** *(pl.)* as required by the question.

◾   Brigitte ist krank, nicht?   *Ja, sie ist sehr krank.*

◾   Trudi und Otto sind glücklich, nicht?   *Ja, sie sind sehr glücklich.*

1. Ursel ist sauer, nicht?
2. Marianne ist zufrieden, nicht?
3. Inge und Thomas sind unglücklich, nicht?
4. Michael und Wolf sind fleißig, nicht?
5. Heidi ist krank, nicht?

Present tense of **haben**

ich **habe**	wir **haben**
du **hast**	ihr **habt**
er/sie **hat**	sie **haben**

G   Frank and his friends are comparing birthdays. Say that the people mentioned were born in the same month as their friends.

> ▪ Du hast im März Geburtstag. (Jens)   *Jens hat auch im März Geburtstag.*

1. Petra hat im Juni Geburtstag. (ich)
2. Wir haben im Februar Geburtstag. (Karin und Urs)
3. Jürgen hat im Mai Geburtstag. (ihr)
4. Ulrike und Thomas haben im September Geburtstag. (wir)
5. Anke hat im März Geburtstag. (du)
6. Ich habe im November Geburtstag. (Ellen)

Specific Questions

Wie alt bist du?	Sechzehn.
Wann hast du Geburtstag?	Im Dezember.
Warum bist du so faul?	Ich bin müde.
Wer ist fleißig?	Christine.
Wieviel ist sechs und sieben?	Dreizehn.

Specific questions begin with interrogatives such as **wie, wann, warum, wer,** or **wieviel,** and require specific answers to supply the desired information.

H   At a crowded party, you can't hear everything Udo is saying. Ask questions to elicit the desired information.

> ▪ Jan ist *vierzehn.*   *Wie alt ist Jan?*
>
> ▪ Das ist *Ingrid Schmidt.*   *Wer ist das?*

1. Das ist *Jens Wagner.*
2. *Frank* hat im Mai Geburtstag.
3. Christa ist *siebzehn.*
4. Monika ist erst *zwölf.*
5. Es geht Inge *gut.*
6. Es geht Ralf *schlecht.*
7. Thomas hat *im Januar* Geburtstag.
8. Paula hat auch *im Januar* Geburtstag.

General questions

Bist du fünfzehn? **Ja.**
Ist Gerda auch fünfzehn? **Nein,** Gerda ist vierzehn.

General questions begin with a verb and require a **ja/nein-**answer.

I Ask whether the statements are really true.

■)) Frank ist vierzehn. *Ist Frank wirklich vierzehn?*

1. Ich bin fünfzehn.
2. Ursel ist elf.
3. Jens ist krank.
4. Gerda ist zufrieden.
5. Udo hat im Dezember Geburtstag.
6. Anke ist fleißig.

Grammatische Übersicht

Subject pronouns (A)

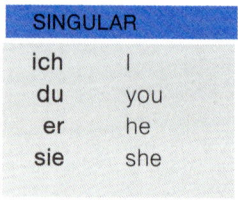
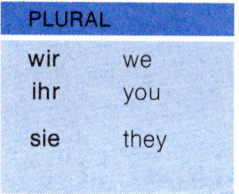

SINGULAR	
ich	I
du	you
er	he
sie	she

PLURAL	
wir	we
ihr	you
sie	they

The plural subject pronouns **wir, ihr,** and **sie** function like the English pronouns *we, you,* and *they.*

The pronouns **sie** (singular) and **sie** (plural) (F)

Ist **sie** müde?   Is *she* tired?
Sind **sie** müde?   Are *they* tired?

Sie may mean *she* or *they*. A singular verb (for example, **ist**) indicates that **sie** means *she.* A plural verb (for example, **sind**) indicates that **sie** means *they.*

Present tense of **sein** (B-E)

SINGULAR	
ich **bin**	I am
du **bist**	you are
er/sie **ist**	he/she is

PLURAL	
wir **sind**	we are
ihr **seid**	you are
sie **sind**	they are

Like the English verb *to be*, the German verb **sein** has several forms in the present tense. The verb forms agree with their subject pronouns.

Present tense of **haben** (G)

ich **habe**	I have
du **hast**	you have
er/sie **hat**	he/she has

wir **haben**	we have
ihr **habt**	you have
sie **haben**	they have

Like the English verb *to have*, the German verb **haben** has several forms in the present tense. The forms must agree with their subject pronouns.

Specific questions and general questions (H-I)

Wie alt bist du?   How old are you?
Wann hast du Geburtstag?   When is your birthday?

A specific question asks for a particular bit of information and begins with an interrogative such as **wie, wieviel, wann, warum,** or **wer.** The voice normally falls at the end of a specific question.

Ist Gerda 15?   Is Gerda 15?
Hat sie im Mai Geburtstag?   Is her birthday in May?

A general question can be answered with **ja** or **nein** and begins with a verb. The voice normally rises at the end of a general question.

Wiederholung

A Answer the questions after the dialogue.

INGRID   Tag, Peter! Wie geht's?
PETER   Sehr schlecht.
INGRID   Was ist denn los? Bist du krank?
PETER   Nein, nur kaputt.

1. Wie geht's Peter?
2. Ist Peter sehr müde?

B Restate the sentences, inserting the flavoring word *denn* where indicated. Then give the English equivalents.

1. Wie alt bist du ____?
2. Wann hast du ____ Geburtstag?
3. Wie geht's ____?
4. Bist du ____ wieder krank?
5. Was ist ____ los?
6. Norbert ist sauer. Warum ____?

C Form complete sentences from the cues below.

▪ Peter / sein / wirklich / sehr fleißig   *Peter ist wirklich sehr fleißig.*
▪ wie / alt / sein / Dieter und Meike /?   *Wie alt sind Dieter und Meike?*

1. wann / haben / du / Geburtstag /?
2. ich / haben / im Juli / Geburtstag
3. wie / alt / du / sein /?
4. sein / Ute / wirklich / unglücklich /?
5. ich / sein / sauer
6. wir / sein / beide / kaputt

D Express in German:

1. See you later!
2. That's correct.
3. I'm only fifteen.
4. I am very lazy.
5. Anja is sick again.

E Answer according to your mood and situation.

1. Wie geht's?
2. Wann hast du Geburtstag?
3. Bist du schon fünfzehn?
4. Wie alt bist du?
5. Bist du alt oder jung?
6. Bist du faul oder fleißig?

F Complete each sentence with an appropriate word from the list below.

aber   denn   los   nicht   nur   wie

1. Du bist auch sechzehn, ____?
2. Das ist ____ sehr alt.
3. Wie alt bist du ____?
4. ____ geht's?
5. Was ist denn ____?
6. Wir sind nicht sauer, ____ sehr müde.

G Choose a logical response or combination of responses from column B for each of the questions in column A.

▪ Du bist schon 17, nicht?   Unsinn. Ich bin erst 15.

A	B
Du bist erst dreizehn, nicht?	Unsinn. / Natürlich.
Du bist sehr jung, nicht?	Ja. / Nein.
Du hast im Juli Geburtstag, nicht?	Richtig. / Du auch, nicht?
Du bist zufrieden, nicht?	Ich bin schon [vierzehn].
Was ist los?	Ich bin erst [fünfzehn].
Bist du denn krank?	Ich bin nur müde.
	Ja, sehr.
	Ich bin krank. / Ich bin sauer.

Vokabeln

VERBEN

haben   to have
sein: wir sind   we are
   ihr seid   you are *(pl.)*
   sie sind   they are

ANDERE WÖRTER

aber   *flavoring word*
alt   old
beide   both
erst   only, first
falsch   wrong
ihr   you *(pl.)*
jung   young

ANDERE WÖRTER

mal   times
Monate   months *(p. 27)*
natürlich   naturally, of course
oder   or
richtig   correct, right
schon   already
sie *(pl.)*   they
wann   when
weniger   minus, less
wer   who
wieviel   how much
wir   we
Zahlen   numbers *(p. 26)*

BESONDERE AUSDRÜCKE

nicht?   isn't that so? *(at the end of a sentence)*
ach so   oh, I see!
wie alt bist du?   how old are you?
ich habe Geburtstag   it's my birthday
im [März]   in [March]

Kapitel 2   35

Kapitel 3
Heute nachmittag

Switzerland (**die Schweiz**), a country about half the size of Maine, is known for its scenery and industrial products. Much of the country is mountainous, and is ideal for skiing and hiking. The capital is Bern.

About 70% of Switzerland's 6½ million people speak a form of German called **Schwyzerdütsch.** The rest speak French, Italian, or Romansch, which is very close to Latin. The Latin name for Switzerland, **Helvetia,** is used on stamps and coins.

Wo wohnst du?

Erik and Sabine live in Bern. School is out. Erik catches up with Sabine as she leaves for home.

ERIK	Gehst du jetzt nach Hause?
SABINE	Ja.
ERIK	Wo wohnst du denn?
SABINE	In der Gartenstraße.
ERIK	Ist das weit von hier?
SABINE	Nein, nur zehn Minuten.

Fragen
1. Wer geht nach Hause?
2. Wohnt Sabine weit von hier?

Du hast das Wort

A. Ask a classmate on what street or in what town he/she lives.

Wo wohnst du?   In der [Garten]straße.
                     In [Bergdorf].

B. Ask how far that place is from where you are.

Ist das weit von hier?   Nein, nicht sehr weit.
                          Nein, nur fünf Minuten.
                          Ja, zehn Kilometer.°
                          Ja, ziemlich° weit.

Kapitel 3 **37**

Marks Fotoalbum

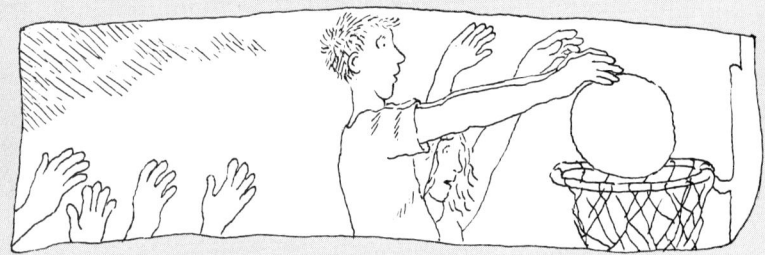

Petra spielt gern Tennis.

Christa und Gerd spielen gern Basketball.

Sie spielt auch gern Volleyball.

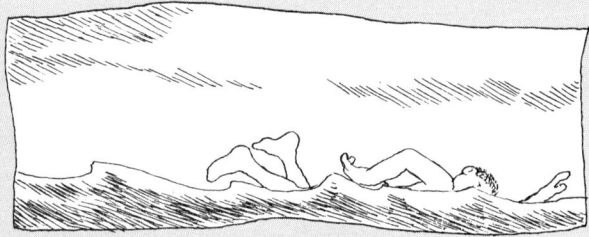

Herbert schwimmt gern.

Ilse wandert viel.

Frank spielt sehr gut Fußball.

Ute und Frank gehen oft spazieren.

Fragen
1. Was macht Herbert gern?
2. Wer spielt Tennis? Basketball?
3. Was machen Ute und Frank?

Du hast das Wort

Ask a classmate whether he/she likes to engage in a particular sport or outdoor activity.

Spielst du gern [Tennis]?	Ja, ich spiele gern [Tennis].
	Ja, aber ich spiele nicht gut.
	Nein, ich spiele nicht gern [Tennis].
Gehst du gern spazieren?	Ja, sehr gern.
	Ja, natürlich.
	Nein, ich gehe nicht gern spazieren.
[Wanderst] du gern?	Ja, du nicht?
	Nein, ich [wandere] nicht gern.

Was machst du?

Jan and Gisela are walking home from school together.

JAN Bleibst du heute nachmittag zu Hause?
GISELA Ja. Natürlich.
JAN Was machst du denn?
GISELA Hausaufgaben. Was sonst?

Du hast das Wort

A classmate asks you when you're going to do your homework. How would you respond?

Machst du	heute nachmittag	Hausaufgaben?	Ja, natürlich.
	heute abend°		Ja, du nicht?
	heute morgen°		Nein, natürlich nicht.
			Nein, ich bin zu° müde.

Hiking and walking are favorite pastimes for Germans of all ages. There are well-maintained trails all over the country. Some are no more than paths through local scenic spots or city parks, while others are part of a vast complex of trails stretching from the Baltic Sea to Lake Constance. Some parks also feature **Trimm-dich-Pfade** (marked jogging paths with obstacles to climb over, and other suggested exercises).

Wortschatzerweiterung

Musikinstrumente

Klavier

Geige

Schlagzeug

Klarinette

Flöte

Gitarre

A Ask a classmate whether he/she plays a particular instrument.

Spielst du [Klavier]?   Ja, natürlich.
Nein, aber° [Geige].
Nein, ich spiele nicht [Klavier].

B Ask your classmate whether he/she plays well.

Spielst du gut?   Ja. Sehr gut.
Ja, nicht schlecht.
Ja, ganz gut.
Nein, nicht sehr gut.

Aussprache

| long vowel [y] | müde, Schüler, Stühle |
| short vowel [Y] | fünf, Günter, Flüsse |

A Practice vertically in columns and horizontally in pairs.

[y]	[Y]
Füßen	Füssen
büßte	Büste
Düne	dünne
Mühle	Müll
fühlen	füllen

B Practice the following words horizontally in pairs.

[i]	[y]	[I]	[Y]
Biene	Bühne	Binde	Bünde
diene	Düne	bitte	Bütte
Kiel	kühl	Kissen	küssen
liegen	lügen	Lifte	Lüfte

C Practice the sounds [y] and [Y]. Read the sentences aloud.

1. Günter, wieviel ist fünf und fünfzehn?
2. Warum seid ihr so müde?
3. Rüdiger ist unglücklich.

In der Kürze liegt die Würze.

Glottal Stop

Say aloud *a nice man* and then say *an ice man.* The second phrase sounds different from the first because you break the stream of air between *an* and *ice.* This process of stopping and starting the air stream in the back of the throat is called a *glottal stop.* Both English and German use the glottal stop before vowels as a device to avoid running together words and parts of words. The glottal stop occurs more frequently in German than in English.

D Read the following sentences aloud. An asterisk (*) indicates a glottal stop.

1. Wo *ist *Erik heute *abend?
2. Wie geht *es *Eva?
3. Wie *alt *ist *Otto?

E Now try reading a few sentences without an asterisk.

1. Guten Abend!
2. Was ist das, Astrid?
3. Ist Udo wieder krank?

Übungen

Present tense of regular verbs

ich / du

ich geh**e**   du geh**st**
ich spiel**e**   du spiel**st**

The endings of regular verbs change according to a pattern. The **ich**-form ends in **-e,** the **du**-form ends in **-st.**

A Sabine is trying to find out more about you and your plans. Answer her questions affirmatively.

■ Gehst du jetzt nach Hause?   *Ja, ich gehe jetzt nach Hause.*

1. Wohnst du weit von hier?
2. Spielst du heute nachmittag Tennis?
3. Bleibst du heute abend zu Hause?
4. Machst du heute abend Hausaufgaben?

B You didn't hear when Petra intends to do certain things. Ask her when it's going to be.

> ▪ Ich spiele heute morgen Fußball. *Wann spielst du Fußball?*

1. Ich gehe heute nachmittag schwimmen.
2. Ich spiele heute nachmittag Tennis.
3. Ich gehe heute abend spazieren.
4. Ich mache heute abend Hausaufgaben.

wir / ihr

wir geh**en**   ihr geh**t**
wir spiel**en**   ihr spiel**t**

The **wir-**form ends in **-en,** the **ihr-**form ends in **-t.**

C Bruno is curious and wants to know what your plans are. Keep him guessing by answering all of his questions in the negative.

> ▪ Geht ihr nach Hause? *Nein. Wir gehen nicht nach Hause.*

1. Bleibt ihr hier?
2. Geht ihr spazieren?
3. Spielt ihr Tennis?
4. Geht ihr schwimmen?
5. Spielt ihr Volleyball?

D Your friends tell you what they're doing today. Ask whether they do these things often.

> ▪ Wir spielen heute Tennis. *Spielt ihr oft Tennis?*

1. Wir spielen heute Fußball.
2. Wir spielen heute Basketball.
3. Wir gehen heute schwimmen.
4. Wir gehen heute spazieren.
5. Wir bleiben heute zu Hause.

er / sie (singular) / sie (plural)

er/sie geh**t**   sie geh**en**
er/sie spiel**t** sie spiel**en**

The **er/sie-**form ends in **-t,** the **sie** *(plural)*-form ends in **-en.**

E Marta asks how well several classmates play their instruments. Answer in each instance that they play either very well or very badly.

■ Spielt Karin gut Klavier?   *Ja, sie spielt sehr gut.*
   Nein, sie spielt sehr schlecht.

1. Spielt Bernhard gut Gitarre?
2. Spielt Astrid gut Klarinette?
3. Spielen Detlev und Erik gut Schlagzeug?
4. Spielt Detlev gut Flöte?
5. Spielen Rita und Christl gut Geige?

F Say that the persons indicated play their instruments well.

■ Frank   *Frank spielt gut Klavier.*

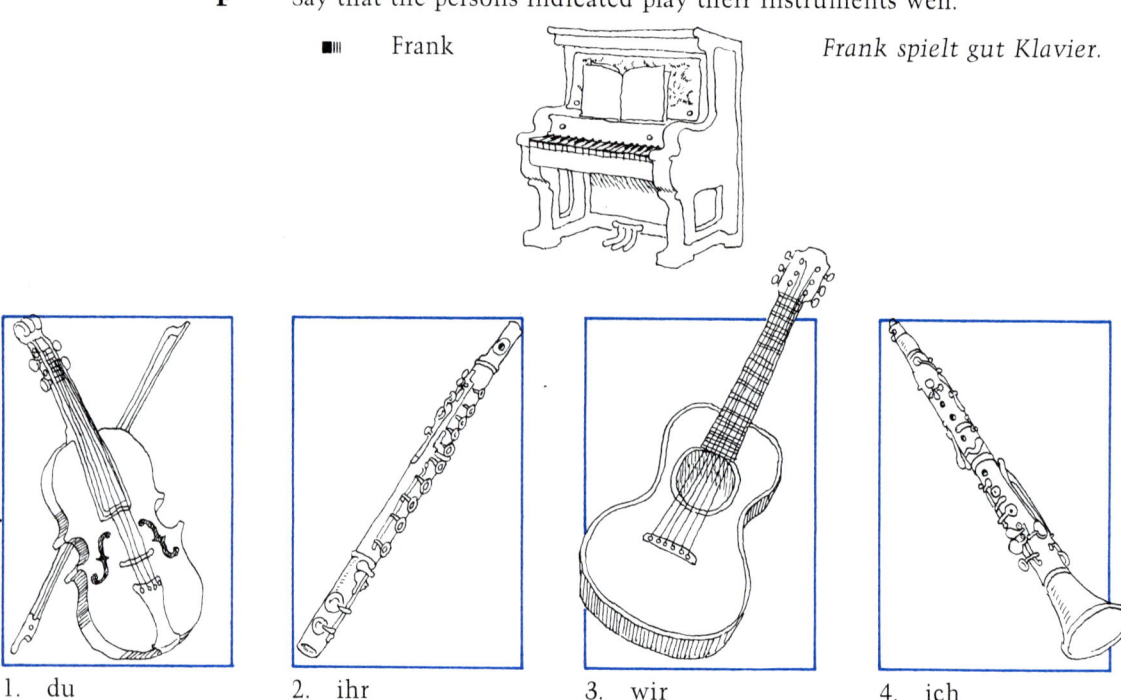

1. du   2. ihr   3. wir   4. ich

Present tense to express future time

Ich mache heute abend Hausaufgaben.
I'm going to do homework tonight.

Spielst du heute nachmittag Tennis?
Are you playing tennis this afternoon?

German, like English, may use the present tense to express action intended or planned for the future. The time reference indicates whether a sentence refers to the present or the future.

G   The following people often engage in sports or outdoor activities. Ask whether they plan to do them this afternoon.

■ Paul spielt oft Fußball.   *Spielt er heute nachmittag?*

1. Gerd und Rita spielen oft Tennis.
2. Gustav und Lutz spielen oft Basketball.
3. Gabi spielt oft Volleyball.
4. Tanja und Birgit spielen oft Volleyball.
5. Kai wandert oft.
6. Ute und Christl schwimmen viel.

Using **gern** with verbs

Ich **spiele gern** Basketball.   I *like to play* basketball.
Ich **spiele nicht gern** Tennis.   I *don't like to play* tennis.

The most common way of saying in German that you like or dislike doing something is to use **gern** or **nicht gern** with the appropriate verb.

H   Sometimes the things you enjoy most are those you don't do very often. Say that you enjoy the activities asked about below.

■ Spielst du viel Tennis?   *Nein, aber ich spiele gern Tennis.*

1. Schwimmst du viel?
2. Spielst du viel Klavier?
3. Spielst du viel Gitarre?
4. Wanderst du viel?
5. Gehst du viel spazieren?

I   When Lutz asks whether various classmates are involved in certain sports and activities, respond in the negative.

■ Schwimmt Frank viel?   *Nein. Er schwimmt nicht gern.*

1. Spielt Wolf oft Tennis?
2. Spielen Luise und Gerda oft Volleyball?
3. Wandert Michael viel?
4. Geht Klaus viel spazieren?
5. Spielt Cornelia oft Geige?

Using **gern** with **haben**

Jens **hat** Kirstin **gern**.   Jens *likes* Kirstin.
Kirstin **hat** Jens **nicht gern**.   Kirstin *doesn't like* Jens.

To express fondness for someone, German uses **gern** with a form of **haben**. **Nicht gern** is used to express a dislike.

J Jochen and his friends are discussing which classmates they like. Form sentences with *haben* and *gern*, using the cues provided.

▪ wir / Martina   *Wir haben Martina gern.*

1. ich / Rolf
2. du / Ingrid / ?
3. Susanne / Rudi
4. ihr / Petra / ?
5. wir / Thomas

The phrases **zu Hause** and **nach Hause**

Gerd bleibt **zu Hause**.   Gerd is staying home.
Inge geht **nach Hause**.   Inge is going home.

When the verb expresses location, **zu Hause** is used.
When the verb expresses direction or movement, **nach Hause** is used.

K Complete the sentences with *zu Hause* or *nach Hause*, as appropriate.

▪ Ich gehe heute nachmittag ____.   *Ich gehe heute nachmittag nach Hause.*

▪ Ich bleibe heute abend ____.   *Ich bleibe heute abend zu Hause.*

1. Wir bleiben heute morgen ____.
2. Petra und Erik gehen ____.
3. Dieter ist ____.
4. Gehst du ____?
5. Meike spielt ____.
6. Wann geht ihr ____?
7. Wann bist du ____?

L Form sentences by supplying an appropriate verb.

bleiben   gehen   sein   spielen

▪ er / zu Hause   *Er ist zu Hause. / Er bleibt zu Hause.*

1. wir / zu Hause
2. wann / du / nach Hause / ?
3. Marta / zu Hause
4. ich / nach Hause
5. ihr / nach Hause / ?
6. wann / du / zu Hause / ?

Grammatische Übersicht

Present tense of regular verbs (A-F)

Infinitive and infinitive stem

INFINITIVE	=	STEM	+	ENDING
bleiben		bleib		en
gehen		geh		en

The basic form of a German verb is the infinitive. Most German infinitives end in **-en;** a few end in **-n.** In vocabularies and dictionaries, verbs are listed under the infinitive form. The infinitive stem is the infinitive minus the **-(e)n** ending.

Present-tense endings of regular verbs

INFINITIVE	SINGULAR			PLURAL		
spielen	ich	spiel	e	wir	spiel	en
	du	spiel	st	ihr	spiel	t
	er/sie	spiel	t	sie	spiel	en

German verb endings change, depending on what the subject of the verb is. The verb endings are added to the infinitive stem. In the present tense most verbs have four different endings: **-e, -st, -t, -en.**

Present-tense meanings

Detlev **spielt** gut.
Detlev *plays* well.
Detlev *is playing* well.

Spielt er gut?
Is he *playing* well?
Does he *play* well?

Notice that German uses one present-tense form to express ideas that require several different present-tense forms in English.

Kapitel 3   **47**

Present tense to express future time (G)

Spielt Jutta heute nachmittag?
Wann **gehst** du nach Hause?

Is Jutta *going to play* this afternoon?
When *are* you *going to go* home?

In German, as in English, the present tense may be used to express action intended or planned for the future. The time reference indicates whether a sentence refers to the present or the future.

Using **gern** with verbs (H-I)

Ich schwimme **gern**.
Ich spiele **nicht gern** Fußball.

I *like* to swim.
I *don't like* to play soccer.

The most common way of saying in German that you like doing something is to use **gern** with a verb. To say that you dislike doing something, use **nicht gern** with a verb.

Using **gern** with **haben** (J)

Jens **hat** Kirstin **gern**.
Sie **hat** aber Jens **nicht gern**.

Jens *likes* Kirstin.
But she *doesn't like* Jens.

One way of expressing fondness for someone in German is to use **gern** with a form of **haben**. One way of saying that you *don't* like someone is to use **nicht gern** with a form of **haben**.

The phrases **zu Hause** and **nach Hause** (K-L)

Erika ist **zu Hause**.
Beate geht **nach Hause**.

Erika is at *home*.
Beate is going *home*.

The phrases **zu Hause** and **nach Hause** both mean *home*, but they are used in somewhat different ways. **Zu Hause** is used to talk about being at home. **Nach Hause** is used to talk about going home.

Wo wohnst du? Above, left: A quiet, residential street in Berlin. Right: A country village in Switzerland. Below: A suburban development near Hannover.

Wiederholung

A Answer the questions based on the following dialogue.

> UTE Tag, Karsten! Was ist denn los? Bist du sauer?
> KARSTEN Ja, sehr. Gisela ist nicht zu Hause.
> UTE Wo ist sie denn?
> KARSTEN Sie spielt wieder Basketball, und ich mache Hausaufgaben.

1. Was macht Gisela?
2. Warum ist Karsten sauer?

B Ask a classmate the following arithmetic problems, beginning each question with *Wieviel ist* . . . .

1. $10 + 6 = ?$
2. $19 - 1 = ?$
3. $3 \times 4 = ?$
4. $15 - 2 = ?$
5. $2 \times 7 = ?$
6. $8 + 9 = ?$

C Begin each question with the appropriate interrogative.

1. ____ ist denn los?
2. ____ bist du so unglücklich?
3. ____ geht's?
4. ____ wohnst du?
5. ____ hast du Geburtstag?

D You and a friend are discussing your plans for the afternoon. Express the following dialogue in German.

> A Hi, [. . .]! What are you doing this afternoon?
> B I'm going to play soccer. You, too?
> A No, I'm going home.
> B But why?
> A I'm going to do homework.

E You are having a negative day. Answer everyone's questions in the negative, and then reinforce what you have to say by using an antonym in your second sentence.

▰ Bist du krank?   *Nein, ich bin nicht krank. Ich bin gesund.*

1. Schwimmt Peter gut?
2. Ist Peter alt?
3. Ist Inge faul?
4. Bist du unglücklich?
5. Seid ihr glücklich?

F A new student is trying to find out more about you. How would you answer her/his questions?

1. Wo wohnst du?
2. Wie alt bist du?
3. Wann hast du Geburtstag?
4. Schwimmst du gern?
5. Spielst du gern Basketball? Spielst du oft?
6. Spielst du Gitarre? Spielst du gut?
7. Was machst du heute abend?

Vokabeln

SUBSTANTIVE (NOUNS)

Der, das, and **die** all mean *the*. The use of these articles will be practiced in Chapter 5.

der Basketball   basketball
die Flöte   flute
das Fotoalbum   photo album
der Fußball   soccer
die Geige   violin
die Gitarre   guitar
die Hausaufgaben (*pl.*)   homework
der Kilometer   kilometer
die Klarinette   clarinet
das Klavier   piano
die Minute   minute
das Musikinstrument   musical instrument
das Schlagzeug   drums
die Straße   street
das Tennis   tennis
der Volleyball   volleyball

VERBEN

bleiben   to remain, to stay
gehen   to go
machen   to do, to make
schwimmen   to swim
spazieren   to walk, to stroll, to go for a walk
spielen   to play
wandern   to hike, to go hiking
wohnen   to live

ANDERE WÖRTER

aber   however, but
gern   gladly, with pleasure
heute   today
hier   here
in   in(to)
jetzt   now
oft   often
viel   much, many, a lot
von   from
weit   far (away)
wo   where
ziemlich   quite
zu   to, too

BESONDERE AUSDRÜCKE

heute nachmittag   this afternoon
heute morgen   this morning
heute abend   tonight; this evening
was sonst?   what else?
nach Hause   home (direction)
zu Hause   (at) home
in der Gartenstraße   on Garden Street
gern haben   to like, to be fond of

Kapitel 4
Ich und meine Familie

In the United States, family names, names of towns, and certain customs recall the many Germans who have immigrated to this country. In cities like New York and Detroit there are still many families who speak German at home. They shop in German stores and keep up with news through German radio programs and newspapers. Many German-speaking communities have clubs that foster social and cultural activities, such as choral singing and dramatics.

Der Brieffreund

Barbara lives in Wisconsin, a state with a large German-speaking population. She has just started corresponding with a pen pal in Germany.

Milwaukee, den 12. Dezember

Lieber Michael!

    Mein Name ist Barbara Braun. Ich bin fünfzehn Jahre alt. Ich bin Schülerin und lerne schon zwei Jahre Deutsch. Mein Hobby ist Musik. Ich spiele gern Klavier, aber nur klassische Musik.
    Mein Bruder heißt Bill. Er ist achtzehn Jahre alt. Er ist groß und schlank. Er spielt Gitarre und singt nicht schlecht. Er spielt oft Rock.
    Meine Schwester heißt Susan. Sie ist erst elf Jahre alt. Sie ist klein und dünn. Sie spielt sehr gut Geige. Oft ist sie doof. Sie ist aber noch ein Kind.
    Meine Mutter ist Apothekerin. Sie arbeitet von Montag bis Donnerstag. Am Freitag, Samstag und Sonntag ist sie zu Hause. Das ist natürlich schön. Sie ist sehr musikalisch. Sie spielt Klavier und Geige.
    Mein Vater ist Elektriker. Er arbeitet viel und kommt oft spät nach Hause. Abends hört er gern Musik, und er kocht (er kocht gern und gut!). Er spielt Klarinette. Am Wochenende machen wir oft Musik, meine Mutter, mein Vater, meine Schwester, mein Bruder und ich. Das macht viel Spaß.
    Was machst Du gern abends? Spielst Du Klavier oder Gitarre? Oder was? Hörst Du gern Musik? Wie findest Du klassische Musik? Treibst Du gern Sport? Tanzt Du gern? Hoffentlich schreibst Du bald.

Herzliche Grüße

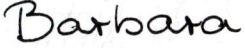

Du hast das Wort

A. Describe Barbara's family.

Wie heißt Barbaras Bruder? Wie alt ist er? Ist er klein oder groß? Ist er musikalisch?
Wie heißt Barbaras Schwester? Wie alt ist sie? Ist sie klein oder groß? Was spielt sie? Warum ist sie oft doof?
Was ist Barbaras Mutter? Von wann bis wann arbeitet sie? Wann ist sie zu Hause? Was spielt sie?
Was ist Barbaras Vater? Was macht er abends? Was spielt er?

B. Invent a family for Barbara's pen pal Michael. Describe the members as Michael would.

Meine Mutter heißt ... Sie ist ... Sie ...
Mein Vater ...
Mein Bruder [Thomas] ...
Meine Schwester [Claudia] ...

C. Ask a classmate for the names of family members (real or imaginary).

Wie heißt | dein Vater? | Er heißt . . .
| dein Bruder? | Er heißt . . .
| deine Mutter? | Sie heißt . . .
| deine Schwester? | Sie heißt . . .

D. A friend asks you what you're going to do this Saturday and Sunday. How would you respond?

Was machst du | am Samstag? | Ich mache meine Hausaufgaben.
| am Sonntag? | Ich spiele [Tennis].
| am Wochenende? | Ich spiele Karten°.
| | Ich schwimme.
| | Ich gehe tanzen.
| | Ich arbeite.

E. Have one of your classmates pretend to be Michael. Ask her/him the questions Barbara asked in her letter.

Was machst du abends?
Spielst du Klavier oder Gitarre?

At least half of the women (married and unmarried) in the Federal Republic work outside the home. In some households the man stays home to take care of the house and children. He cannot be known as the **Hausfrau,** so he is called the "**Hausmann.**"

Families often share leisure activities. When children are young, these activities include visits to friends and relatives, Sunday afternoon walks, outings to the country or to nearby cities and towns, and vacations. While teen-agers may choose not to go on the Sunday afternoon walks, they often participate in other kinds of family outings. They almost always join the family on vacation.

Wortschatzerweiterung

Berufe

Herr Schwarz ist **Geschäftsmann**.
Frau Schwarz ist **Geschäftsfrau**.

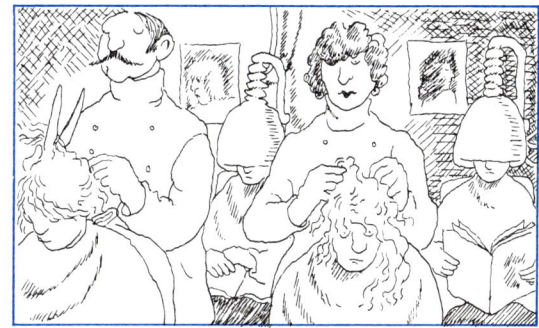

Herr Stein ist **Friseur**.
Fräulein Kneip ist **Friseuse**.

Herr Schmidt ist **Arbeiter**.
Frau Meier ist **Arbeiterin**.

Herr Weiß ist **Verkäufer**.
Fräulein Klein ist **Verkäuferin**.

Herr Wagner ist **Lehrer**.
Frau Wagner ist **Lehrerin**.

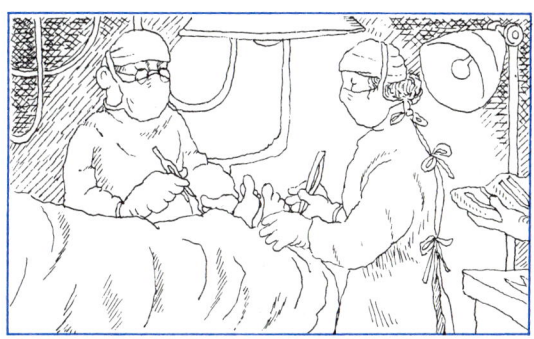

Herr Müller ist **Arzt**.
Frau Müller ist **Ärztin**.

In German there are usually different forms of a noun to indicate a man and a woman in the same profession. Often, the feminine equivalent simply adds **-in** to the masculine form. Occasionally, an umlaut must also be added to the feminine form.

A Complete the sentences to say what the following people's parents do for a living.

■ Ritas Mutter ist Friseuse; Franks Vater ist ____. *Friseur*

1. Utes Mutter ist Lehrerin; Jans Vater ist ____.
2. Peters Mutter ist Arbeiterin; Trudis Vater ist ____.
3. Ottos Vater ist Arzt; Elkes Mutter ist ____.
4. Georgs Mutter ist Geschäftsfrau; Ursels Vater ist ____.
5. Ritas Vater ist Apotheker; Gerds Mutter ist ____.
6. Sabines Mutter ist Verkäuferin; Werners Vater ist ____.
7. Franks Vater ist Friseur; Sylvias Mutter ist ____.

Zahlen: 20–1.000

20	zwanzig	50	fünfzig	80	achtzig	200	zweihundert
30	dreißig	60	sechzig	90	neunzig	500	fünfhundert
40	vierzig	70	siebzig	100	hundert	1.000	tausend

Dreißig ends in **-ßig** instead of **-zig**.
Sechzig loses the final **-s** of **sechs**.
Siebzig loses the final **-en** of **sieben**.
Hundert und **tausend** are generally used instead of **einhundert** und **eintausend**.

B You're at an auction. Each time a bid is made you raise it by 10.

■ 40 (vierzig)   (50) *fünfzig*

1. 90   3. 70   5. 60
2. 30   4. 20   6. 80

21	einundzwanzig	79	neunundsiebzig
22	zweiundzwanzig	101	hunderteins
34	vierunddreißig	121	hunderteinundzwanzig
57	siebenundfünfzig	265	zweihundertfünfundsechzig

The German numbers within the twenties, thirties, and so on, follow the number pattern used in the English nursery rhyme "four-and-twenty blackbirds."

In compound numbers with **eins**, the **-s** of **eins** is dropped:

eins > **einundzwanzig**

C Your friends are trying to guess the numbers you're thinking of. Each time their guess is one short. Correct them.

▪ 24 (vierundzwanzig)? *Nein, fünfundzwanzig.*

1. 75?
2. 98?
3. 37?
4. 68?
5. 120?
6. 782?
7. 998?
8. 1.206?
9. 1.300?

Zentimetermaß

1 Meter (1 m) = 39,37 in.
1 Zentimeter (1 cm) = 0,39 in.
2,54 Zentimeter (2,54 cm) = 1,0 in.

In German, a comma is used to write decimals.

Wie groß bist du? 1,62 m | Ein Meter zweiundsechzig.
Eins zweiundsechzig.

There are several ways to express height in German.

m/cm	ft/in.
1,95	6'5"
1,90	6'3"
1,85	6'1"
1,80	5'11"
1,75	5'9"
1,70	5'7"
1,65	5'5"
1,60	5'3"
1,55	5'1"
1,50	4'11"
1,45	4'9"
1,40	4'7"
1,35	4'5"
1,30	4'3"

D Ask a classmate how tall he/she is.

▪ Wie groß bist du? [*Ein Meter fünfundvierzig.*]

E Ask a classmate how tall various friends and relatives are.

▪ Wie groß ist dein Vater? dein Freund? deine Freundin? dein Bruder? deine Schwester?

Kapitel 4

Aussprache

long vowel [ø] schön, Flöte
short vowel [œ] zwölf, Wörter

A Practice vertically in columns and horizontally in pairs.

[ø]	[œ]
Höhle	Hölle
Öfen	öffnen
fröhlich	Frösche
König	können
lösen	löschen

B Practice the following words horizontally in pairs.

[e]	[ø]	[ɛ]	[œ]
lesen	lösen	kennte	könnte
hehlen	Höhlen	helle	Hölle
bete	böte	stecke	Stöcke
flehe	Flöhe	fällig	völlig

C Practice the sounds [ø] and [œ]. Read the sentences aloud.

1. Jörg hört gern klassische Musik.
2. Petra spielt schön Flöte.
3. Sie wohnt in der Goethestraße.

Viele Köche verderben den Brei.

Übungen

Verbs with stem ending in -d or -t

finden	
ich finde	wir finden
du findest	ihr findet
er/sie findet	sie finden

arbeiten	
ich arbeite	wir arbeiten
du arbeitest	ihr arbeitet
er/sie arbeitet	sie arbeiten

Verbs with stem ending in **-d** or **-t** have an **-e** before the **-st** and **-t** endings in the present tense.

A Inform Gabi that all of the people she mentions work in the evenings.

◼ Was macht Inge abends?   *Sie arbeitet.*

1. Was macht Herr Klein abends?
2. Was machst du abends?
3. Was machen Hans und Volker abends?
4. Was macht Frau Kluge abends?
5. Was macht ihr abends?

B Hans-Jürgen asks what you and others think of rock music. Say that everyone finds it great.

◼ Wie findet Claudia Rockmusik?   *Sie findet Rockmusik schön.*

1. Und Dieter?
2. Frau Lenz?
3. Und du?
4. Margit?
5. Ihr?

Verbs with stem ending in a sibilant

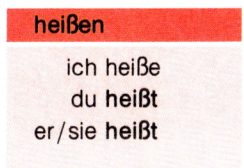
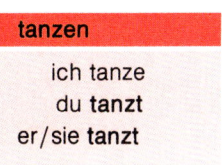

heißen
ich heiße
du heißt
er/sie heißt

tanzen
ich tanze
du tanzt
er/sie tanzt

The **-st** of the **du**-form ending contracts to **-t** when the verb stem ends in any sibilant (**-s, -ss, -ß, -z,** or **-tz**).

C Ask whether each of the following persons likes to dance.

▪III Petras Bruder   *Tanzt Petras Bruder gern?*

1. Inges Schwester
2. Dieters Bruder
3. du
4. ihr
5. Ritas Schwester

Position of the verb in statements

1	2	3	4
Wir	arbeiten	abends	nicht.
Abends	arbeiten	wir	nicht.
Heute abend	arbeiten	wir	nicht.

In a German statement, the verb is always in second position, even when an element other than the subject is in the first position. When words other than the subject begin a sentence, the subject follows the verb.

D Günther asks you what your interests are. Say that of course you do each of the things he asks about.

▪III Spielst du Klavier?   *Natürlich spiele ich Klavier!*

1. Spielst du Tennis?
2. Hörst du gern Musik?
3. Arbeitest du viel?
4. Tanzt du gut?
5. Gehst du oft spazieren?
6. Kochst du gern?

E Say that you don't do any of the following things. Begin each sentence with *Nein* and the emphasized word or phrase.

▪III Gehst du *abends* spazieren?   *Nein, abends gehe ich nicht spazieren.*

1. Arbeitest du *heute abend*?
2. Arbeitest du *am Samstag*?
3. Spielst du *Tennis*?
4. Singst du *gut*?
5. Bist du *musikalisch*?
6. Spielst du *klassische Musik*?

Original Mozart manuscript

Possession with proper names

Ist das **Inges** Gitarre?   Is that *Inge's* guitar?
Wie alt ist **Utes** Bruder?   How old is *Ute's* brother?

In German, an **-s** is usually added to a proper name to show possession or other close relationship.

Ist das **Thomas'** Mutter?   Is that *Thomas's* mother?

If the name already ends in an **s**-sound, no **-s** is added. In written German, an apostrophe is used after a name ending in an **s**-sound.

F   The students mentioned below each have a brother who plays the same instrument. Point that out to a friend.

■   Gerda spielt Klavier.   *Gerdas Bruder spielt auch Klavier.*

1. Bernd spielt Geige.
2. Petra spielt Klarinette.
3. Hans spielt Gitarre.
4. Thomas spielt Schlagzeug.
5. Inge spielt Flöte.
6. Karin spielt Klavier.

Possessive adjectives

mein/dein

Mein Vater arbeitet viel.   **Dein** Vater auch?
Meine Mutter arbeitet viel.   **Deine** Mutter auch?

The possessive adjectives **mein** and **dein** are equivalent to *my* and *your* (sg.). Possessive adjectives end in **-e** when they modify nouns referring to females.

G   Gisela tells you about the activities in which various friends and relatives participate. Ask to make sure you heard the right person.

■   Mein Freund schwimmt gern.   *Wer? Dein Freund?*

1. Meine Freundin schwimmt gut.
2. Mein Vater wandert gern.
3. Mein Bruder spielt Fußball.
4. Meine Schwester spielt Basketball.
5. Meine Mutter spielt Tennis.
6. Mein Freund spielt Volleyball.

H Ute asks you questions about various people. Check to make sure you know which person she's asking about, and then confirm her judgment.

▪ Ist deine Mutter jung?   *Meine Mutter? Ja, sehr.*

1. Ist dein Vater jung?
2. Ist dein Bruder faul?
3. Ist deine Schwester fleißig?
4. Ist dein Freund Hans-Dieter groß?
5. Ist deine Freundin Inge glücklich?

sein / ihr

Seine Mutter ist Apothekerin.   *His* mother is a druggist.
Ihr Vater ist Geschäftsmann.   *Her* father is a businessman.

I At a school event Ilse is trying to identify a number of spectators. Confirm Ilse's identifications.

▪ Das ist Jochens Mutter, nicht?   *Ja, das ist seine Mutter.*

1. Das ist Volkers Vater, nicht?
2. Das ist Utes Schwester, nicht?
3. Das ist Giselas Bruder, nicht?
4. Das ist Walters Freund, nicht?
5. Das ist Heidis Freundin, nicht?

J Rolf asks about the occupation of a number of acquaintances. Say that his guesses are wrong.

▪ Ist Martas Mutter Lehrerin?   *Ihre Mutter Lehrerin? Nein.*

▪ Ist Martas Vater Lehrer?   *Ihr Vater Lehrer? Nein.*

1. Ist Ritas Freund Verkäufer?
2. Ist Ritas Freundin Geschäftsfrau?
3. Ist Rudis Mutter Ärztin?
4. Ist Rudis Vater Arzt?
5. Ist Franks Bruder Apotheker?

unser / euer

Unser Arzt ist gut.   *Our doctor is good.*
Unsere Ärztin ist gut.

Ist **euer** Arzt auch gut?   *Is your doctor good, too?*
Ist **eure** Ärztin auch gut?

When **euer** has an ending, the **-e** before the **-r** is usually omitted.

K You've just moved to a new town, and your relatives are curious about the professional people you've found there. Answer that they're good.

▪ Wie ist eure Ärztin?   *Unsere Ärztin ist gut.*

1. Wie ist euer Apotheker?
2. Wie ist euer Lehrer?
3. Wie ist eure Friseuse?
4. Wie ist euer Elektriker?

L You are talking to a pair of twins. Inquire why their friends and relatives feel or act as they do.

▪ Bruder / müde   *Warum ist euer Bruder so müde?*

1. Schwester / faul
2. Vater / sauer
3. Mutter / glücklich
4. Freund / doof
5. Freundin / unglücklich

ihr (singular) and ihr (plural)

Hier ist **Gerda.** Und das ist **ihre** Mutter.
Here's *Gerda.* And that's *her* mother.

Hier sind **Trudi and Jens.** Und das ist **ihre** Mutter.
Here are *Trudi and Jens.* And that's *their* mother.

Ihr can mean *their* as well as *her*. Context usually makes the meaning clear.

M You and Heike are at a band concert. Heike asks about the identity of a number of people in the audience. Say that she has guessed correctly.

▪ Ist das Elkes Schwester?   *Ja, das ist ihre Schwester.*

1. Ist das Juttas Bruder?
2. Ist das Ottos und Pauls Lehrer?
3. Ist das Helgas und Eriks Lehrerin?
4. Ist das Evas Vater?
5. Ist das Günters und Tanjas Mutter?

N Gerd asks you a number of questions about your friends and relatives. Answer him in the negative.

▪ Tanzt Gerdas Bruder gut?   *Ihr Bruder? Nein.*

1. Spielt Tanjas Schwester Tennis?
2. Kocht dein Bruder gut?
3. Spielt deine Schwester Geige?
4. Ist Stefans Vater Arzt?
5. Ist Volkers Mutter Geschäftsfrau?
6. Ist euer Arzt jung?
7. Ist eure Lehrerin alt?

Du hast das Wort — Describe some friends and members of your family by answering the following questions.

Ist deine Mutter jung oder alt?
Ist dein Vater jung oder alt?
Ist dein Bruder [Volker] prima oder doof?
Ist deine Schwester [Erika] faul oder fleißig?
Ist dein Freund [Hannes] groß oder klein? Und deine Freundin [Barbara]?
Ist deine Freundin [Cordula] glücklich oder unglücklich? Und dein Freund [Alex]?
Ist deine Freundin [Petra] oft sauer? Und dein Freund [Hans-Dieter]?
Ist dein Freund [Stefan] faul oder fleißig? Und deine Freundin [Angelika]?

Grammatische Übersicht

Verbs with stem ending in **-d** or **-t** (A–B)

finden	
ich finde	wir finden
du **findest**	ihr **findet**
er/sie **findet**	sie finden

arbeiten	
ich arbeite	wir arbeiten
du **arbeitest**	ihr **arbeitet**
er/sie **arbeitet**	sie arbeiten

Verbs with stem ending in **-d** or **-t** require an **-e** before the present-tense endings **-st** or **-t**.

Verbs with stem ending in a sibilant (C)

heißen	
ich heiße	wir heißen
du **heißt**	ihr heißt
er/sie **heißt**	sie heißen

tanzen	
ich tanze	wir tanzen
du **tanzt**	ihr tanzt
er/sie **tanzt**	sie tanzen

The sounds represented by the letters **s, ss, ß, z,** and **tz** are called sibilants. When a verb stem ends in a sibilant, the **-st** of the **du-**form ending contrasts to **-t**, making the **du-** and **er/sie-**forms identical.

Position of the verb in statements (D-E)

1	2	3	4
Brigitte	arbeitet	am Samstag	zu Hause.
Am Samstag	arbeitet	Brigitte	zu Hause.

In a German statement, the verb is always in second position, even when an element other than the subject (for example, an adverb or a prepositional phrase) is in first position. When a word or phrase other than the subject begins the sentence, the subject follows the verb.

Possession with proper names (F)

Das ist **Bettinas** Gitarre.   That's *Bettina's* guitar.
Wie alt ist **Peters** Schwester?   How old is *Peter's* sister?

In German, as in English, possession and other close relationships are expressed by adding **-s** to proper names. In written German, no apostrophe is used before the **-s.**

Ist das **Hans'** Vater?   Is that *Hans's* father?
Wie alt ist **Franz'** Bruder?   How old is *Franz's* brother?

Unlike English, German does not add an **-s** if a name already ends in an **s-**sound. In written German, an apostrophe is used after a name ending in an **s-**sound.

Possessive adjectives (G-N)

SUBJECT PRONOUN	POSSESSIVE ADJECTIVE	
ich	mein/meine	my
du	dein/deine	your
er	sein/seine	his
sie	ihr/ihre	her
wir	unser/unsere	our
ihr	euer/eure	your
sie	ihr/ihre	their

Mein Bruder arbeitet viel.
Meine Schwester arbeitet auch viel.

Possessive adjectives add no special ending when they modify nouns referring to males. They end in **-e** when they modify nouns referring to females.

Hier ist **Rita.** Und das ist **ihr** Vater.
Here's *Rita.* And that's *her* father.

Hier sind **Inge und Jens.** Und das ist **ihr** Vater.
Here are *Inge and Jens.* And that's *their* father.

Context usually makes clear whether **ihr(e)** means *her* or *their*.

Wie alt ist **euer** Vater?
Wie alt ist **eure** Mutter?

When **euer** has an ending, the **-e** before the **-r** is usually omitted: **euere>eure.**

Capitalization of du and dein / ihr and euer in letters

Lieber Michael!

... Was machst **Du** am Samstag? Was macht **Dein** Bruder Jens?
Geht **Ihr** tanzen? ... Hoffentlich schreibst **Du** bald ...

In letters or notes the German equivalents for *you* and *your* are capitalized: **Du, Dein(e), Ihr(e),** and **Euer(e).**

Wiederholung

A Identify the occupations shown in the drawings. Use the German name for each occupation in a brief sentence.

Meine Mutter ist Ärztin.
Ist deine Freundin Ärztin?

1.

2.

3.

4.

B You're showing some snapshots of people to Kurt, who tries to identify them. Confirm or deny his guesses, as in the model.

■ Das ist Gerdas Vater, nicht?   *Ja, das ist ihr Vater.*
Nein, das ist nicht ihr Vater.

1. Das ist Brunos Schwester, nicht?
2. Das ist Petras Bruder, nicht?
3. Das ist Andreas' Mutter, nicht?
4. Das ist Lottes Freund, nicht?
5. Das ist deine Freundin Katja, nicht?
6. Das ist dein Freund Stefan, nicht?
7. Das ist Kurts Vater, nicht?
8. Das ist euer Lehrer, nicht?
9. Das ist Jans and Ellens Mutter, nicht?

C Choose the phrase that best completes each statement based on the following paragraph.

Meine Schwester Inge hat am Samstag Geburtstag. Am Samstag abend kommen ihr Freund Hans und seine Schwester Gabi. Hans ist Verkäufer, und Gabi ist Friseuse. Sie sind beide sehr musikalisch. Gabi spielt gut Klavier. Hans spielt sehr gut Schlagzeug. Inge spielt nicht schlecht Gitarre. Ich spiele Klarinette — nicht gut, nur gern. Hoffentlich spielen wir am Samstag. Das macht wirklich Spaß.

1. Am Samstag ...
   a. arbeitet Inge.
   b. kommen Inges Freund und seine Schwester.
   c. geht Inge nach Hause.
2. Gabi ...
   a. spielt nicht gern Klavier.
   b. spielt Klavier, und Hans spielt Schlagzeug.
   c. ist die Freundin von Hans.
3. Inges Bruder ...
   a. spielt auch Schlagzeug.
   b. spielt gern Klarinette.
   c. spielt gut Klarinette.

D Use a centimeter ruler to measure the following things. Give your measurements in German.

1. the length of your pencil (pen)
2. the width of this book
3. the length of your thumb
4. the length of a blackboard eraser
5. the width of your hand

Use a meterstick to measure larger items.

6. the circumference of your desk
7. the width of a blackboard
8. the length of the classroom
9. the length of a yardstick

E Form questions, using the cues provided.

▄▄▄ warum / du / arbeiten / nicht / ?   *Warum arbeitest du nicht?*

1. dein Vater / arbeiten / abends / ?
2. du / tanzen / gern / ?
3. wie / deine Schwester / heißen / ?
4. wann / wir / gehen / nach Hause / ?
5. wann / Rita / arbeiten / ?

F Say in German that . . .

1. your friend likes to play tennis
2. in the evening, you play cards
3. that's fun
4. Peter's brother is home
5. he plays the piano well

Vokabeln

SUBSTANTIVE

der Apotheker/die Apothekerin pharmacist
der Arbeiter/die Arbeiterin worker
der Arzt/die Ärztin doctor, physician
der Brief letter
der Brieffreund/die Brieffreundin pen pal
der Bruder brother
das Deutsch German language
der Donnerstag Thursday
der Elektriker/die Elektrikerin electrician
die Familie family
(die) Frau Mrs.
(das) Fräulein Miss
der Freitag Friday
der Freund/die Freundin friend
der Friseur/die Friseuse hairdresser
der Geschäftsmann/die Geschäftsfrau businessman/businesswoman
(der) Herr Mr.
das Hobby hobby
das Jahr year

SUBSTANTIVE

die Karten (*pl.*) (playing) cards
das Kind child
der Lehrer/die Lehrerin teacher
der Meter meter
der Montag Monday
die Musik music
die Mutter mother
der Name name
(der) Rock rock (music)
der Samstag Saturday
der Schüler/die Schülerin student
die Schwester sister
der Sonntag Sunday
der Vater father
der Verkäufer/die Verkäuferin salesperson
das Wochenende weekend
der Zentimeter centimeter

(Continued)

VERBEN

arbeiten　to work
finden　to find
hören　to hear
kochen　to cook
kommen　to come
lernen　to learn, to study
schreiben　to write
singen　to sing
tanzen　to dance

ANDERE WÖRTER

abends　evenings, in the evening
bald　soon
bis　till, until
dein　your *(sg.)*
doof　goofy, dumb, stupid
dünn　thin
euer　your *(pl.)*
groß　tall, big
hoffentlich　I hope, let's hope
ihr　her, their
klassisch　classical
klein　small, short, little
lieber/liebe　dear *(opening in letters)*
mein　my
musikalisch　musical
noch　still, yet
schlank　slender, slim
schön　nice
sein　his
spät　late; **zu spät**　too late, tardy
unser　our

BESONDERE AUSDRÜCKE

ich lerne schon zwei Jahre Deutsch　I've been studying German for two years
ich bin fünfzehn Jahre alt　I'm fifteen years old
sie ist aber noch ein Kind　she's still a child
wie groß bist du?　how tall are you?
treibst du Sport?　are you active in sports?
das macht Spaß!　that's fun!
herzliche Grüße　best wishes, kind regards, sincerely *(closing in letters)*
am Samstag　on Saturday

noch einmal

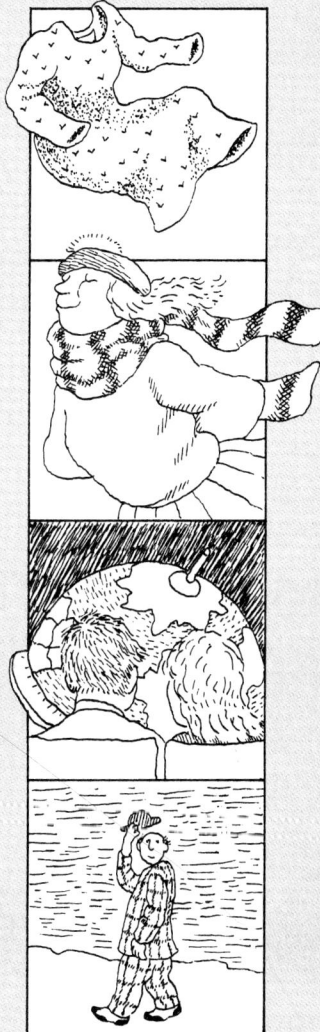

A **Wer bin ich?** Prepare a short autobiography. It may include information about your age, birthday, appearance, address, family members, parents' occupation, work habits, hobbies. The autobiographies are divided between two panels of five members each. First one team of panel members takes turns reading the information provided in the autobiographies, while the other team tries to identify the writer. The panels then switch roles. The team that guesses the most students wins. The quiz continues with new panels until all students have participated.

B **Deutsche Teenager.** Look at the pictures of the young people in the photographs on pages 1–7 and describe two or three of them in German as completely as you can (name, age, height, personality, hobbies, family); or, select several of the teen-agers you have met in the dialogues of chapters 1–4 and discuss them, based on the dialogue material. In either case, you may wish to invent some additional information.

C **Deutsche in der Welt.** Gather information on the German influence in the United States. Look through a telephone directory and list 25 names of people who might be of German origin. From a state map, see how many names of towns indicate they may have been settled by Germans. Collect magazine pictures that pertain to German-speaking people around the world. Report your findings.

D **Guten Tag!** With a partner, prepare a skit in which you introduce yourself to a teen-ager from a German-speaking country who is visiting your school and who speaks no English. You will probably want to say hello, introduce yourself, and tell about your interests and activities. Don't forget to ask your guest for information as well.

So leben wir

2

Arbeit . . . Traditional arts and crafts are still practiced in many parts of Germany — hand-woven baskets are for sale in Rothenburg, and violins are handmade in Mittenwald, for example — but modern, large-scale industry is also very much part of German life today. Hamburg's massive harbor helps tie Germany to the rest of the world.

. . . und Freizeit. Whether it's camping on Lake Constance, boating in a park in Cologne, playing chess in Bern, or going to an amusement park like this one in Munich, German-speaking people have a great variety of leisure-time activities.

Land und Stadt. Much European land has long been under cultivation, but in the cities, modern apartment complexes blend with older buildings while flowers add a touch of country color.

Kapitel 5
Brauchst du neue Sachen?

Das ist zu teuer

Astrid, Gisela, and Erik are window-shopping, looking at clothes.

ASTRID	Wie teuer ist das Kleid da?
GISELA	20 Mark, und das ist zu teuer.
ASTRID	Wie meinst du das?
GISELA	Ich finde, es ist häßlich.
ERIK	Die Jeans da sind wirklich klasse.
ASTRID	Meinst du? Wieviel kosten sie?
ERIK	50 Mark.
ASTRID	50 Mark! Das ist aber preiswert. Kaufst du sie?
ERIK	Ja.

Fragen

1. Ist das Kleid teuer?
2. Ist es schön?
3. Wie sind die Jeans?
4. Wieviel kosten sie? Ist das teuer?

Toll! Für Mädchen und Jungen!

1. das Hemd DM 19,–
2. die Jacke DM 68,–
3. die Hose DM 28,–
4. die Socken DM 5,–
5. die Bluse DM 25,–
6. der Gürtel DM 15,–
7. die Jeans DM 70,–

Schick! Für Damen und Herren!

1. der Pulli
   DM 47,–
2. der Rock
   DM 45,–
3. die Schuhe
   DM 65,–
4. der Anzug
   DM 150,–
5. die Krawatte
   DM 12,–
6. der Mantel
   DM 200,–
7. die Handschuhe
   DM 24,–

Fragen

1. Wieviel kostet das Hemd? die Jacke? der Rock?
2. Wieviel kosten die Jeans? die Schuhe? die Socken?

Du hast das Wort

A. What is your reaction to the price of each item of clothing mentioned below?

Das Hemd kostet DM 30,–.   Das ist furchtbar° teuer.
Die Krawatte kostet DM 7,–.   Das ist (sehr) teuer.
Der Mantel kostet DM 500,–.   Das ist preiswert.
Die Handschuhe kosten DM 4,–.   Das ist billig°.
Die Jacke kostet DM 99,–.   Das ist spottbillig°.
Die Bluse kostet DM 23,–.
Das Kleid kostet DM 80,–.
Der Gürtel kostet DM 15,–.
Die Hose kostet DM 30,–.
Der Anzug kostet DM 350,–.

B. A friend asks you to react to some of the clothes pictured on pages 81–82. How would you respond?

Wie ist	die Jacke?	Toll!
	der Rock?	Klasse!
	das Hemd?	(Sehr) schön.
		(Sehr) hübsch°.
		Nicht schlecht.
		Häßlich.
		Doof.

German fashion magazines are filled with terms that an American would recognize. Many German young people seem to be fascinated by things American or British, and as a result quite a bit of English has crept into the fashion language, especially in advertisements.

Sometimes English is used to describe various pieces of clothing, such as **T-Shirt, Blazer, Sweatshirt,** or **Jeans.** Jeans in particular seem to be under the influence of the American West, with labels such as **Pioneer, Bronco, Mustang,** or **Explorer.**

Styles or trends also often bear English names. A woman can buy **Make-up im College-Look** to go with her new **Overalls.** A man who doesn't go in for the leisurely **Sportswear-Look** can buy a **Cord-Anzug** or a **Tweed-Anzug.** A couple might want to buy coordinated outfits — they can be found in the catalogue under the heading **Er und sie im Partner-Look.** And to finish off their wardrobe, the fashion-conscious people can buy **Schuhe-Creationen mit viel Pep!**

Kapitel 5

KONFEKTIONSGRÖSSEN: EUROPA/USA													
Kleidung für Damen							**Kleidung für Herren**						
Blusen, Röcke, Kleider, Mäntel, Hosen							*Anzüge, Jacken, Mäntel, Hosen*						
Europa	32	34	36	38	40	42	Europa	40	42	44	46	48	50
USA	4	6	8	10	12	14	USA	30	32	34	36	38	40
Pullis							*Hemden*						
Europa	38	40	42	44	46	48	Europa	35	36	37	38	39	40
USA	30	32	34	36	38	40	USA	13½	14	14½	15	15½	16
Schuhe							*Schuhe*						
Europa	36	37	38	39	40	41	Europa	38	39	40	41	42	43
USA	5	6	7	8	9	10	USA	5	6½	7½	8½	9	10

Welche Größe trägst du?

Astrid is helping Erik look for a new coat.

ASTRID Hier ist ein Mantel in Braun. Schön, nicht?
ERIK   Ja, toll. Er ist auch schön warm.
ASTRID Paßt er?
ERIK   Leider nicht. Er ist zu groß.
ASTRID Welche Größe trägst du denn?
ERIK   Größe 40.
ASTRID Hier ist deine Größe.
ERIK   Das ist aber kein Mantel. Das ist eine Jacke.
ASTRID Ach ja. Schade.

Du hast das Wort

A. Name an article of clothing you'd like to buy for a friend or relative. Give the size you need according to the chart.

   Jacke   Er/sie trägt Größe . . .

B. Take the role of a salesperson trying to help a customer in a clothing store.

   Paßt [der Mantel]?   Ja.
                                  Ja, [er] paßt sehr gut.
                                  Nein, [er] ist zu groß.
                                  Nein, [er] ist zu klein°.
                                  Nein, ich brauche Größe [40].

Wortschatzerweiterung

Die Farben

Can you guess these colors? The cognates in the following sentences should help you.

blau	Die See ist blau.
braun	Die Schokolade ist braun.
gelb	Die Banane ist gelb.
grau	Die Maus ist grau.
grün	Das Gras ist grün.
rot	Die Tomate ist rot.
schwarz	Die Kohle ist schwarz.
weiß	Das Papier ist weiß.

A Ask a classmate about the color of the clothes he/she is wearing.

Welche Farbe hat dein Pulli? *Mein Pulli ist [rot].*
dein Hemd?
dein Gürtel?
dein Kleid?
deine Jacke?
deine Bluse?
deine Hose?

Aussprache

| long vowel [u] | g**u**t, Bl**u**se, Sch**uh** |
| short vowel [U] | **u**nd, P**u**lli |

A Practice vertically in columns and horizontally in pairs.

[u]	[U]
B**u**ße	B**u**sse
B**u**ch	B**u**cht
H**uh**ne	H**u**nne
B**uh**le	B**u**lle
M**u**s	m**u**ß

B Practice the following words horizontally in pairs.

[u]	[y]	[U]	[Y]
F**u**ße	F**ü**ße	m**u**ßte	m**ü**ßte
H**u**te	H**ü**te	B**u**sche	B**ü**sche
Z**u**ge	Z**ü**ge	j**u**nger	j**ü**nger
F**u**hre	f**ü**hre	kr**u**mmen	kr**ü**mmen
g**u**te	G**ü**te	d**u**nkel	D**ü**nkel

C Practice the sounds [u] and [U]. Read the sentences aloud.

1. Wieviel kosten die Bluse und der Pulli?
2. Warum trägt Utes Bruder keine Schuhe?
3. Der Junge spielt gut Fußball.

Ende gut, alles gut.

Übungen

Verbs with stem-vowel change a>ä

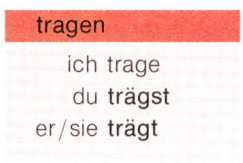

tragen
 ich trage
 du trägst
 er/sie trägt

Tragen has a stem-vowel change **a>ä** in the **du-** and **er/sie-**forms of the present tense.

A Find out what your friends are wearing to the party tonight.

■ Paula   Was trägt Paula heute abend?

1. Rita   3. Stefan   5. Birgit und Ute
2. Günter   4. du   6. ihr

The singular definite articles **der, das, die**

der Mann   **das** Mädchen   **die** Frau
der Gürtel **das** Kleid   **die** Bluse

The definite articles **der, das,** and **die** are used with nouns, and are equivalent to the English definite article *the*.

Kapitel 5   **87**

B Inquire about the price of each article of clothing.

> ▪ der Pulli *Wieviel kostet der Pulli?*

1. die Jacke
2. das Hemd
3. die Bluse
4. der Anzug
5. die Krawatte
6. der Gürtel

C Give your opinion of each of the following articles of clothing.

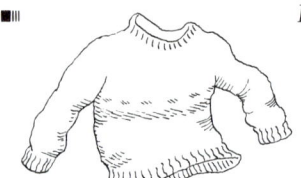

> ▪ *Der Pulli ist klasse [häßlich, schön, etc.]*

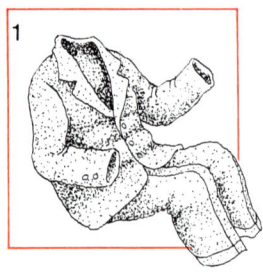

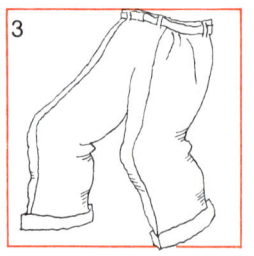
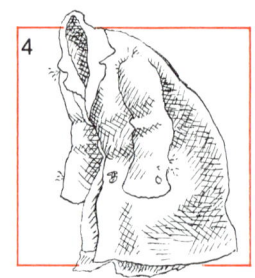
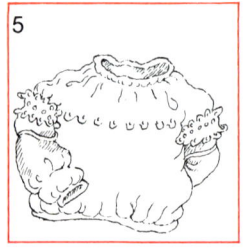
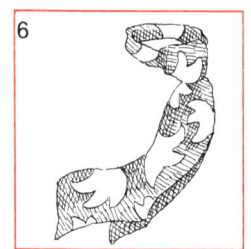
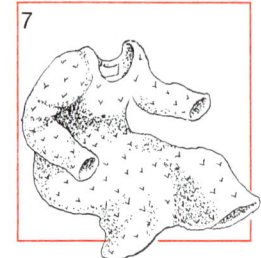
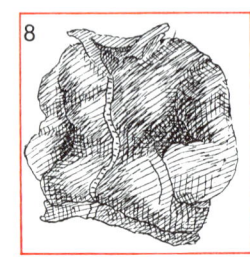

D You don't recognize a number of people at a school event. Ask a friend to identify them.

> ▪ die Frau da *Wie heißt die Frau da?*

1. die Lehrerin da
2. der Lehrer da
3. das Mädchen da
4. der Junge da
5. der Mann da
6. das Kind da

Noun plurals

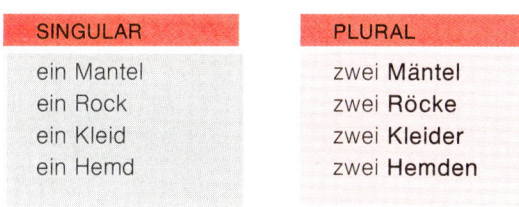

There is no simple way of predicting the plural form of a noun. German noun plurals are formed according to several basic patterns. The patterns are listed in the **Grammatische Übersicht** on pages 95–96.

E You and a friend are applying basic multiplication patterns to practical situations. Tell what the following purchases would cost.

> ■ Ein Kleid kostet 200 Mark.   *Zwei Kleider kosten 400*
> Was kosten zwei Kleider?   *Mark.*

1. Ein Mantel kostet 300 Mark. Was kosten zwei Mäntel?
2. Ein Gürtel kostet 20 Mark. Was kosten vier Gürtel?
3. Ein Hemd kostet 30 Mark. Was kosten drei Hemden?
4. Eine Jacke kostet 100 Mark. Was kosten zwei Jacken?
5. Eine Krawatte kostet 15 Mark. Was kosten drei Krawatten?
6. Ein Anzug kostet 250 Mark. Was kosten zwei Anzüge?

The plural definite article **die**

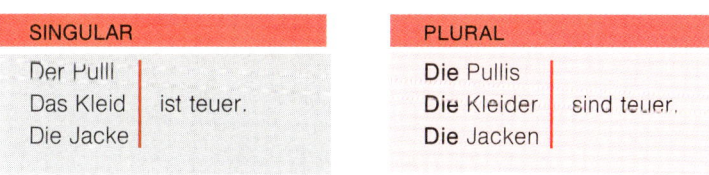

The definite article **die** is used with plural nouns.

F You're shopping in a department store with Mark. Tell him what you think about the following items.

> ■ Schuhe / klasse   *Die Schuhe sind klasse.*

1. Jeans / preiswert
2. Socken / schön warm
3. Hemden / häßlich
4. Pullis / toll
5. Gürtel / spottbillig

Noun-pronoun relationship

Singular

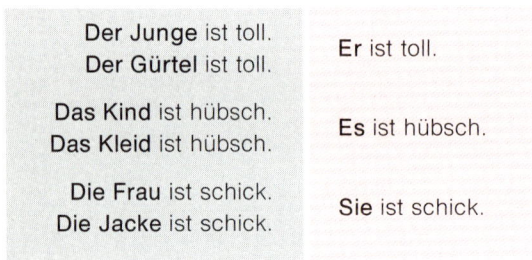

G Confirm Ute's guesses about the following articles of clothing.

▪ Ist der Pulli teuer? *Ja, er ist sehr teuer.*

1. Ist der Anzug billig?
2. Ist der Rock hübsch?
3. Ist der Mantel schick?
4. Ist der Gürtel preiswert?

H Say that the following people are good at certain sports.

▪ Spielt dein Bruder Fußball? *Ja, und er spielt auch gut.*

1. Spielt dein Vater Tennis?
2. Spielt dein Freund Dieter Basketball?
3. Spielt dein Lehrer Volleyball?
4. Spielt Erik Fußball?

I Tell Frank that each item is the opposite of what he thinks.

▪ Ist das Hemd alt? *Nein, es ist neu.*

1. Ist das Kleid billig?
2. Ist das Hemd schön?
3. Ist das Klavier gut?
4. Ist das Schlagzeug neu?

J Erna tells you which instruments various friends and relatives play. Ask whether they play well.

▪ Meine Lehrerin spielt Klavier. *Spielt sie gut?*

1. Meine Mutter spielt Geige.
2. Meine Freundin Birgit spielt Flöte.
3. Meine Schwester spielt Klarinette.
4. Ilse spielt Gitarre.

K   Agree with Manfred about the following articles of clothing.

       ▪   Die Bluse da ist schick, nicht?   *Ja, sie ist wirklich schick.*

1. Die Jacke da ist teuer, nicht?
2. Die Hose da ist spottbillig, nicht?
3. Die Krawatte da ist häßlich, nicht?
4. Die Hose da ist preiswert, nicht?

Plural

     Die Jeans sind klasse.   **Sie** sind wirklich toll.
     Die Hemden sind klasse.   Und **sie** sind billig.

L   You are at a flea market with Katrin. Say that you agree more or less with her opinions.

       ▪   Die Schuhe da sind teuer, nicht?   *Ja, sie sind ziemlich teuer.*

1. Die Handschuhe da sind preiswert, nicht?
2. Die Jeans da sind billig, nicht?
3. Die Hemden da sind gut, nicht?
4. Die Jacken da sind alt, nicht?

M   Thomas is pointing out various items in a clothing catalogue. Ask him whether they're reasonably priced.

       ▪   Der Mantel ist schön.   *Ist er preiswert?*

       ▪   Die Socken sind warm.   *Sind sie preiswert?*

1. Der Rock ist schick.   5. Der Gürtel ist schön.
2. Das Kleid ist klasse.   6. Die Schuhe sind schick.
3. Die Bluse ist hübsch.   7. Die Jeans sind klasse.
4. Das Hemd ist toll.   8. Die Handschuhe sind warm.

Nominative case of ein

Der Anzug kostet 900 Mark.	**Ein Anzug** kostet wirklich 900 Mark?
Das Hemd kostet 100 Mark.	**Ein Hemd** kostet wirklich 100 Mark?
Die Jacke kostet 300 Mark.	**Eine Jacke** kostet wirklich 300 Mark?
Die Schuhe kosten 250 Mark.	**Schuhe** kosten wirklich 250 Mark?

The indefinite articles **ein** and **eine** are equivalent to English *a* or *an*. **Ein** and **eine** have no plural form.

N You're trying to find out how much clothing costs in Germany. Ask your teacher about the price of the following things.

■ Anzug *Wieviel kostet ein Anzug?*

1. Pulli
2. Bluse
3. Kleid
4. Hemd
5. Jacke
6. Rock
7. Krawatte
8. Gürtel
9. Hose

O Some acquaintances brag about how much their clothes cost. You find the prices ridiculous. Say that the things *can't* be that expensive.

■ Meine Jacke kostet DM 200.   *Unsinn! Eine Jacke kostet nicht soviel!*

1. Meine Hose kostet DM 500.
2. Mein Hemd kostet DM 300.
3. Mein Mantel kostet DM 900.
4. Petras Bluse kostet DM 200.
5. Ellens Kleid kostet DM 800.
6. Hugos Jacke kostet DM 600.

Nominative case of kein

Ist das **ein Pulli?**	Nein, das ist **kein Pulli,** das ist ein Hemd.
Ist das **ein Hemd?**	Nein, das ist **kein Hemd,** das ist ein Pulli.
Ist das **eine Bluse?**	Nein, das ist **keine Bluse,** das ist eine Jacke.
Sind das **Blusen?**	Nein, das sind **keine Blusen,** das sind Hemden.

Kein and **keine** are equivalent to English *not a, not an, not any,* or *no*. **Kein** is used before **der-** and **das-**nouns. **Keine** is used before **die-**nouns and plural nouns.

P   Andreas is guessing the price of clothes in a catalogue. Disagree with his guesses.

■▮   Was kostet der Mantel? 2000 Mark?   *Nein, kein Mantel kostet 2000 Mark.*

1. Was kostet der Pulli? 400 Mark?
2. Was kostet die Jacke? 500 Mark?
3. Was kostet das Hemd? 100 Mark?
4. Was kostet die Bluse? 150 Mark?
5. Was kostet die Krawatte? 50 Mark?
6. Was kosten die Handschuhe? 70 Mark?
7. Was kosten die Socken? 40 Mark?
8. Was kosten die Jeans? 120 Mark?

Grammatische Übersicht

Verbs with stem-vowel change a > ä (A)

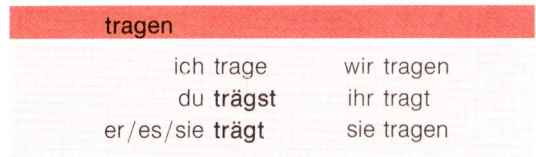

tragen	
ich trage	wir tragen
du **trägst**	ihr tragt
er/es/sie **trägt**	sie tragen

A number of German verbs have a stem-vowel change (for example **a > ä**) in the **du-** and **er/sie-**forms of the present tense. In the vocabularies of this text, the stem-vowel change of the **du-** and **er/sie-**forms is shown in parentheses directly after the infinitive: **tragen (ä)**.

Nominative case

Meine Schwester spielt Klavier.
Spielt **dein Freund** Klarinette?

German nouns show different cases depending on how they are used in a sentence. When a noun is used as the subject of a sentence, it is in the nominative case.

SUBJECT		PREDICATE NOMINATIVE
Das Mädchen	ist	meine Schwester.
Der Junge da	ist	der Bruder von Inge.

When a noun is used in the predicate after the verb **sein,** it is also in the nominative case.

The singular definite articles **der, das, die**   (B-D)

der Mann	**das** Mädchen	**die** Frau
der Gürtel	**das** Kleid	**die** Bluse

The singular definite articles **der, das,** and **die** function like the English definite article *the*. They are used with singular nouns in the nominative case.

There are three groups of nouns in German: **der**-nouns, **das**-nouns, and **die**-nouns. Most nouns referring to males are **der**-nouns; most nouns referring to females are **die**-nouns. (**Das Mädchen** is an exception.) Objects may belong to any group, for example **der Gürtel, das Kleid, die Bluse.** Since there is no simple way of predicting which group a noun belongs to, it is very important to learn the definite article when you learn the noun. Learn **der Gürtel,** not just **Gürtel.**

The plural definite article **die**   (F)

SINGULAR		PLURAL	
Der Rock		Die Röcke	
Das Hemd	ist klasse.	Die Hemden	sind klasse.
Die Bluse		Die Blusen	

The definite article used with plural nouns is **die.**

Noun plurals (E)

In German, noun plurals are formed according to five basic patterns. There is no simple way of predicting the plural form of a noun. You will, however, gradually discover that there is a kind of system to these patterns.

This "system" depends partly on whether the noun is a **der-, das-** or **die-**noun, and partly on how many syllables it has. From now on, learn the plural of the noun when you learn the singular form.

Pattern 1

no change in plural

    das Mädchen   **die Mädchen**
    der Gürtel   **die Gürtel**

plural adds umlaut

    der Vater   **die Väter**
    der Mantel   **die Mäntel**

Pattern 2

plural adds **-e**

    der Freund   **die Freunde**
    der Schuh   **die Schuhe**

plural adds **-e** *and umlaut*

    der Anzug   **die Anzüge**
    der Rock   **die Röcke**

Pattern 3

plural adds **-er**

    das Kind   **die Kinder**
    das Kleid   **die Kleider**

plural adds **-er** *and umlaut*

    der Mann   **die Männer**
    das Buch   **die Bücher**

Pattern 4

plural adds **-n**

der Junge	**die Jungen**
die Schwester	**die Schwestern**

plural adds **-en**

das Hemd	**die Hemden**

plural adds **-nen**

die Lehrerin	**die Lehrerinnen**
die Ärztin	**die Ärztinnen**

Pattern 5

plural adds **-s**

das Hobby	**die Hobbys**
der Pulli	**die Pullis**

In the vocabularies of this text, the plural of most nouns will be indicated directly after the singular. For example:

der Lehrer, – indicates that there is no change in the plural form of the noun: **der Lehrer > die Lehrer.**

der Rock, ⸚e indicates that an **-e** is added in the plural, and an umlaut is added to the appropriate vowel: **der Rock > die Röcke.**

Here are the plurals of some other familiar nouns.

der Apotheker, –	die Friseuse, –n
die Apothekerin, –nen	der Geschäftsmann, ⸚er
der Arbeiter, –	die Geschäftsfrau, –en
die Arbeiterin, –nen	das Jahr, –e
der Arzt, ⸚e	die Minute, –n
der Brief, –e	die Mutter, ⸚
der Bruder, ⸚	der Schüler, –
der Elektriker, –	die Schülerin, –nen
die Elektrikerin, –nen	die Straße, –n
die Familie, –n	der Tag, –e
die Freundin, –nen	der Verkäufer, –
der Friseur, –e	die Verkäuferin, –nen

Noun-pronoun relationship (G-M)

SINGULAR	
Der Mann ist alt. Der Anzug ist alt.	Er ist alt.
Das Kind ist schön. Das Hemd ist schön.	Es ist schön.
Die Frau ist hübsch. Die Jacke ist hübsch.	Sie ist hübsch.

PLURAL	
Die Männer sind schick. Die Jeans sind schick.	Sie sind schick.

The pronouns **er, es, sie** (sg.) and **sie** (pl.) may refer to either persons or things.

In the singular, **er** replaces **der**-nouns.
  es replaces **das**-nouns.
  sie replaces **die**-nouns.

In the plural, **sie** replaces all nouns.

Nominative case of **ein** and **kein**   (N-P)

Das ist **ein** Hemd.   That's *a* shirt.
Das ist **kein** Pulli.   That's *not a* sweater.
Das ist **keine** Jacke.   That's *not a* jacket.

The indefinite articles **ein** and **eine** are equivalent to English *a* or *an*. The negative forms **kein** and **keine** are equivalent to English *not a (not an)*, *not any*, or *no*.

SINGULAR	
der Pulli	Das ist ein Pulli. / kein
das Hemd	Das ist ein Hemd. / kein
die Bluse	Das ist eine Bluse. / keine

Ein and **kein** are used before **der-** and **das-**nouns in the nominative case. **Eine** and **keine** are used before **die-**nouns in the nominative case.

PLURAL	
die Jeans	Das sind Jeans.
	Das sind keine Jeans.

Ein and **eine** have no plural form.
Keine is used before plural nouns in the nominative case.

Kein and nicht

Ist das **ein Hemd?**   Nein, das ist **kein Hemd.**
Trägst du **Jeans?**   Nein, ich trage **keine Jeans.**

Ist das **die Jacke?**   Nein, das ist **nicht die Jacke.**
Ist das **dein Hemd?**   Nein, das ist **nicht mein Hemd.**

Kein is used to negate a noun that would be preceded by **ein** or by no article at all in an affirmative sentence. **Nicht** is used in a negative sentence when the noun is preceded by a definite article or a possessive adjective.

Wiederholung

A Jan and Paul are talking about the forthcoming party on Saturday. Answer the questions, based on the dialogue.

> JAN Trägst du am Samstag eine Jacke?
> PAUL Nein, ich trage keine Jacke. Ich trage nur ein Hemd.
> JAN Warum?
> PAUL Ich trage nicht gern Jacken. Und eine Jacke ist auch zu warm.

1. Was trägt Paul am Samstag?
2. Warum trägt er keine Jacke?

B Form sentences, using the cues provided.

1. Petra / treiben / gern / Sport
2. tanzen / du / viel / ?
3. was / tragen / Paula / am Samstag / ?
4. ich / tragen / oft / Jeans
5. wie / heißen / der Junge da / ?

C You are in a negative mood, so you find fault with everything Susanne says. Use *er, es,* or *sie* in your answers, as appropriate.

> ■ Das Hemd ist schick, nicht?
>
> Nein, ich finde, es ist häßlich.
> Unsinn! Die Farbe ist furchtbar.
> Ja, aber es ist furchtbar teuer.

1. Die Bluse ist toll, nicht?
2. Claudias Kleid ist schön, nicht?
3. Ihr Rock ist hübsch, nicht?
4. Volkers Schuhe sind klasse, nicht?
5. Sein Pulli ist prima, nicht?

A sweater put on over the head can be called either a **Pullover** or a **Pulli.** Generally **der Pullover** is used for a heavier sweater with long sleeves. **Pulli** is the shortened form of **Pullover,** but is used mostly for lighter sweaters, often short-sleeved or even sleeveless.

Kapitel 5

D Make up at least two sentences about the objects in each picture.

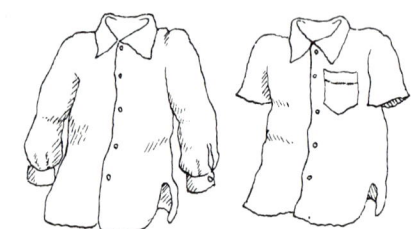

Hier sind zwei Hemden.
Sie sind preiswert.
Sie sind ziemlich neu.

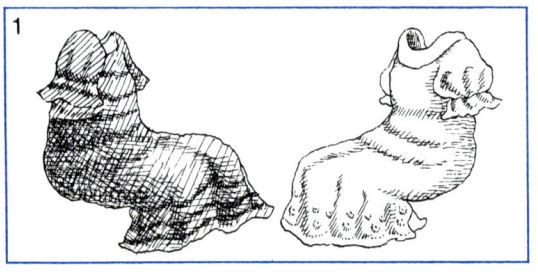

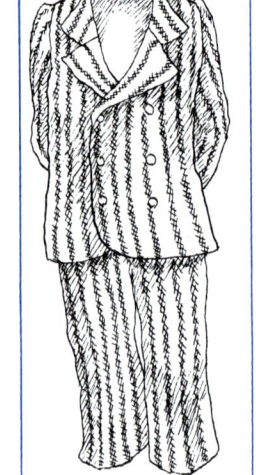
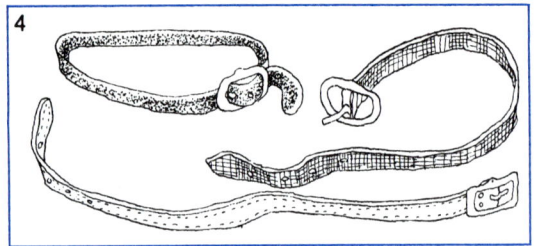
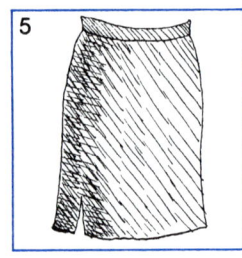

E Complete each sentence with an appropriate antonym.

1. Die Jeans sind nicht zu teuer; sie sind ____ .
2. Der Rock ist nicht häßlich; er ist sehr ____ .
3. Der Pulli ist nicht zu groß; er ist zu ____ .
4. Die Jacken da sind nicht alt; sie sind ____ .
5. Die Schuhe sind nicht gut; sie sind sehr ____ .
6. Das Kleid ist nicht billig; es ist furchtbar ____ .

F Express the following in German.

1. Is Jörg going home?
2. He's going to play basketball this afternoon.
3. Does he play well?
4. Will you play tennis this afternoon?
5. When are we going to go swimming?
6. Why are they going?

G Column A consists of questions or comments about clothing. Choose an appropriate response to each one from column B.

A	B
Ist der Rock teuer?	Schade.
Die Mäntel da sind wirklich klasse.	DM 12,45.
Wieviel kostet die Krawatte da?	Nein, er ist ziemlich billig.
Das Hemd hier kostet nur DM 5,–.	Meinst du?
Wie findest du die Jacke?	Das ist ja spottbillig!
Die Jeans passen leider nicht.	Wirklich klasse.

H Express the following two-line conversational exchanges in German.

1. What's the name of that girl (over there)?
   Her name is [...].
2. What color is her dress?
   It's [...].
3. How expensive is the sweater?
   It's a very good buy.
4. How much do the shoes cost?
   They cost [...].
5. What size does your friend wear?
   Size [...].

German stores are permitted by law to have a clearance sale (**Ausverkauf**) twice a year: a winter sale (**Winterschlußverkauf**) at the end of January and a summer sale (**Sommerschlußverkauf**) at the end of July. In addition, there may be special offers (**Sonderangebote**) periodically.

Kapitel 5

Kulturlesestück

Geld° money

Das ist eine Mark.
Eine Mark hat hundert Pfennig.

Das sind zehn Mark (DM 10,—).
Das ist ein Zehnmarkschein°. 10–Mark bill

Das sind auch zehn Mark (DM 10,—).
Das sind aber zwei Fünfmarkstücke°. 5–Mark pieces (coins)

Was bekommt° man für zehn Mark? get
Zum Beispiel°: zum Beispiel: for example
  Zwei Tassen° Kaffee   DM 3,60 cups
  Zwei Stück Torte   DM 5,60
                        DM 9,20

Kaffee ist teuer in Deutschland. Torte auch.

A Say how long the following people have to work in order to earn enough money for the items they want.

1. Ingrid verdient *(earns)* zehn Mark die Stunde *(an hour)*. Sie kauft neue Schuhe zu *(for)* DM 40,–. Wieviel Stunden arbeitet sie für die Schuhe?
2. Jan verdient sechs Mark die Stunde. Er kauft ein Polohemd zu DM 12,–. Wieviel Stunden arbeitet er für das Polohemd?
3. Peter verdient neun Mark die Stunde. Er kauft eine Gitarre zu DM 270,–. Wieviel Stunden arbeitet er für die Gitarre?

While German-speaking countries are similar in many ways, they do not share a common monetary system. The **BRD's** basic unit is the **Mark.** The **DDR** also uses a **Mark,** although its value is somewhat different from that of the Federal Republic's.

Switzerland's basic unit is the **Franken,** roughly equal in value to the **Mark** of the Federal Republic. There are 100 **Rappen** in a **Franken.**

Austria's basic unit is the **Schilling.** The **Schilling** is a much smaller unit than the **Mark:** a piece of cake would cost about twenty **Schilling.** There are 100 **Groschen** in a **Schilling.**

_____ Vokabeln _____

SUBSTANTIVE

der Anzug, ⁻e   man's suit
die Bluse, -n   blouse
die Dame, -n   lady, woman
die Farbe, -n   color
die Frau, -en   woman
die Größe, -n   size
der Gürtel, -   belt
der Handschuh, -e   glove
das Hemd, -en   shirt
der Herr, -en   gentleman
die Hose, -n   pants, slacks
die Jacke, -n   suit coat, jacket
die Jeans *(pl.)*   jeans
der Junge, -n   boy

SUBSTANTIVE

das Kleid, -er   dress
die Krawatte, -n   tie
das Mädchen, -   girl
der Mann, ⁻er   man
der Mantel, ⁻   coat
die Mark   German coin **(DM = Deutsche Mark** = 100 **Pfennig)**
der Pulli, -s   pullover
der Rock, ⁻e   skirt
die Sache, -n   thing; **Sachen**   clothes
der Schuh, -e   shoe
die Socke, -n   sock

(Continued)

Kapitel 5   **103**

VERBEN

brauchen to need
kaufen to buy
kosten to cost
meinen to think; to mean
passen to fit; to match
tragen (ä) to wear

ANDERE WÖRTER

billig inexpensive, cheap
blau blue
braun brown
da here, there
das that, the
für for
furchtbar terribly
gelb yellow
grau gray
grün green
häßlich ugly
hübsch pretty, nice
kein not a, not any

ANDERE WÖRTER

klasse terrific
leider unfortunately
neu new
preiswert worth the money, reasonably priced
rot red
schick chic, stylish
schön beautiful
schwarz black
spottbillig dirt-cheap
teuer expensive
warm warm
weiß white
welcher which, what

BESONDERE AUSDRÜCKE

wieviel kostet der Pulli? how much is the sweater?
welche Farbe hat dein Pulli? what color is your sweater?
ein Mantel in Braun a coat in brown
schade too bad

Kapitel 6
Der Schultag

Ingrids Stundenplan

Ingrid Wagner						Klasse 10
Zeit	Montag	Dienstag	Mittwoch	Donnerstag	Freitag	Samstag
8.00- 8.45	Sport	Physik	—	Deutsch	—	—
8.50- 9.35	Sport	Mathe	Chemie	Erdkunde	Geschichte	Physik
9.35 - 9.55	1. große Pause					
9.55 - 10.40	Englisch	Englisch	Latein	Chemie	Mathe	Deutsch
10.45 - 11.30	Geschichte	Latein	Deutsch	Geschichte	Mathe	—
11.30 -11.50	2. große Pause					
11.50- 12.35	Mathe	Erdkunde	Englisch	Kunst	Latein	—
12.45 -13.30	Biologie	Musik	Biologie	Kunst	Deutsch	—

Fragen

1. Was hat Ingrid Montag um acht Uhr? Dienstag um 9.45 Uhr (neun Uhr fünfundvierzig)? Donnerstag um 11.50 Uhr (elf Uhr fünfzig)?
2. Was hat Ingrid am Samstag?

Du hast das Wort

A. A classmate asks you which subjects you have today. How would you respond?

Welche Fächer° hast du heute?   Heute habe ich [Bio, Chemie und Deutsch].

B. Ask a classmate which subjects he/she has this year.

Welche Fächer hast du dieses° Jahr?   [Deutsch, Mathe, Bio, Englisch und Geschichte.]

Im Klassenzimmer

Gisela and Dieter are waiting for class to begin.

GISELA   Was haben wir um neun? Chemie?
DIETER   Nein, heute haben wir keine Chemie. Wir haben Mathe.
GISELA   Oh, prima!
DIETER   Mathe und „prima"?
GISELA   Ja, ich finde Mathe interessant. Mathe ist mein Lieblingsfach.

Fragen

1. Was hat Gisela um neun Uhr?
2. Was ist Giselas Lieblingsfach?
3. Findet Dieter Mathe interessant?

Du hast das Wort

A. Ask a classmate which subjects he/she likes and why.

     Was ist dein Lieblingsfach?   [Englisch].

     Warum?   Ich finde [Englisch] | toll.
  interessant.
  prima.
  leicht°.

B. Ask a classmate which subject he/she does not like and why.

     Welches Fach hast du nicht gern?   [Bio].

     Warum?   Es ist | langweilig°.
                                                                                                                                                                                                  zu schwer°.

Most German students go to school from 8 A.M. to around 1 P.M. six days a week, although some now have school on Saturday only twice a month. Since classes do not meet every day, students often take ten or more subjects in one term. There are several recess periods during the day: one or two twenty-minute **große Pausen,** and often a ten-minute **kleine Pause** as well. These breaks usually occur after two class periods have been completed. During the breaks the students go outside (weather permitting) to relax and have a snack.

In der Pause

Karin and Norbert are in the school yard, discussing homework. Norbert is unhappy about the news he hears.

KARIN	Hast du deine Hausaufgaben schon fertig?
NORBERT	Welche? Die Matheaufgaben?
KARIN	Nein, die Chemieaufgaben.
NORBERT	Die mache ich heute abend. Was machst du heute nachmittag?
KARIN	Ich mache Bio.
NORBERT	Mensch! Bioaufgaben haben wir auch?
KARIN	Klar!

Fragen
1. Wann macht Norbert Chemie?
2. Was macht Karin am Nachmittag°?
3. Haben Norbert und Karin auch Bioaufgaben?

Du hast das Wort

Ask a classmate when he/she intends to do homework.

Wann machst du deine	Matheaufgaben?	Heute nachmittag.
	Bioaufgaben?	Heute abend.
	Deutschaufgaben?	Jetzt.
		Später.
		Morgen.

Wieviel Uhr ist es?

Dieter is always late for class. Sabine doesn't seem to find that a serious problem.

DIETER	Wie spät ist es?
SABINE	Es ist fünf nach zehn.
DIETER	Mensch! Ich komme wieder zu spät.
SABINE	Ist ja nicht so schlimm. Du bist ja gut in Chemie.

Fragen
1. Ist es schon zehn Uhr?
2. Wie spät ist es?
3. Welches Fach hat Dieter jetzt?
4. Wer ist gut in Chemie?

Wortschatzerweiterung

The flavoring word ja

DIETER	Mensch! Ich komme wieder zu spät!	Oh no! I'm going to be late again!
SABINE	Ist **ja** nicht so schlimm.	That's not so bad.
	Du bist **ja** gut in Chemie.	You're good in chemistry (after all).

In Sabine's statements, the implication is that she and Dieter both know that Dieter is good in chemistry, so there's no need to worry. As a flavoring word, **ja** is often used to point out that both the speaker and the listener are aware of the circumstances to which the utterance refers. **Ja** also often has a reassuring tone.

A Restate the sentences, inserting the flavoring word *ja* where indicated. Then give the English equivalents.

■)) Was? Der Mantel kostet nur 50 Mark?   *Das ist ja spottbillig!*

1. Natürlich hat sie Mathe gern. Mathe ist ___ ihr Lieblingsfach.
2. Jan geht jetzt schwimmen. Er hat seine Hausaufgaben ___ fertig.
3. Diese Schuhe kaufe ich nicht. Sie sind ___ viel zu klein!
4. Du gehst auch Tennis spielen? Das ist ___ toll!
5. Meine Mutter spielt gut Tennis. Sie spielt ___ auch viel.

Schulsachen

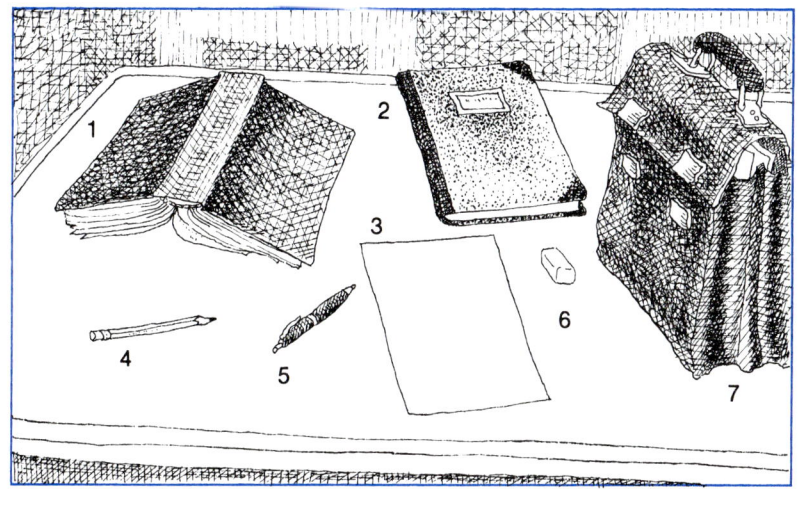

1. das Buch
2. das Heft
3. das Papier
4. der Bleistift
5. der Kugelschreiber (der Kuli)
6. der Radiergummi
7. die Mappe

Adjectives

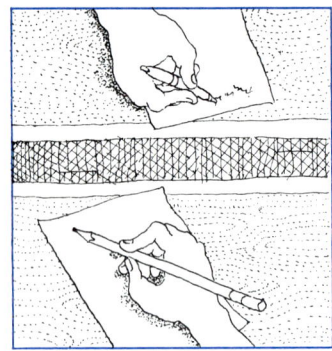
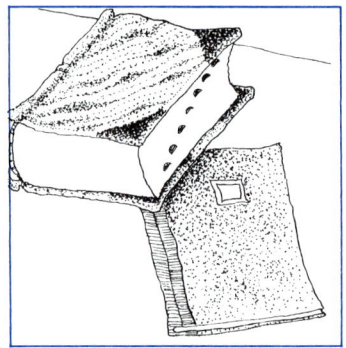
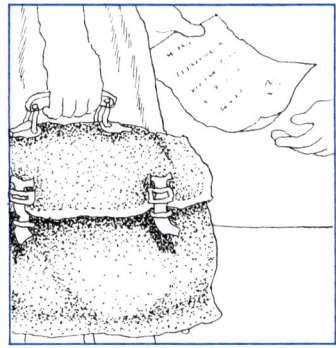

Der Kuli ist **kurz**.
Der Bleistift ist **lang**.

Das Buch ist **dick**.
Das Heft ist **dünn**.

Die Mappe ist **schwer**.
Das Papier ist **leicht**.

B Think of an object in the classroom. Have your classmates ask questions until they guess which object you've picked.

Ist es lang?	Ja.	Ist es dünn?	Ja.
Ist es alt?	Nein.	Ist es blau?	Ja.
Ist es teuer?	Ja.	Ist es ein Kuli?	Ja.

Das Alphabet

The German alphabet has 26 regular letters and 4 special letters.

a	ah	f	eff	k	kah	p	peh	u	uh	z	tsett
b	beh	g	geh	l	ell	q	kuh	v	fau	ä	äh
c	tseh	h	hah	m	emm	r	err	w	weh	ö	öh
d	deh	i	ih	n	enn	s	ess	x	iks	ü	üh
e	eh	j	jot	o	oh	t	teh	y	üpsilon	ß	ess-tset

In speech, capital letters are indicated by using the word **groß: großes B, großes W**. Lower-case letters are referred to as **klein: kleines b, kleines w**.

C Pronounce the following abbreviations.

VW (Volkswagen)   **BMW** (Bayerische Motorenwerke)
BRD (Bundesrepublik Deutschland)   **DDR** (Deutsche Demokratische Republik)   **USA** (U.S.A.)

D Spell the following words.

Physik   preiswert   billig   Farbe   Hose   häßlich

Aussprache

long vowel [o] so, wohnen, Hose, Boot
short vowel [ɔ] kommen, Socke

A Practice vertically in columns and horizontally in pairs.

[o]	[ɔ]
bog	Bock
Schote	Schotte
Moos	Most
Tone	Tonne
Ofen	offen
Sohne	Sonne

B Practice the following words horizontally in pairs.

[o]	[ø]	[ɔ]	[œ]
große	Größe	Kopfe	Köpfe
Hofe	Höfe	konnte	könnte
stoße	Stöße	Stocke	Stöcke
Gote	Goethe	Hocker	Höcker
Ofen	Öfen	Topfe	Töpfe

C Practice the sounds [o] and [ɔ]. Read the sentences aloud.

1. Kommt Otto am Sonntag oder am Montag?
2. Lotte und Monika hören gern Rockmusik.
3. Hoffentlich kostet die Hose nicht sehr viel.

Doof bleibt doof, da helfen keine Pillen!

Übungen

Telling time

Es ist zwei.   Es ist eins.
Es ist zwei Uhr.   Es ist ein Uhr.

A Various friends want to know when you're coming to visit on Saturday. Inform them that you'll come an hour later than they expected.

▪ Kommst du um vier?   *Nein, um fünf.*

1. Kommst du um drei?   4. Kommst du um elf?
2. Kommst du um sechs?   5. Kommst du um neun?
3. Kommst du um eins?

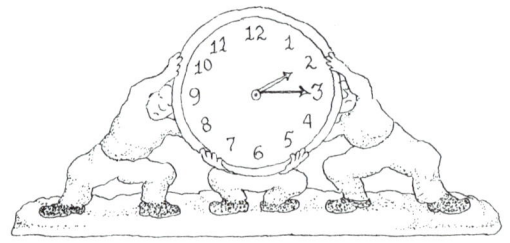 

Es ist Viertel nach zwei.   Es ist Viertel vor drei.

B Tell Axel that you have classes a quarter hour later than he thinks.

▪ Hast du um drei Bio?   *Nein, um Viertel nach drei.*

1. Hast du um acht Deutsch?   4. Hast du um eins Englisch?
2. Hast du um neun Mathe?   5. Hast du um zehn Chemie?
3. Hast du um elf Geschichte?

C Inform Inge that you have classes a quarter hour earlier than she thinks.

▪ Hast du um acht Musik?   *Nein, um Viertel vor acht.*

1. Hast du um zehn Kunst?   4. Hast du um eins Erdkunde?
2. Hast du um zwölf Sport?   5. Hast du um elf Physik?
3. Hast du um neun Latein?

Es ist zehn vor fünf. Es ist zehn nach sechs.
Es ist zehn Minuten vor fünf. Es ist zehn Minuten nach sechs.

D Tell your friends that it's five minutes later than they thought.

■» Ist es Viertel nach acht?   *Nein, es ist schon zwanzig nach acht.*

1. Ist es fünf nach elf?
2. Ist es sieben Uhr?
3. Ist es zehn nach sechs?
4. Ist es fünf vor neun?
5. Ist es zwanzig vor eins?
6. Ist es Viertel vor zwölf?
7. Ist es zehn vor acht?

Es ist halb drei.
Es ist zwei Uhr dreißig.

E Tell each friend who asks that you're going home a half hour later than the time mentioned.

■» Gehst du um vier nach Hause?   *Nein, um halb fünf.*

1. Gehst du um elf nach Hause?
2. Gehst du um sieben nach Hause?
3. Gehst du um eins nach Hause?
4. Gehst du um neun nach Hause?
5. Gehst du um sechs nach Hause?
6. Gehst du um drei nach Hause?

Du hast das Wort   Find out when a classmate has various classes.

Hast du um acht [Bio]?
Wann hast du [Chemie]?
Du hast um halb zehn [Englisch], nicht?
Um wieviel Uhr hast du [Mathe]?

Accusative case of **der, das, die**

NOMINATIVE
Der Mantel ist preiswert.
Das Hemd ist toll.
Die Hose ist klasse.
Die Schuhe sind spottbillig.

ACCUSATIVE
Meinst du **den** Mantel da?
Meinst du **das** Hemd da?
Meinst du **die** Hose da?
Meinst du **die** Schuhe da?

The direct object of a verb is in the accusative case. **Der** is the only definite article that has a different form before nouns in the accusative case: **der > den.**

F You are shown some clothing. Say you find each article attractive.

■ der Pulli   *Ich finde den Pulli hübsch.*

1. die Krawatte   3. das Kleid   5. der Mantel
2. der Gürtel   4. der Rock   6. die Bluse

G Ute reacts favorably to a number of items in a clothing store. Ask her to specify which ones she means.

■ Der Anzug ist preiswert.   *Meinst du den Anzug da?*

1. Der Gürtel ist klasse.   4. Das Hemd ist schön.
2. Die Bluse ist toll.   5. Der Mantel ist teuer.
3. Der Rock ist spottbillig.   6. Das Kleid ist hübsch.

Accusative case of **ein** and **kein**

NOMINATIVE
Da ist **ein** Bleistift.
Da ist **kein** Bleistift.
Da ist **ein** Buch.
Da ist **kein** Buch.
Da ist **eine** Mappe.
Da ist **keine** Mappe.
Da sind Bleistifte.
Da sind **keine** Bleistifte.

ACCUSATIVE
Hast du **einen** Bleistift?
Hast du **keinen** Bleistift?
Hast du **ein** Buch?
Hast du **kein** Buch?
Hast du **eine** Mappe?
Hast du **keine** Mappe?
Hast du Bleistifte?
Hast du **keine** Bleistifte?

The indefinite article **ein** and its negative form **kein** become **einen** and **keinen** before **der-**nouns in the accusative singular. **Ein** has no plural forms.

H You've misplaced several of your school supplies. Try to borrow the following articles from various friends.

> ▪▮   ein Bleistift   *Hast du einen Bleistift?*

1. ein Kuli
2. ein Radiergummi
3. ein Heft
4. eine Mappe
5. ein Buch
6. ein Bleistift

I Christa asks what you and your friends are wearing to the party. Tell her you all don't plan to wear what she expects.

> ▪▮   Trägst du heute abend eine Jacke?   *Nein, ich trage keine Jacke.*

1. Trägst du heute abend einen Pulli?
2. Trägt Erik einen Anzug?
3. Trägt Gisela ein Kleid?
4. Trägt sie einen Rock?
5. Trägt Günter Jeans?
6. Trägt er Schuhe?
7. Trägt er Socken?

Accusative case of possessive adjectives

Ich habe **einen** Bleistift.
Ich habe **ein** Heft.
Ich habe **eine** Mappe.
Ich habe Bücher.

Ich habe **meinen** Bleistift.
Ich habe **mein** Heft.
Ich habe **meine** Mappe.
Ich habe **meine** Bücher.

J You're always picking up after absent-minded Erik. When he asks where his school supplies are, say that you have them.

■ Wo ist mein Kuli? *Ich habe deinen Kuli.*

1. Wo ist mein Radiergummi?
2. Wo ist mein Heft?
3. Wo ist meine Mappe?
4. Wo ist mein Bleistift?
5. Wo sind meine Bücher?
6. Wo ist mein Papier?

K After an afternoon of swimming, everyone's clothes have become mixed up. Answer that you and Ulf have them.

■ Wer hat unsere Socken? *Wir haben eure Socken.*

1. Wer hat unsere Schuhe?
2. Wer hat unsere Hemden?
3. Wer hat unsere Jacken?
4. Wer hat unsere Gürtel?

L   Ilse points out that some of her friends are wearing new clothes. Ask what she thinks of them.

> ▪   Astrids Kleid ist neu.   *Wirklich? Wie findest du ihr Kleid?*

1. Christas Bluse ist neu.
2. Kirstins Rock ist neu.
3. Jochens Jacke ist neu.
4. Kurts Pulli ist neu.
5. Thomas' Hemd ist neu.
6. Gerdas Mantel ist neu.
7. Herberts Schuhe sind neu.

Du hast das Wort   Play a guessing game with your classmates. Think of a student in your class and name two or three articles of clothing that he/she is wearing. Your classmates will try to guess whom you have in mind.

Ich trage Hose und Hemd und einen Pulli.
Meine Hose ist braun.
Mein Pulli ist rot.
Wer bin ich?

Using **der, das, die** as pronouns

Kaufst du **den Gürtel** da?	Are you going to buy that belt?
Nein, **der** ist zu teuer.	No, it is too expensive.
Wie findest du **den Mantel** da?	How do you like that coat?
Den finde ich schön.	I think that one is nice.

Der, das, die are often used as pronouns to replace nouns. The forms of these pronouns are the same as the forms of the definite articles.

M   You and Gabi are shopping. For some reason you don't seem to agree with any of her opinions.

> ▪   Ich finde den Pulli schön. Du auch?   *Nein, den finde ich nicht schön.*

1. Ich finde das Kleid hübsch. Du auch?
2. Ich finde die Bluse toll. Du auch?
3. Ich finde das Hemd teuer. Du auch?
4. Ich finde den Rock billig. Du auch?
5. Ich finde die Jacke hübsch. Du auch?
6. Ich finde den Mantel schön. Du auch?

Grammatische Übersicht

Telling time (A-E)

Time is expressed in the following ways:

1. on the hour: 1.00 Es ist eins.
   Es ist ein Uhr.

Notice that the **-s** of **eins** is dropped before the noun **Uhr.** Notice also that in written German a period is used after the numeral indicating the hour.

2. past the hour: 1.10 Es ist zehn (Minuten) nach eins.
   1.15 Es ist Viertel nach eins.
   1.30 Es ist ein Uhr dreißig.
   Es ist halb zwei.

Notice that the expression with **halb** names the hour to come, not the preceding hour: **1.30 = halb zwei.**

3. before the hour: 1.40 Es ist zwanzig (Minuten) vor zwei.
   1.45 Es ist Viertel vor zwei.

Official time

Ingrid hat **um 13 Uhr 30** Bio.   Ingrid has biology at 1:30 P.M.

Official time, used for concerts, train and plane schedules, and schools, is indicated on a twenty-four-hour basis: 8 Uhr = 8 A.M.
20 Uhr = 8 P.M.

Accusative case

Kaufst du **den Mantel**? Are you buying the coat?
Ich kaufe **eine Jacke**. I'm buying a jacket.
Petra trägt heute **keinen Pulli**. Petra isn't wearing a sweater today.

A German noun has different cases, depending on how it is used in a sentence. When a noun is used as the direct object of a verb, it is in the *accusative case*.

Accusative case of **der, das, die** (F-G)

NOMINATIVE	ACCUSATIVE
Der Anzug ist billig.	Meinst du **den** Anzug da?
Das Kleid ist schick.	Meinst du **das** Kleid da?
Die Jacke ist klasse.	Meinst du **die** Jacke da?
Die Schuhe sind teuer.	Meinst du **die** Schuhe da?

Den is used instead of **der** in the accusative case. The other articles, **das** and **die**, have identical nominative and accusative forms.

Accusative case of **ein** and **kein** (H-I)

NOMINATIVE	ACCUSATIVE
Da ist **ein** Bleistift.	Sie hat **einen** Bleistift.
Da ist **kein** Bleistift.	Er hat **keinen** Bleistift.
Da ist **ein** Heft.	Sie hat **ein** Heft.
Da ist **kein** Heft.	Er hat **kein** Heft.
Da ist **eine** Mappe.	Sie hat **eine** Mappe.
Da ist **keine** Mappe.	Er hat **keine** Mappe.
Da sind Bleistifte.	Sie hat Bleistifte.
Da sind **keine** Bleistifte.	Er hat **keine** Bleistifte.

Ein changes to **einen** before a **der**-noun in the accusative singular. **Ein** has no plural forms.

Kein follows the pattern of **ein**, except that **kein** has plural forms. In the plural, the nominative and accusative forms are identical. They are both **keine**.

Accusative case of possessive adjectives (J-L)

NOMINATIVE		
Wo ist	ein mein	Kuli?
Wo ist	ein mein	Heft?
Wo ist	eine meine	Mappe?
Wo sind	meine	Bücher?

ACCUSATIVE		
Wer hat	einen meinen	Kuli?
Wer hat	ein mein	Heft?
Wer hat	eine meine	Mappe?
Wer hat	meine	Bücher?

The possessive adjectives **(mein, dein, sein, ihr, unser, euer)** have the same endings as the indefinite article **ein.**

Using **der, das, die** as pronouns (M)

Kaufst du **die Jacke** da? Are you going to buy *that jacket?*
Nein, **die** ist zu teuer. No, *it* is too expensive.

Der, das, die are often used as pronouns to replace nouns. They are then called demonstrative pronouns. Demonstrative pronouns usually occur at or near the beginning of a sentence. The English equivalent is usually a personal pronoun.

	SINGULAR			PLURAL
Nominative	der	das	die	die
Accusative	den	das	die	die

The forms of the demonstrative pronouns are the same as the forms of the definite articles.

Grades are based on class performance, written tests called **Klassenarbeiten,** and frequent quizzes called **Kurzarbeiten.** Pressure to achieve good grades is very strong because admission to a university (and to some jobs) depends primarily on the applicant's secondary school grades.

Extracurricular activities such as clubs, organizations, and sports are limited in German schools. Where such activities do exist, they are not really part of the school day.

Wiederholung

A Choose the phrase that best completes each statement, based on the dialogue.

PAUL Tag, Ursel! Wie geht's?
URSEL Es geht. Ich habe heute nachmittag viel Hausaufgaben.
PAUL Das ist ja doof. Ich spiele jetzt Tennis.
URSEL Du, Paul . . . Wie spät ist es denn?
PAUL Erst eins.
URSEL Na gut. Ich spiele bis zwei.
PAUL Das ist ja prima.

1. Es geht Ursel . . .
   a. gut.
   b. prima.
   c. nicht so gut.
2. Paul . . .
   a. geht jetzt nach Hause.
   b. macht Hausaufgaben.
   c. treibt heute nachmittag Sport.
3. Paul und Ursel . . .
   a. haben jetzt Schule.
   b. gehen jetzt nach Hause.
   c. spielen jetzt Tennis.

Kapitel 6   **121**

B Explain to Gabi that things are not as she thinks, but rather exactly the opposite.

▪▥ Ist dein Buch interessant?   *Nein, es ist nicht interessant; es ist langweilig.*

1. Sind deine Matheaufgaben leicht?
2. Ist dein Kuli billig?
3. Ist deine Mappe neu?
4. Sind deine Englischaufgaben lang?
5. Ist dein Klassenzimmer groß?

C Take the role of the person in each picture. Tell what you are wearing.

▪▥     *Ich trage keine Jacke; ich trage einen Pulli.*

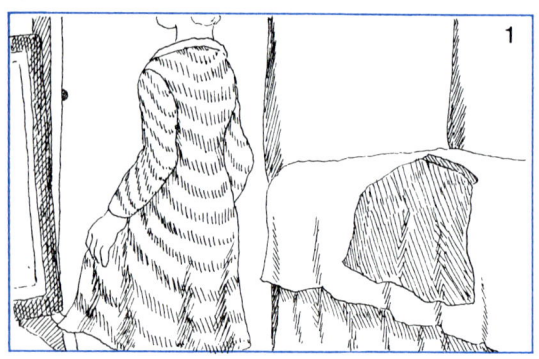 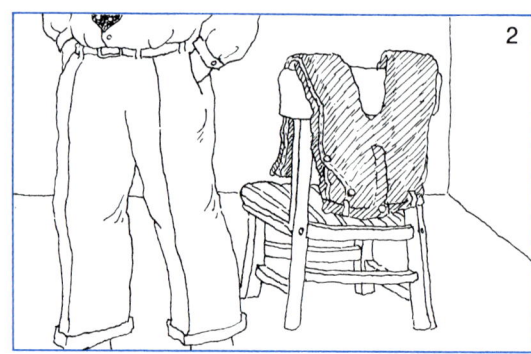

D Supply additional information to each of the following sentences by beginning with one of the words or expressions below.

abends   heute nachmittag   hoffentlich

jetzt   natürlich   morgens um halb neun

▪ Mein Brieffreund wohnt in   *Jetzt wohnt mein*
Bergdorf.   *Brieffreund in Bergdorf.*

1. Er geht da in die Schule.
2. Er hat Chemie.
3. Er spielt Fußball.
4. Er macht seine Hausaufgaben.
5. Er schreibt bald.

E A German student is visiting your school. You overhear various snatches of conversation during lunch. Tell your German friend what people are saying.

1. Ingrid: I have math this afternoon.
   Math is my favorite subject.
2. Mark: I'm going to do my chemistry homework this afternoon.
   I think chemistry is interesting.
3. Erik: It's already a quarter after twelve.
   I'm going to be late again.
4. Christl: Gerd likes Petra.
   Sabine: Yes, but Petra doesn't like Gerd.
5. Robert: Does your pen pal live in Kiel?
   Tanja: No. He lives in Stuttgart now.

F Find out from a classmate what he/she does after school on certain days.

▪ Was machst du am [Montag]?   Ich [spiele Fußball].

G Interview a classmate about school. You may want to ask some of the following questions. Summarize your findings.

Was ist dein Lieblingsfach?
Wann hast du [Deutsch]?
Wie findest du [Erdkunde]?
  Ist es leicht? schwer?
Hast du viel Hausaufgaben?
Machst du gern [Chemie]aufgaben?
  Wann machst du sie?
Welches Fach hast du nicht gern?

You may wish to begin: *Gerdas Lieblingsfach ist Bio. Sie . . .*

Kulturlesestück

1 = sehr gut

2 = gut

3 = befriedigend

4 = ausreichend

5 = mangelhaft

6 = ungenügend

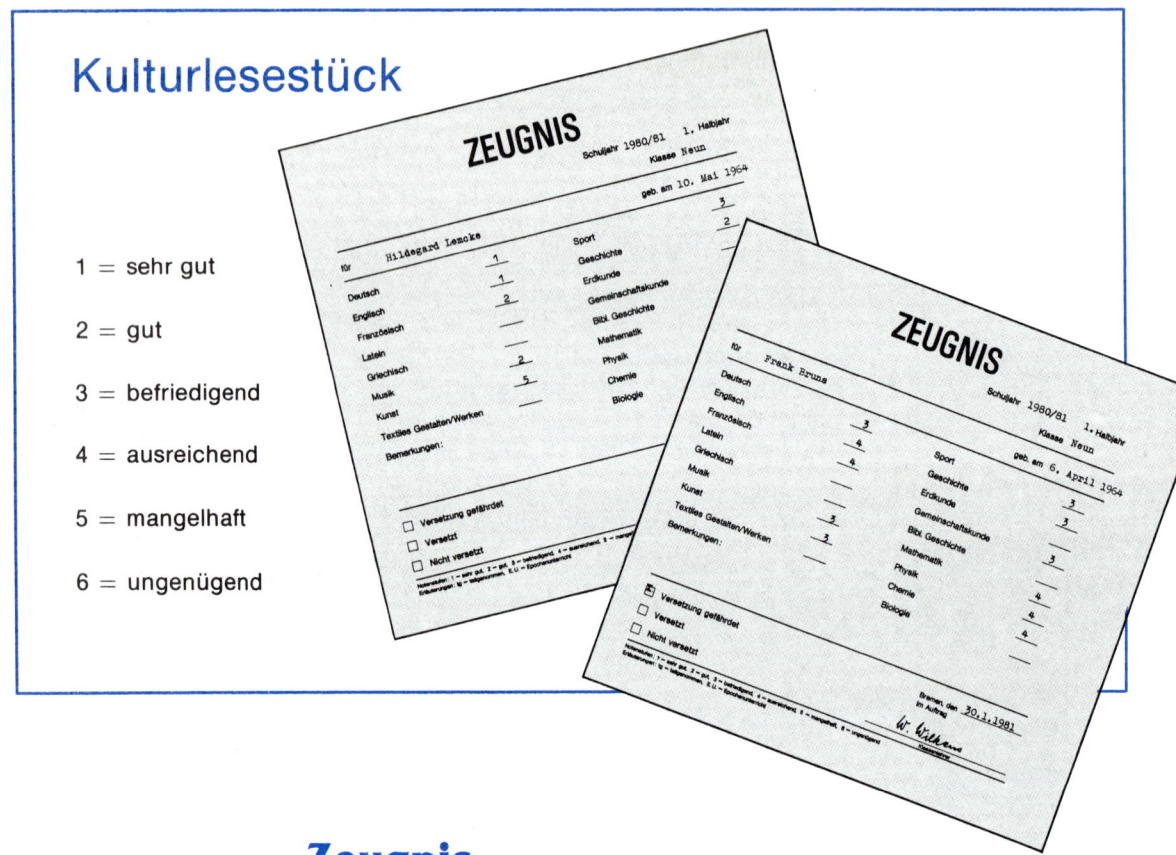

Zeugnis

Hilde geht in Bremen zur Schule. Sie ist in Klasse Neun. Links° ist ihr Zeugnis. In Deutsch und Englisch hat sie eine Eins. Das sind ihre Lieblingsfächer. Da ist sie sehr gut. In Mathe und Physik ist sie gut. Sie hat in beiden° eine Zwei. Nur in Kunst ist sie wirklich schlecht. Da hat sie eine Fünf. Sie findet Kunst langweilig.

Hildes Freund Frank ist nicht so gut. Er hat viele Dreien und Vieren. Er arbeitet nicht gern. Hoffentlich bekommt° er nächstes Mal° nicht nur Vieren und Fünfen. Mit° drei Fünfen zum Beispiel oder mit zwei Fünfen und ohne° Dreien bleibt er sitzen°. Dann° geht Hilde in Klasse Zehn, und er macht die ganze Klasse Neun noch einmal°.

on the left

in beiden: in both

gets / nächstes Mal: next time
with
without / bleibt . . . sitzen: he repeats a year / then
noch einmal: again

A Answer the following questions, based on the reading.

1. Wo hat Hilde eine Zwei?
   a. in Englisch
   b. in Deutsch
   c. in Mathe
   d. in Kunst
2. Wie findet Hilde Kunst?
   a. interessant
   b. leicht
   c. nicht interessant
   d. schwer
3. Warum ist Franks Zeugnis nicht gut?
   a. Er findet alle Fächer langweilig.
   b. Er ist faul.
   c. Die Fächer sind zu schwer.
   d. Er spielt zuviel Fußball.

Vokabeln

SUBSTANTIVE

die Aufgabe, -n homework, lesson; **die Chemieaufgabe** chemistry homework
die Biologie biology; **die Bio** bio
der Bleistift, -e pencil
das Buch, ¨er book
die Chemie chemistry
der Dienstag Tuesday
das Englisch English
die Erdkunde geography
das Fach, ¨er (school) subject
die Geschichte history
das Heft, -e notebook
die Klasse, -n grade, class
das Klassenzimmer, - classroom
der Kugelschreiber, - (der Kuli, -s) ballpoint pen
das Lieblingsfach, ¨er favorite subject
die Mappe, -n briefcase, book bag

SUBSTANTIVE

die Mathematik mathematics; **die Mathe** math
der Mittwoch Wednesday
der Nachmittag, -e afternoon; **am ~** in the afternoon
das Papier paper
die Pause, -n break, intermission
die Physik physics
der Plan, ¨e plan; schedule
der Radiergummi, -s eraser
die Schule, -n school
der Sport sport
die Stunde, -n hour; class
der Stundenplan, ¨e class schedule
die Uhr, -en clock, watch
das Viertel, - quarter

(Continued)

Kapitel 6 **125**

ANDERE WÖRTER

ach oh
dick fat, thick
dieser this
fertig ready, finished
halb half
interessant interesting
ja *flavoring word (see p. 109)*
kurz short
lang long
langweilig boring
leicht easy, light
schlimm bad
schwer difficult, heavy
um at, around
vor before

BESONDERE AUSDRÜCKE

Mensch! wow! brother! oh, boy!
klar! sure! of course!
wie spät ist es? what time is it?
wieviel Uhr ist es? what time is it?
es ist zehn Uhr it's ten o'clock
um wieviel Uhr? at what time?
um ein Uhr at one o'clock

Kapitel 7
Willst du ins Konzert?

The **Litfaßsäule** (a thick column on which advertising posters are displayed) was introduced to Germany in 1854 by Ernst Litfaß, a printer from Berlin. Litfaß had seen similar columns in other countries and recognized their value in advertising. The Berlin police gave Litfaß a monopoly on the poster columns; they saw them as a way of controlling the location of posters put up throughout the city. The **Litfaßsäulen** soon spread through the rest of Germany and are still in use today.

Fragen

1. Wo gibt es ein Konzert°?
2. Wie heißt die Rock Band°?
3. Wieviel Tage spielen die *Frankfurter Hot Dogs*?
4. Wann beginnt° die Vorstellung°?
5. Wieviel kosten die Karten?

Du hast das Wort

A. Ask a classmate to name the rock group he/she likes best.

   Wie heißt deine Lieblingsgruppe?   [Die *Hot Dogs*.]

B. Ask a friend whether he/she would like to hear a concert by a certain rock group.

   Möchtest° du [die *Hot Dogs*] hören?

   Ja, [sie sind] toll.
   Ja, und wie!
   Klar!
   Ja, hast du Karten?
   Vielleicht°.
   Nein, ich habe keine Lust°.

Konzert im Jugendzentrum

Dieter and Ingrid are trying to find a time when they can both go to the Hot Dogs *concert.*

INGRID	Du, Dieter, die *Hot Dogs* spielen heute abend.
DIETER	Das ist ja dumm. Ich kann leider heute abend nicht.
INGRID	Und morgen abend?
DIETER	Morgen abend geht's. Meinst du, wir bekommen noch Karten?
INGRID	Wir können's ja mal versuchen.

Fragen
1. Wer spielt heute abend?
2. Wann kann Dieter ins Konzert gehen?
3. Können die beiden noch Karten bekommen?
4. Hören sie die *Hot Dogs* gern?

Du hast das Wort   Create a dialogue between you and a friend. Try to make plans to go to a movie, play, or concert.

DU
Was macht ihr ╎ heute abend? / am Samstag?

FREUND(IN)
Wir wollen ╎ ins Kino°. / ins Theater°. / ins Konzert.

DU
Wann?
Um wieviel Uhr?

FREUND(IN)
Um [8] Uhr. ╎ Kommst du auch? / Hast du Lust zu kommen?

DU
Nein, ich habe ╎ keine Zeit°. / kein Geld°.
Nein, ich muß Hausaufgaben machen.
Ich habe schon Lust, aber keine Zeit.
Nein, ich darf° nicht.

FREUND(IN)
Schade.
Das tut mir leid.

DU
Ja, gern. Gibt° es noch Karten?

FREUND(IN)
Ich glaube° ja.
Vielleicht, vielleicht auch nicht.
Wir können ja mal fragen°.

American music and rock groups are popular in German-speaking countries. German teen-agers listen to rock, disco, and country-western. American songs performed by European artists are usually sung in English. Even songs written by German artists often have English lyrics.

PRETTY BABY

Du bist so schön.
Ich muß dich seh'n,
Heute noch seh'n,
Oh, pretty baby!

Du hast mein Herz.
Das ist kein Scherz.
Oh, welcher Schmerz
Ohne dich, baby!

Glücklich zu sein,
Mit dir allein,
Immer zu zwei'n,
Oh, pretty baby!

Es kann nicht sein.
Ich bin allein,
Immer allein
Ohne dich, baby.

An der Kasse

The Hot Dogs *are a popular group. Ingrid and Dieter have a hard time getting tickets.*

INGRID Haben Sie noch Karten für morgen abend?
HERR Es tut mir leid. Für morgen abend ist nichts mehr da. Ich habe noch ein paar Karten für übermorgen.
INGRID *(zu Dieter)* Was meinst du?
DIETER Ich kann ja. Aber mußt du dann nicht arbeiten?
INGRID Das schon. Aber ich bekomme sicher frei. Ich muß die *Hot Dogs* einfach hören.
DIETER Also gut.

Fragen
1. Gibt es noch Karten für morgen abend?
2. Für wann gibt es noch Karten?
3. Warum will Ingrid übermorgen nicht arbeiten?

Du hast das Wort With a partner, make up a short dialogue about buying tickets to a performance. Use some of the questions and responses below.

DU	FRAU
Haben Sie noch Karten für heute abend? morgen°? übermorgen?	Es tut mir leid. Es ist alles ausverkauft°. Für [heute abend] haben wir nichts mehr. Für [heute abend] ist noch alles° da. Für [übermorgen] haben wir noch Karten.
Was kosten die Karten?	Wir haben Karten zu [5, 8, 12 und 16] Mark. Wir haben noch ein paar Karten zu [8] Mark.
Ich nehme° [2] Karten zu [8] Mark. Danke.	Bitte. Das macht° [16] Mark.
Oh, noch eine Frage°. Wann beginnt die Vorstellung?	Um [20] Uhr.

Wortschatzerweiterung

Noun compounds

German has many noun compounds. Their meaning can often be guessed from their component parts.

    der Abend + die Vorstellung = die Abendvorstellung
    das Theater + die Karten   = die Theaterkarten

A noun compound takes the definite article of the last noun in the compound.

A   What do the italicized words mean?

1. Die *Abendvorstellung* beginnt um acht Uhr.
2. Gibt es für heute noch *Theaterkarten*?
3. Welche *Schuhgröße* hast du?
4. Hast du morgen *Klavierstunde*?
5. Wann machst du deine *Hausaufgaben*?
6. Am *Wochenende* mache ich meine *Matheaufgaben*.
7. Wie heißt dein *Deutschlehrer*?
8. Wo ist das *Deutschbuch*?
9. Was sind deine *Lieblingsfächer*?

Flavoring word **mal**

Wir können's ja **mal** versuchen.	Let's at least give it a try. (We can try it sometime.)
Du kannst ja **mal** ins Kino gehen.	You can go to the movies for a change.
Bernd will **mal** in Hamburg arbeiten.	Bernd wants to work in Hamburg someday.

The flavoring word **mal** is often used in commands, suggestions, or in statements of intent. The time for carrying out the intended action is not stated precisely. To express the same idea in English one often uses *sometime* or *someday*.

B Choose a German response to complete each conversational exchange, based on the English guidelines.

a. Was können wir denn mal machen?
b. Möchtest du die *Hot Dogs* mal hören?
c. Das möchte ich auch mal machen.
d. Das muß ich auch mal lernen.
e. Ich muß bald mal neue Schuhe kaufen.
f. Ich muß Gerda auch mal schreiben.

1. *Jens says he also has to learn English someday.*
   Torsten: Dieses Jahr lerne ich Englisch.
   Jens: ...
2. *Gerda would like to play more tennis.*
   Erika: Im Sommer spiele ich viel Tennis.
   Gerda: ...
3. *Mark casually remarks that he needs new shoes soon.*
   Frank: Deine Schuhe sind kaputt.
   Mark: Ja. ...
4. *Ursel asks what she and Barbara can do to relieve their boredom on a rainy afternoon.*
   Barbara: Es ist heute so langweilig.
   Ursel: ...
5. *Gerd asks whether Uwe wants to play a different record for a change.*
   Uwe: Du, diese Gruppe ist furchtbar langweilig.
   Gerd: ...
6. *Barbara has been corresponding regularly with Gerda. Renate remembers that she owes Gerda a letter, too.*
   Barbara: Morgen muß ich wieder an Gerda schreiben.
   Renate: ...

Aussprache

long vowel [a]　Vater, St**aa**t, Fr**a**ge
short vowel [A]　K**a**sse, **a**lles, M**a**nn

A　Practice vertically in columns and horizontally in pairs.

[a]	[A]
B**ah**n	B**a**nn
k**a**m	K**a**mm
St**aa**t	St**a**dt
Schl**a**f	schl**a**ff
l**ah**m	L**a**mm

B　Practice the following words horizontally in pairs.

[a]	[ɔ]	[A]	[ɔ]
B**ah**n	B**o**nn	B**a**nn	B**o**nn
k**a**m	k**o**mm	K**a**mm	k**o**mm
st**ah**len	St**o**llen	M**a**tte	M**o**tte
Sp**a**ten	sp**o**tten	kn**a**lle	Kn**o**lle
f**ah**l	v**o**ll	f**a**lle	v**o**lle

C　Practice the sounds [a] and [A]. Read the sentences aloud.

1. Hast du Astrids Mappe?
2. Ich habe noch eine Karte zu acht Mark.
3. Kannst du heute abend tanzen gehen?

Ein Spatz in der Hand ist besser als eine Taube auf dem Dach.

Die Hot Dogs *sind toll, nicht?*

--- **Übungen** ---

The subject pronouns **du, ihr, Sie**

The pronouns **du, ihr,** and **Sie** are all equivalent to English *you.*

> Tag, **Elke!** Was machst **du** denn?
> Tag, **Inge!** Tag, **Gerd!** Was macht **ihr** denn?

The familiar forms **du** and **ihr** are used in addressing relatives, close friends, and persons under about fifteen.

> Tag, **Herr Wagner!** Gehen **Sie** heute ins Konzert?
> Tag, **Frau Braun!** Tag, **Fräulein Schneider!** Gehen **Sie** auch ins Konzert?

Sie is a more formal form of address and is used in addressing strangers or adults whom the speaker doesn't know as close friends. **Sie** can refer to one or more persons.

A   Ask Mrs. Wagner the same questions you recently asked Günter.

▪ Gehst du heute abend ins Theater, Günter?
     Gehen Sie heute abend ins Theater, Frau Wagner?

1. Bekommst du noch Karten?
2. Was meinst du?
3. Hörst du gern Rockmusik?
4. Gehst du morgen ins Konzert?
5. Wie findest du die *Hot Dogs?*

Kapitel 7   **135**

The possessive adjectives **dein, euer, Ihr**

Hast du **deinen** Mantel, Inge? — Do you have *your* coat, Inge?

Habt ihr **eure** Mäntel, Kinder? — Do you have *your* coats, children?

Haben Sie **Ihren** Mantel, Herr Lenz? — Do you have *your* coat, Mr. Lenz?

German has three possessive adjectives meaning *your*:

    dein (familiar singular)
    euer (familiar plural)
    Ihr (formal, singular and plural)

B Mrs. Wagner is straightening up the classroom. She asks whether various objects belong to you. They don't. Express surprise that they're not hers.

◼ Ist das dein Buch? — *Nein, ist das nicht Ihr Buch?*

1. Ist das dein Heft?
2. Ist das dein Radiergummi?
3. Ist das dein Kugelschreiber?
4. Ist das deine Mappe?
5. Sind das deine Bleistifte?

C Check to make sure all your friends and acquaintances have their tickets for the concert you're going to tonight.

◼ Karin — *Hast du deine Karte?*
◼ Inge und Klaus — *Habt ihr eure Karten?*
◼ Frau Lenz — *Haben Sie Ihre Karte?*

1. Hans
2. Jens und Thomas
3. Gabi
4. Herr Hansen
5. Petra und Claudia
6. Frau Schneider

Verbs with stem-vowel change e>i

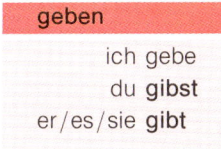
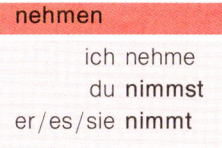

Geben and **nehmen** have a stem-vowel change **e>i** in the **du-** and **er/sie-**forms of the present tense.

D Stefan is selling off a block of tickets to a soccer game. Ask whether the following people are taking some tickets.

▪ Braucht ihr Karten? *Nehmt ihr Karten?*

1. Braucht Frau Lange Karten?
2. Braucht Fräulein Roth Karten?
3. Braucht Bernd Karten?
4. Brauchen wir Karten?
5. Braucht Herr Wagner Karten?
6. Brauchst du Karten?

E Marita wonders how Christa can afford to go to so many concerts. Tell her that various people give her tickets.

▪ Erik *Erik gibt Christa oft Karten.*

1. Inge
2. mein Bruder
3. ihre Schwester
4. du
5. ihre Freunde
6. ihr

Modal auxiliaries

können can, to be able to

ich **kann**		wir **können**
du **kannst**	Sie **können**	ihr **könnt**
er/es/sie **kann**		sie **können**

Ich **kann** es mal **versuchen.**   *I can try it.*

Modal auxiliaries are irregular in the present-tense singular. They are usually used with dependent infinitives. The infinitive is in last position.

Kapitel 7 **137**

F The library seems very noisy today. Say that the following people can't work.

> ▪▥ Ich arbeite nicht.   *Ich kann nicht arbeiten.*

1. Bernd arbeitet nicht.
2. Ingrid arbeitet nicht.
3. Wir arbeiten nicht.
4. Du arbeitest nicht.
5. Frau Lange arbeitet nicht.
6. Ihr arbeitet nicht.

G Say who can (or can't) do the following things.

> ▪▥ Wir können es machen. (Susanne)   *Susanne kann es machen.*

1. Die Jungen können es machen. (du)
2. Du kannst das Buch nehmen. (ihr)
3. Ihr könnt gut singen. (ich)
4. Ich kann die Vokabeln nicht lernen. (Erika)
5. Inge kann die Musik nicht hören. (wir)
6. Wir können heute nicht arbeiten. (Gisela)
7. Ich kann heute nicht ins Kino gehen. (Ute und Jens)

sollen to be supposed to

ich soll		wir sollen
du sollst	Sie sollen	ihr sollt
er/es/sie soll		sie sollen

Du **sollst** jetzt **beginnen**.   You're supposed to begin now.

H Decide which parts the members of your band should take.

■ Wer soll Klarinette spielen? Jürgen?   *Ja, Jürgen soll Klarinette spielen.*

1. Wer soll Gitarre spielen? Ich?
2. Wer soll Schlagzeug spielen? Jutta und Rainer?
3. Wer soll Klavier spielen? Kirstin?
4. Wer soll singen? Ich?
5. Wer soll Geige spielen? Stefan und Ute?

müssen must, to have to

ich muß		wir müssen
du mußt	Sie müssen	ihr müßt
er/es/sie muß		sie müssen

Sie **muß** es bald **tun**.   She has to do it soon.

I It's late. Say that the following people have to leave now

■ Gabi   *Gabi muß jetzt gehen.*

1. Hans-Jürgen
2. du
3. wir
4. ich
5. ihr
6. Stefan und Barbara

J Report to the class all the things you must do in the next few days.

■ schwer arbeiten   *Ich muß schwer arbeiten.*

1. Mathe und Englisch machen
2. Vokabeln lernen
3. Briefe schreiben
4. Schuhe kaufen

Kapitel 7   **139**

dürfen   may, to be permitted to

ich **darf**	wir **dürfen**
du **darfst** Sie dürfen	ihr **dürft**
er/es/sie **darf**	sie dürfen

Wir **dürfen** jetzt **gehen.**   We're allowed to go now.

K   Ask whether your friends really have permission to do what they plan.

▪   Ich gehe heute ins Kino.   *Darfst du denn heute ins Kino gehen?*

1. Ich gehe morgen ins Konzert.
2. Ich gehe übermorgen ins Theater.
3. Inge spielt heute Volleyball.
4. Bruno spielt heute Fußball.
5. Stefan und Bettina gehen morgen abend tanzen.

L   It's against the rules! Respond to the following questions by saying the actions are not permitted.

▪   Warum spielst du nicht?   *Ich darf nicht spielen.*

1. Warum beginnst du nicht?
2. Warum schwimmst du nicht?
3. Warum kommt Ute nicht?
4. Warum bleibt Jens nicht?
5. Warum geht ihr nicht?

wollen   to want, wish; to intend to

ich **will**	wir **wollen**
du **willst** Sie wollen	ihr **wollt**
er/es/sie **will**	sie wollen

Ihr **wollt** hoffentlich **arbeiten.**   You want to work, I hope.

M   Say who is planning to do the following things.

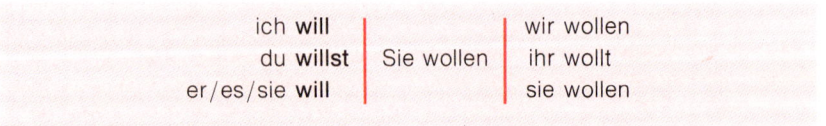

▪   Will Erik Musik hören? (du)   *Willst du Musik hören?*

1. Greta will heute nicht arbeiten. (wir)
2. Wir wollen Tennis spielen. (ich)
3. Ich will morgen schwimmen gehen. (Monika)
4. Will Ute Englisch lernen? (ihr)
5. Wollt ihr das Buch kaufen? (Hans-Jürgen)

möchte would like to

ich **möchte**		wir **möchten**
du **möchtest**	Sie **möchten**	ihr **möchtet**
er/es/sie **möchte**		sie **möchten**

Sie **möchten** es **kaufen.**   They would like to buy it.

Ich möchte, du möchtest, etc., are special forms of the verb **mögen** *(to like)* and are equivalent to *I would like, you would like*, etc.

N   Tell your teacher that you would like to do the following things.

■▥   jetzt Karten spielen   *Ich möchte jetzt Karten spielen.*

1. heute nachmittag Mathe machen
2. heute abend ins Kino gehen
3. morgen schwimmen gehen
4. am Wochenende wandern
5. die *Hot Dogs* hören

Du hast das Wort   Ask your teacher some questions about her/his leisure activities.

Können Sie [Klavier] spielen?
Möchten Sie am Wochenende [wandern]?
Wollen Sie heute abend [ins Kino] gehen?
Können Sie gut [schwimmen]?

Omission of the dependent infinitive with modals

Ich kann es nicht.   =   Ich kann es nicht tun.
Ich muß nach Hause. =   Ich muß nach Hause gehen.

In sentences with a modal, the dependent infinitive is often **omitted** when its meaning is clear.

O   Give the English equivalents of the following conversational exchanges.

1. Es ist schon spät.
   Mußt du wirklich nach Hause?
2. Wir wollen ins Kino. Hast du Zeit?
   Nein, heute kann ich nicht. Ich muß arbeiten.
3. Ich kann die Aufgabe nicht machen. Ich habe keinen Bleistift.
   Möchtest du meinen Kuli?
4. Ist das nicht Christl Wagner da?
   Ja, was will sie denn hier?

Street musicians in German-speaking countries entertain their listeners with many different kinds of music. Town squares and pedestrian shopping streets make ideal gathering places for audiences. Facing page, top: A casual jam session in Vienna. Middle: One can hear classical music on the streets in Munich. Bottom: Students of medieval music perform on the steps of the town hall in Rothenburg. Right: Organ grinders can still be heard on the Kurfürstendamm in Berlin. Below: Passing the hat at a street concert in Nürnberg.

Grammatische Übersicht

The subject pronouns **du, ihr, Sie** (A)

Tag, Frank! Was machst **du** heute?
Tag, Inge! Tag, Claudia! Was macht **ihr** heute?

Tag, Herr Wagner! Was machen **Sie** heute?
Tag, Frau Lenz! Tag, Frau Becker! Was machen **Sie** heute?

There are three ways to express *you* in German: **du, ihr,** and **Sie.** The familiar forms **du** (singular) and **ihr** (plural) are used in addressing relatives, close friends, or persons under about fifteen. **Du** and **ihr** are also used frequently among members of a group such as students, athletes, laborers, or soldiers. **Du** is used to address a single individual. **Ihr** is used to address two or more individuals.

Sie is a more formal form of address. It is used in addressing strangers or adults whom the speaker doesn't consider close friends. **Sie** may be either singular or plural.

Often people agree to use **du** with each other once a relationship has become more familiar. Addressing someone with **du** is called **duzen.** Addressing someone with **Sie** is called **siezen.**

Historically speaking, **sie sind** *(they are)* and **Sie sind** *(you are)* are the same form. It was considered polite to address someone as **sie** *(they)* and to capitalize the pronoun in writing.

The development of formal pronouns to address a person was common to a number of European languages. English used to distinguish singular *thou/thee* from plural *ye/you; thou/thee* was restricted to informal usage, and *ye/you* was used both as informal plural and formal singular and plural. Today only *you* survives as our all-purpose pronoun.

The meanings and uses of **sie** and **Sie**

Glaubt **sie** das?   Does *she* believe that?
Glauben **sie** das?   Do *they* believe that?
Glauben **Sie** das?   Do *you* believe that?

In spoken German, the meanings of **sie** *(she),* **sie** *(they),* and **Sie** *(you)* can be distinguished with the help of the corresponding verb form and the context.

sie + singular verb form = *she*
sie + plural verb form = *they*
Sie + plural verb form = *you* (formal)

In written German, **Sie** *(you)* is always capitalized.

The possessive adjectives **dein, euer, Ihr** (B-C)

Hast **du deinen** Mantel, Erik?
Habt **ihr eure** Mäntel, Kinder?
Haben **Sie Ihren** Mantel, Frau Lenz?

German has three possessive adjectives that correspond to the subject pronouns meaning *you*.

	SUBJECT PRONOUN	POSSESSIVE ADJECTIVE
familiar singular	du	dein/deine
familiar plural	ihr	euer/eure
formal, singular and plural	Sie	Ihr/Ihre

The meanings and uses of **ihr** and **Ihr**

Hat sie **ihren** Mantel?	Does she have *her* coat?
Haben sie **ihre** Mäntel?	Do they have *their* coats?
Haben Sie **Ihren** Mantel?	Do you have *your* coat?

Context usually makes clear the meanings of **ihr** *(her)*, **ihr** *(their)*, and **Ihr** *(your)*. Note that **Ihr** *(your)* is always capitalized, like the corresponding subject pronoun **Sie**.

Verbs with stem-vowel change **e > i** (D-E)

geben			
ich gebe		wir geben	
du **gibst**	Sie geben	ihr gebt	
er/es/sie **gibt**		sie geben	

nehmen			
ich nehme		wir nehmen	
du **nimmst**	Sie nehmen	ihr nehmt	
er/es/sie **nimmt**		sie nehmen	

Geben and **nehmen** have a stem-vowel change **e > i** in the **du-** and **er/sie-**forms. Note that an additional spelling change occurs in **nehmen: er/sie nimmt, du nimmst.**

Modal auxiliaries (F-O)

Er **muß** jetzt arbeiten.   He *must* work now.
Sie **kann** es tun.   She *can* do it.

English has modal auxiliary verbs such as *must* and *can* that indicate an attitude about an action, rather than expressing the action itself.

German also uses modal auxiliary verbs. German modals are irregular in the present-tense singular. They lack endings in the **ich-** and **er/sie-** forms, and most modals show stem-vowel change.

	dürfen	können	müssen	sollen	wollen	möchte
ich	darf	kann	muß	soll	will	möchte
du	darfst	kannst	mußt	sollst	willst	möchtest
er/es/sie	darf	kann	muß	soll	will	möchte
wir	dürfen	können	müssen	sollen	wollen	möchten
ihr	dürft	könnt	müßt	sollt	wollt	möchtet
sie	dürfen	können	müssen	sollen	wollen	möchten
Sie	dürfen	können	müssen	sollen	wollen	möchten

Soll ich die Karten **kaufen?**
Frank **will** nicht **arbeiten.**

Modal auxiliaries in German are usually used with dependent infinitives. The infinitive is in last position.

Ich **muß** nach Hause.   =   Ich **muß** nach Hause gehen.
Ich **will** mein Geld.   =   Ich **will** mein Geld haben.

The dependent infinitive may be omitted when the meaning of the sentence is clear from the context.

Meanings of modals

INFINITIVE/MEANING		EXAMPLES	ENGLISH EQUIVALENTS
dürfen	permission	Ich **darf** arbeiten.	I'm *allowed to* work.
können	ability	Ich **kann** arbeiten.	I *can* work.
müssen	compulsion	Ich **muß** arbeiten.	I *must (have to)* work.
sollen	obligation	Ich **soll** arbeiten.	I'm *supposed to* work.
wollen	wishing, wanting, intention	Ich **will** arbeiten.	I *want (intend) to* work.
möchte	desire	Ich **möchte** arbeiten.	I *would like to* work.

Das Metropol Theater ist in Ost-Berlin.

The modal **mögen**

Ich möchte, du möchtest, and so on, are special forms of the modal **mögen.** They are used frequently and are equivalent to English *would like.*

Mögen also has regular present-tense forms which are not used as often **(ich mag, du magst, er/sie mag, wir mögen, ihr mögt, sie mögen, Sie mögen).** The present-tense forms can be used to express a fondness or dislike for someone or something. **Mögen** rarely occurs in the affirmative. It is usually used in the interrogative or in the negative, without a dependent infinitive:

      Mögen Sie Frau Lenz?   Do you like Mrs. Lenz?
      Ich **mag** Rockmusik nicht.   I don't like rock music.

At this point, you will be expected only to recognize the present-tense forms of **mögen.**

Negative of **müssen**

      Du **mußt nicht** arbeiten.   You *don't have to* work (if you don't want to).

The negative of **müssen** means *not to have to.* Note that **Du mußt nicht arbeiten** means *You don't have (you're not forced) to work,* whereas English *You mustn't work* means *You are forbidden to work.*

The German movie industry was extremely important during the era of silent films and early "talkies" (1919–1932). Directors like Fritz Lang, F. W. Murnau, and G. W. Pabst were considered among the finest in the world, and the German use of the "moving camera" was very influential.

During the 1930's and 1940's many great German filmmakers moved to other countries — mainly the United States — and there was a long period of mediocrity in German cinema due to this loss of talent. Since the early 1970's there has been a rebirth of German film, led by directors like Werner Herzog, Rainer Werner Fassbinder, and Wim Wenders, to name only the best-known of a large and growing group. Their films explore profound issues relating to politics, art, and human nature.

Wiederholung

A Christl and Peter are discussing the *Hot Dogs* concert. Answer the questions, based on the following dialogue.

CHRISTL Die *Hot Dogs* geben morgen abend ein Konzert hier!
PETER Das ist ja prima, aber ich kann sie nicht hören.
CHRISTL Warum denn nicht? Mußt du arbeiten?
PETER Nein. Ich habe kein Geld, und die Karten sind sehr teuer.
CHRISTL Kein Problem! Mein Bruder arbeitet an der Kasse. Ich habe zwei Karten für das Konzert. Ich bekomme eine, und du bekommst eine.
PETER Das ist ja klasse. Vielen Dank!

1. Wann geben die *Hot Dogs* ein Konzert?
2. Warum kann Peter nicht ins Konzert?
3. Wer arbeitet an der Kasse?
4. Wer gibt Peter eine Karte für das Konzert?

B Inform Ingrid that you're going to do the same things she is doing this week.

■ Ich mache heute abend Hausaufgaben. (sollen)   *Ich soll heute abend auch Hausaufgaben machen.*

1. Ich spiele heute nachmittag Tennis. (können)
2. Ich gehe am Samstag ins Kino. (dürfen)
3. Ich kaufe morgen einen Pulli. (wollen)
4. Ich treibe am Sonntag Sport. (möchten)
5. Ich mache am Montag Chemie. (müssen)

C For each set of words below, pick out the three words that fit best into one category.

■ Mark, tragen, kosten, wieviel   *Mark, kosten, wieviel*

1. Jugendzentrum, Konzert, Band, Lieblingsfach
2. wohnen, Karte, Kasse, ausverkauft
3. Stunde, Theater, Zeit, Uhr
4. Lust, Aufgabe, Geschichte, Englisch
5. Bleistift, Kuli, Geld, Radiergummi
6. Anzug, Schlagzeug, Größe, Farbe
7. Freund, Bruder, Schwester, Vater
8. Gitarre, Flöte, Geige, Fußball
9. Wochenende, Nachmittag, Café, Abend

D It's Inge's birthday. Tell what she is getting from her family and friends.

> ▪ Erna/Bluse   *Erna gibt Inge eine Bluse.*

1. Carola/Kleid
2. Hans-Dieter/Pulli
3. ihr Vater/Schulmappe
4. ihre Mutter/Gitarre
5. Thomas/Kuli
6. Rüdiger/Buch

E Udo isn't speaking loudly enough. Ask about the part of the sentence you didn't hear.

> ▪ Ich gehe *heute abend* ins Konzert.   *Wann gehst du ins Konzert?*

1. *Meine Freundin Ute* kommt auch.
2. *Die Hot Dogs* spielen.
3. Sie spielen *im Jugendzentrum*.
4. Die Vorstellung beginnt *um halb acht*.
5. Die Karten kosten *DM 12,50*.

F Take the role of the ticket-seller in the illustration and answer the customers' questions.

1. Wer gibt das Rock-Konzert am Samstag abend?
2. Wieviel kosten die Karten?
3. Haben Sie noch Karten zu 8 Mark?
4. Wann beginnt die Vorstellung?
5. Wer spielt morgen abend hier?
6. Kann ich noch Karten für morgen abend bekommen?

Kulturlesestück

Wer geht ins Kino?

Deutsche Teenager gehen gern ins Kino. Einige° Filme sind sehr gut und laufen° zum Beispiel° auch in Amerika. Aber die Deutschen sehen° auch amerikanische Filme gern. Amerikanische Stars sprechen° in deutschen Kinos Deutsch. Die Deutschen mögen Untertitel° nicht.

    Die Karten für gute Plätze° sind teuer — sie können sieben Mark oder mehr kosten. Natürlich kann man auch billige Karten bekommen. Die guten Plätze sind hinten°, die billigen Plätze vorne°.

    Meistens° gibt es eine Vorstellung am Nachmittag und zwei Vorstellungen am Abend, zum Beispiel um 19 und um 21 Uhr. Und man muß dann auch um 7 oder um 9 Uhr kommen.

°some / run
°for example
°see, watch
°speak
°subtitles
°seats
°in the back
°in the front
°usually

A Decide whether each statement is true *(richtig)* or false *(falsch)* based on the reading.

1. Deutsche Teenager dürfen nicht ins Kino gehen.
2. Deutsche sehen amerikanische Filme gern.
3. In deutschen Kinos haben amerikanische Filme Untertitel.
4. In deutschen Kinos kosten alle Karten sieben Mark.
5. Die Plätze vorne kosten mehr als *(more than)* die Plätze hinten.
6. Die Filme in deutschen Kinos laufen meistens nicht den ganzen Tag.

B Separate the following statements into two categories — those most typical of German movies and those most typical of American movies. If the statement is generally true of both German and American movies, put it in both categories: *deutsch und amerikanisch*.

1. Teenager gehen gern ins Kino.
2. Amerikanische Filme sind populär.
3. Die amerikanischen Stars sprechen Deutsch.
4. Die Stars sprechen Deutsch, aber der Film hat Untertitel.
5. Karten sind teuer.
6. Die Plätze vorne sind billig, denn *(because)* sie sind nicht so gut.
7. Die Vorstellung beginnt um sieben, aber man kann auch oft um acht hineingehen *(go in)*.
8. Es gibt eine Vorstellung am Nachmittag.

Vokabeln

SUBSTANTIVE

die Band, -s   band
die Frage, -n   question
das Geld   money
die Gruppe, -n   group
das Jugendzentrum   youth center, club
die Karte, -n   ticket
die Kasse   box office
das Kino, -s   movie theater
das Konzert, -e   concert
die Lust   pleasure, enjoyment
das Theater, -   theater
die Vorstellung, -en   performance
die Zeit   time

VERBEN

beginnen   to start, to begin
bekommen   to get, to receive
dürfen (darf)   may, to be permitted to
fragen   to ask
geben (i)   to give; **es gibt** (+ *acc.*)   there is, there are
glauben   to believe
können (kann)   can, to be able to
möchte   would like to
mögen (mag)   to like
müssen (muß)   must, to have to
nehmen (nimmt)   to take
sollen (soll)   should, to be supposed to
tun   to do
versuchen   to try
wollen (will)   to want, to intend to, to wish

ANDERE WÖRTER

alles   all, everything
an   at
ausverkauft   sold out
bei   at
bitte   please; you're welcome
bitte schön   please; you're welcome
dann   then
dumm   dumb, stupid
ein paar   a few, some
einfach   simple, simply
frei   free, not busy
mal   *flavoring word (see p. 133)*
mehr   more
morgen   tomorrow; ~ **abend**   tomorrow evening
nichts   nothing
noch nicht   not yet
sicher   sure, certain(ly)
Sie   you (*formal*)
übermorgen   the day after tomorrow
vielleicht   maybe

BESONDERE AUSDRÜCKE

hast du Lust?   do you feel like . . . ?
ich habe keine Lust   I don't feel like it
ja, und wie!   sure, I do (I am)
es geht   it's possible
ich bekomme frei   I'll get (the day) off
das schon   that's true
Karten zu drei Mark   tickets for three marks
das macht sechzehn Mark   that's sixteen marks
nichts mehr   nothing left

Ansichtskarten sind interessant

Thomas is curious about Petra's choice of a hobby. He thinks old postcards are dull.

THOMAS Sag mal, warum sammelst du gerade Ansichtskarten?
PETRA Ich weiß nicht. Es macht Spaß.
THOMAS Wirklich? Das verstehe ich nicht.
PETRA Sehr einfach. Alte Ansichtskarten sind interessant und auch wertvoll.

Fragen
1. Was ist Petras Hobby?
2. Wie findet Thomas Petras Hobby?
3. Warum sammelt Petra alte Ansichtskarten?

Du hast das Wort

Ask a classmate whether he/she collects anything.

Sammelst du etwas°?   Nein, ich sammle nichts.
                     Ja. Ich sammle | Briefmarken°.
                                    | Schallplatten°.
                                    | Poster°.
                                    | Ansichtskarten.
                                    | Bierdeckel°.

Thomas braucht ein Hobby

Petra and Gerd think maybe Thomas needs a hobby, too.

GERD Der Thomas ist wirklich eine lahme Ente.
PETRA Ja, er ist immer müde. Und er findet immer alles langweilig.
GERD Er hat aber auch zu nichts Lust.
PETRA Was er braucht, ist ein Hobby.
GERD Radioamateur vielleicht.
PETRA Oder Keramik.

Richtig oder falsch?
1. Thomas ist immer müde.
2. Er findet alles interessant.
3. Er hat zu nichts Lust.
4. Er hat ein Hobby.
5. Er ist Radioamateur.

Sammelst du auch Briefmarken?

Du hast das Wort

A. A classmate asks you whether you have a hobby. How would you respond?

Hast du ein Hobby?   Ja, ich spiele [Tennis].
Ja, ich fotografiere° sehr gern.
Ja, ich sammle Briefmarken.
Ja, ich lese° viel.
Ja, ich gehe gern spazieren.
Ja, ich repariere° alte Autos°.
Nein, ich habe kein Hobby.

B. A friend suggests that you need a hobby. What are your excuses for not choosing the hobby he/she suggests?

| Du brauchst ein Hobby. | Ja, ich habe oft nichts zu tun.
Ja, ich habe oft Langeweile°.
Meinst du? |

Keramik	ist	vielleicht	Ach, [Keramik] ist zu schwer.
Radioamateur		interessant.	Ach, [Radios°] sind zu kompliziert°.
Ansichtskarten	sind		Ach, [Ansichtskarten] sind so langweilig.
Briefmarken			Ach, [Briefmarken] sind zu teuer.

Was habt ihr heute vor?

Astrid would like to know what Klaus and his friends have planned for the afternoon.

ASTRID   Du, Klaus, was habt ihr heute nachmittag vor?
KLAUS   Wir fahren nach Hamburg.
ASTRID   Kauft ihr ein?
KLAUS   Ja, wir kaufen Gerds Geburtstagsgeschenk.
ASTRID   Wo?
KLAUS   Ich weiß noch nicht. Bei Karstadt vielleicht.

Fragen

1. Wohin° fahren Klaus und seine Freunde?
2. Was wollen sie machen?
3. Wo kaufen sie ein?

Du hast das Wort

A classmate inquires about your plans. How would you respond?

| Was hast du | heute / heute nachmittag / heute abend / am Wochenende | vor? |

Ich muß [arbeiten].
Ich muß [Deutsch] machen.
Ich gehe [ins Kino].
Ich spiele [Tennis].
Ich weiß noch nicht.
Nichts.
Ich habe zu nichts Lust.
Ich repariere mein Auto.

The government of the **BRD** regulates store hours to prevent competitors from taking advantage of each other and to maintain reasonable working hours. Monday through Friday stores are permitted to be open only between 7:00 A.M. and 6:30 P.M. On Saturdays stores must close by 2:00 P.M., with the exception of the first Saturday of the month **(langer Samstag),** when they may remain open until 6:00 P.M.

Stores in small towns and some city neighborhoods generally close for two or three hours during lunchtime on weekdays.

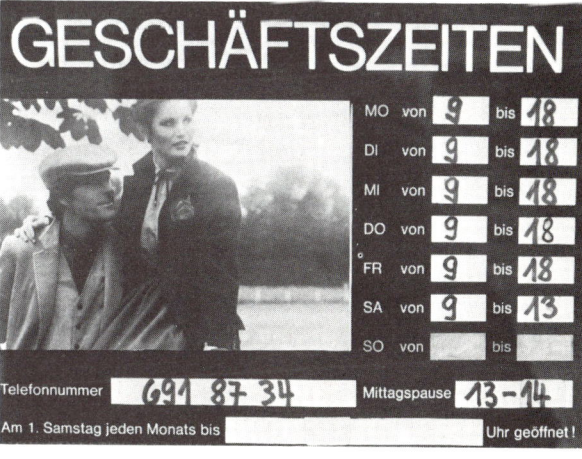

Komm doch mit!

Astrid tries to persuade Erik to go shopping with her.

ASTRID   Kommst du heute nachmittag mit?
ERIK   Wohin?
ASTRID   In die Stadt. Zum Musikhaus Schumann.
ERIK   Heute, am Samstag?
ASTRID   Ja, heute ist doch langer Samstag.
ERIK   Ach ja, stimmt. Da machen die Geschäfte erst um fünf zu. Was willst du denn bei Schumann?
ASTRID   Die neue Platte von Katja Peters kaufen. Also, willst du nun mitkommen oder nicht?
ERIK   Ich habe eigentlich keine Zeit.
ASTRID   Ach, komm doch mit!
ERIK   Na gut.

Du hast das Wort

You have plans for this evening. Invite a friend to come along and inform her/him where you're going.

Kommst du heute abend mit?   Wohin?

In die Disco°.   Ja, gern.
In die Stadt.   Wann gehen wir?
Ins Café°.   Danke, ich kann nicht.
Ins Kino.
Ins Konzert.
Ins Jugendzentrum.
Ins Theater.

Frag!

Ask a friend to obtain certain information from someone else. Note that when someone tells you to ask someone else a question, the verb comes at the end. In your question, however, regular word order is used.

■ Frag [Ute], wie sie alte An-   Ute, wie findest du alte Ansichtskarten findet!   sichtskarten?

1. Frag [Kai], was er sammelt!
2. Frag [Ute], was sie heute nachmittag macht!
3. Frag [Kai], was er bei Schumann kaufen will!
4. Frag [Ute], welche Platte sie kaufen möchte!
5. Frag [Kai], wann er ins Kino geht!
6. Frag [Ute], wieviel die Kinokarten kosten!

In recent years the downtown areas of many cities in German-speaking countries have been converted to traffic-free pedestrian zones **(Fußgängerzonen).** In addition to attractive shops and boutiques, the **Fußgängerzone** has many restaurants and outdoor cafés. The streets are frequently lined with flowers or trees, and they often lead into small squares with fountains or sculpture. Throughout the **Fußgängerzone** there are benches where people can rest their tired feet or simply sit and watch the others go by.

Wortschatzerweiterung

Musikhaus Schumann

1. der Cassetten-Recorder
2. das Radio
3. die Cassette
4. der Fernseher
5. die Schallplatte (die Platte)
6. die Stereoanlage
7. der Plattenspieler

A Answer the following questions based on the illustration.

1. Wie teuer ist die Stereoanlage?
2. Was kostet mehr — das Radio oder der Cassetten-Recorder?
3. Ist der Fernseher preiswert?
4. Ist eine Schallplatte billig oder teuer?

Du hast das Wort Compare your preferences with a classmate's.

Möchtest du einen Cassetten-Recorder kaufen oder hast du schon einen?
Kaufst du viele Platten? Cassetten?
Hörst du gern Radio?
Siehst du oft fern°?

Some useful commands

Mach die Tür bitte zu!	Please close the door.
Mach das Fenster bitte auf!	Please open the window.
Mach das Licht bitte an!	Please turn on the light.
Mach das Licht bitte aus!	Please turn out the light.
Steh bitte auf!	Please stand up.

B Carry out the commands as your teacher gives them.

C Tell a friend to carry out some of the commands above.

Flavoring word **mal** in commands

Sag **mal,** warum sammelst du gerade Ansichtskarten?	Say (Tell me), why do you collect post cards?
Schreib doch **mal!**	Why don't you write (sometime)?

Mal is frequently used to soften commands. The speaker leaves the time for carrying out the command vague and up to the receiver of the command.

Flavoring word **doch**

Komm **doch** mit!	Why don't you come along?
Ja, heute ist **doch** langer Samstag.	Today's the first Saturday of the month (remember?).

As a flavoring word **doch** has several meanings. In the first example the speaker uses **doch** to persuade the listener to do something. In the second example the speaker uses **doch** to imply that what is said is obvious and reminds the listener of something they both know.

D Give the English equivalents.

1. Sag mal! Gehen wir heute einkaufen oder nicht?
2. Hör mal! Das tut man doch nicht.
3. Wir gehen abends oft schwimmen. Komm doch mal mit!
4. Was machst du heute abend?
   Das weißt du doch.
5. Möchtest du mal die *Hot Dogs* hören?
6. Wir können es ja mal versuchen.
7. Schreib doch mal an Barbara.

Aussprache

[ai] m**ei**n, M**ai**er
[ɔi] h**eu**te, H**äu**ser
[ao] br**au**n

A Practice the following words horizontally in pairs.

[ai]	[ɔi]	[ao]	[ɔi]
l**ei**te	L**eu**te	L**au**te	L**eu**te
h**ei**ser	H**äu**ser	bl**au**e	Bl**äu**e
S**ei**le	S**äu**le	s**au**re	S**äu**re
B**ei**le	B**eu**le	B**au**m	B**äu**me
H**ai**	H**eu**	H**au**fen	h**äu**fen

[i]	[ai]
L**ie**be	L**ei**be
W**ie**se	W**ei**se
s**ie**de	S**ei**de
B**ie**l	B**ei**l
W**ie**n	W**ei**n

B Practice the sounds [ai], [ɔi], and [ao]. Read the sentences aloud.

1. Meine Brüder spielen beide viel Fußball.
2. Das kleine Kind lernt fleißig Deutsch.
3. Warum gibt es so viele graue Häuser hier?

Aus den Augen, aus dem Sinn.

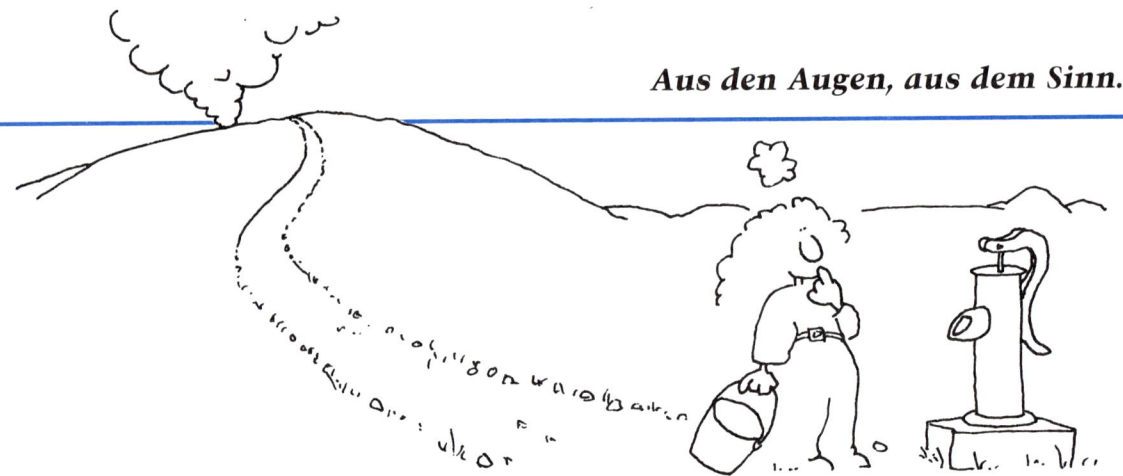

Übungen

The interrogatives **wo** and **wohin**

Wo ist Martina? Where is Martina?
Wohin geht sie? Where is she going?

Wo is used to ask about location. **Wohin** is used to ask about direction.

A You didn't hear the last part of the following statements. Ask to have the information repeated, using *wo* or *wohin*.

■ Martina wohnt in München. *Wo wohnt Martina?*
■ Sie fährt morgen nach Bremen. *Wohin fährt sie morgen?*

1. Utes Freund wohnt in Frankfurt.
2. Ilse geht jetzt nach Hause.
3. Tanja und Günter gehen ins Kino.
4. Herr Fleischer arbeitet zu Hause.
5. Frau Kaufmann fährt in die Stadt.

Verbs with stem-vowel change **e>ie**

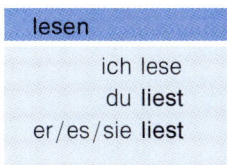
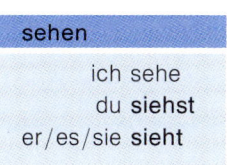

lesen	sehen
ich lese	ich sehe
du liest	du siehst
er/es/sie liest	er/es/sie sieht

Lesen and **sehen** have a stem-vowel change **e>ie** in the **du-** and **er/sie-**forms of the present tense.

B Report on the leisure activities of the following people.

■ Dieter *Dieter liest viel.*

1. Frau Weiß 3. Monika 5. wir
2. ich 4. du 6. ihr

C Say that the following people often watch television.

■ Marita *Marita sieht oft fern.*

1. Herr Hübner 3. Torsten 5. wir
2. ich 4. du 6. ihr

Present tense of **wissen**

ich **weiß**	wir **wissen**
du **weißt** Sie **wissen**	ihr **wißt**
er/es/sie **weiß**	sie **wissen**

Wissen is irregular in the singular forms of the present tense.

D You and your friends are going to a disco. Confirm that everyone knows when you're going.

■) Jutta weiß, wann wir in die Disco gehen. Und Jürgen?   *Er weiß das auch.*

1. Und Benno?
2. Und Christl?
3. Und du?
4. Und Ulf und Jochen?
5. Und ihr?

Du hast das Wort

A. Answer according to your personal knowledge or experience. Use *Ja, das weiß ich* or *Nein, das weiß ich nicht.*

Weißt du, wie alt deine Mutter ist?
Weißt du, wann dein Vater Geburtstag hat?
Weißt du, wann deine Freunde Geburtstag haben?
Weißt du, wieviel Jeans kosten?
Weißt du, wieviel eine Mappe kostet?
Weißt du, wieviel Kinokarten kosten?

B. Ask your teacher some of the questions in Exercise A.

The imperative forms: **du, ihr, Sie**

Imperative forms are used to express commands. In both German and English, the verb is in first position.

du-imperative

Inge! **Frag(e)** bitte Frau Held!	Inge, ask Mrs. Held, please.
Dirk! **Arbeite** bitte jetzt!	Dirk, work now, please.

The **du**-imperative consists of the stem of a verb plus **-e**. The **-e** is often dropped in informal usage: **frage!** > **frag!** The **-e** may not be omitted if the stem ends in **-d** or **-t: arbeite!**

E Frank is trying to put off repairing your car until tomorrow. Try to convince him to do it today.

▪▪▪ Ich repariere es morgen.   *Ach, repariere es doch heute!*

1. Ich versuche es morgen.
2. Ich mache es morgen.
3. Ich beginne morgen.
4. Ich komme morgen.

Petra! **Nimm** bitte das Buch da!	Petra, please take that book.
Lies es heute abend!	Read it this evening.

If the stem vowel of a verb changes from **e** to **i** or **ie**, the imperative has the same vowel change and has no final **-e: nehmen** > **nimm!**

F Monika is working with you in the library. Order her to do the things she asks about.

▪▪▪ Soll ich das Buch da nehmen?   *Ja, nimm das Buch da!*

1. Soll ich das Buch lesen?
2. Soll ich das Heft nehmen?
3. Soll ich Ute das Buch geben?
4. Soll ich Jan das Heft geben?

Interessante Ansichtskarten

ihr-imperative

Günter! Peter! **Fragt** bitte Frau Held!	Günter and Peter, please ask Mrs. Held.
Arbeitet bitte jetzt!	Please work now.

The **ihr**-imperative is identical with the **ihr**-form of the present tense, except that the pronoun **ihr** is omitted.

G You and your friends are in a record store. Advise them to do the things they ask about.

    ▪ Sollen wir die Platte hier kaufen?   *Ja, kauft die Platte!*

1. Sollen wir auch die Cassette nehmen?
2. Sollen wir die Platte spielen?
3. Sollen wir jetzt beginnen?
4. Sollen wir es versuchen?

Sie-imperative

Herr Schmidt! **Fragen Sie** Frau Held!	Mr. Schmidt, ask Mrs. Held.
Arbeiten Sie bitte jetzt!	Please work now.

The **Sie**-imperative is identical with the **Sie**-form of the present tense. The pronoun **Sie** is always stated and follows the verb directly.

H Frau Wagner is to pick up some theater tickets for you. Give her precise instructions as to what to do.

    ▪ Soll ich jetzt zur Theaterkasse gehen?   *Ja, gehen Sie bitte jetzt zur Theaterkasse!*

1. Soll ich drei Karten kaufen?
2. Soll ich die Karten zu 30 Mark nehmen?
3. Soll ich heute abend ins Theater gehen?
4. Soll ich um sieben kommen?
5. Soll ich mit Frau Lange fahren?

Du hast das Wort Lead your class in a team game. Give various orders to individual members of each team. If they obey you, their teams gain a point. You may wish to use some of the commands from page 161.

Mach das Licht aus!   Steh auf!
Mach das Fenster auf!   Nimm [Utes] Buch!
Mach die Tür zu!   Gib [Erik] das Buch!

Welche Platte soll ich denn kaufen?

Imperative forms of the verb **sein**

Inge!	**Sei** um sieben da!	
Günter! Peter!	**Seid** um sieben da!	Be here at seven.
Frau Lange!	**Seien Sie** um sieben da!	

I Urge the following people to change their attitudes.

▪ Andrea, du bist aber faul.   *Sei nicht so faul!*

1. Astrid, du bist aber sauer.
2. Anton, du bist aber doof.
3. Bernd, du bist aber wirklich langweilig.

▪ Claudia! Gerd! Ihr seid ja so sauer.   *Seid nicht so sauer!*

4. Regina! Hugo! Ihr seid aber sehr faul.
5. Elke! Paul! Ihr seid so doof.
6. Inge! Franz! Ihr seid wirklich langweilig.

▪ Herr Kurz! Sind Sie sicher?   *Seien Sie nicht so sicher!*

7. Frau Lutz! Sie sind ja so fleißig.
8. Fräulein Weiß! Sie sind ja so fleißig.
9. Herr Lehner! Warum sind Sie so langweilig?

Separable-prefix verbs

The separable prefix

mitkommen	Ingrid **kommt** heute **mit**.	Ingrid is coming along today.
zumachen	Wann **macht** das Geschäft **zu**?	When does the store close?

Many German verbs begin with prefixes such as **mit** and **zu**. Some prefixes are separable: in the present tense, they are separated from the base form of the verb and are in last position.

Möchtest du heute **mitkommen?**   Would you like to come along today?

Kannst du die Tür **zumachen?**   Can you shut the door?

In the infinitive form, the prefix is attached to the base form of the verb.

J Ingrid asks what you and your friends have planned today. Verify her guesses.

■ Kommst du heute nachmittag mit?   Ja, ich komme heute nachmittag mit.

1. Kommt Axel auch mit?
2. Hat Helga etwas vor?
3. Kaufst du bei Karstadt ein?
4. Macht Karstadt um fünf zu?

Nicht with separable-prefix verbs

mitkommen	Ingrid kommt heute **nicht** mit.	
aufmachen	Warum machst du das Fenster **nicht** auf?	

In a negative sentence, the adverb **nicht** usually comes directly before the separable prefix.

K Werner wants to know what plans you and Trudi have. Keep him guessing by answering his questions in the negative.

■ Kommt ihr heute nachmittag mit?   Nein, wir kommen nicht mit.

1. Kauft ihr heute nachmittag ein?
2. Kommt ihr heute abend mit?
3. Seht ihr heute abend fern?
4. Habt ihr vor, ins Kino zu gehen?

Imperative forms of separable-prefix verbs

Gerd! **Mach** die Tür bitte **zu!**
Peter! Claudia! **Kommt** jetzt **mit!**
Frau Stein! **Machen Sie** bitte das Fenster **auf!**

In an imperative sentence, the separable prefix is in last position.

L You're getting the room ready for a party at the youth center. Tell each of your assistants what to do.

◼ Türen aufmachen *Mach die Türen auf!*

1. Fenster aufmachen
2. Licht anmachen
3. bei Karstadt einkaufen
4. Fenster wieder zumachen
5. Türen wieder zumachen
6. Licht ausmachen

Grammatische Übersicht

Interrogatives **wo** and **wohin** (A)

Wo ist Ingrid? *Where* is Ingrid?
Wohin geht Dieter? *Where* is Dieter going?

English uses the single word *where* for the two meanings *in what place* and *to what place*. German always distinguishes between these two meanings. **Wo** is used for *in what place* and **wohin** is used for *to what place*.

Verbs with stem-vowel change **e > ie** (B-C)

lesen		
ich lese		wir lesen
du **liest**	Sie lesen	ihr lest
er/es/sie **liest**		sie lesen

sehen		
ich sehe		wir sehen
du **siehst**	Sie sehen	ihr seht
er/es/sie **sieht**		sie sehen

Lesen and **sehen** have a stem-vowel change **e>ie** in the **du-** and **er/sie-**forms of the present tense. Note that because the stem of **lesen** ends in a sibilant, the **-st** ending of the **du-**form contracts to **-t: du liest.**

Kapitel 8

Present tense of **wissen** (D)

ich **weiß**	wir **wissen**
du **weißt** Sie **wissen**	ihr **wißt**
er/es/sie **weiß**	sie **wissen**

Wissen is irregular in the singular forms of the present tense.

The imperative forms: **du, ihr, Sie** (E-H)

Ernst!	**Schreib** bald!	
Peter! Inge!	**Schreibt** bald!	Write soon.
Herr Schmidt!	**Schreiben Sie** bald!	

The imperative forms are used to express commands. As in English, the verb is in first position. In written German an exclamation point is always used after a command.

du-imperative

INFINITIVE	IMPERATIVE	PRESENT
beginnen	**Beginn(e)** jetzt!	Beginnst du jetzt?
arbeiten	**Arbeite** jetzt!	Arbeitest du jetzt?
nehmen	**Nimm** das Papier!	Nimmst du das Papier?

The **du-**imperative consists of the stem of a verb plus **-e,** but the **-e** is often dropped in informal usage. If the stem of the verb ends in **-d** or **-t,** the **-e** may not be omitted in written German: **arbeite!**

If the stem vowel of a verb changes from **e** to **i** or **ie,** the **du-**imperative has the same vowel change and has no final **-e.** The pronoun **du** is not used in the imperative.

ihr-imperative

INFINITIVE	IMPERATIVE	PRESENT
beginnen	**Beginnt** jetzt!	Beginnt ihr jetzt?
nehmen	**Nehmt** das Papier!	Nehmt ihr das Papier?

The **ihr-**imperative is identical with the **ihr-**form of the present tense, except that the pronoun **ihr** is not used in the imperative.

Sie-imperative

INFINITIVE	IMPERATIVE	PRESENT
beginnen	**Beginnen Sie** jetzt!	Beginnen Sie jetzt?
nehmen	**Nehmen Sie** das Papier!	Nehmen Sie das Papier?

The **Sie-**imperative is identical with the **Sie-**form of the present tense. The pronoun **Sie** is always stated and follows the verb immediately.

In speech, one differentiates a command from a question by intonation. The voice falls at the end of a command and rises at the end of a general question.

Imperative forms of the verb **sein** (I)

Inge!	**Sei** um sieben Uhr da!	
Petra! Uwe!	**Seid** um sieben Uhr da!	Be here at seven
Herr Braun!	**Seien Sie** um sieben Uhr da!	o'clock.

Note that the **Sie-**imperative of **sein** is different from the **Sie-**form of the present tense.

Spinnen ist ein interessantes Hobby.

Separable-prefix verbs (J-L)

to get up	I *get up* early.
to call up	Did you *call* your friend *up*?
to write down	Let me *write down* your address.

English has many two-word verbs, such as *to get up, to call up,* and *to write down.* These two-word verbs consist of a verb and a particle (for example, *up, down*). In sentences the particle is sometimes separated from the verb.

aufstehen	Warum **stehst** du nicht **auf?**
mitkommen	Erik **kommt** heute **mit.**
zumachen	**Mach** die Tür **zu!**

German has a large number of *separable-prefix verbs* that function like certain English two-word verbs. Examples are **aufstehen, mitkommen, zumachen.** In present-tense statements and questions and in imperative forms, the separable prefix (**auf, mit, zu,** and so on) is separated from the verb and is in last position.

> Ute kann nicht **mitkommen.**

In the infinitive form, the prefix is attached to the base form of the verb.

> Inge kommt heute **nicht** mit.

The adverb **nicht** usually comes directly before a separable prefix.

> Frank möchte **mit'kommen.**
> Petra kommt nicht **mit'.**

In spoken German, the stress falls on the prefix of separable-prefix verbs. In the vocabularies of this text, separable-prefix verbs are indicated by a raised dot between the prefix and the verb: **auf·stehen, ein·kaufen, mit·kommen, fern·sehen, vor·haben, zu·machen.**

Infinitives ending in **-eln**

sammeln		
ich **sammle**		wir sammeln
du **sammelst**	Sie sammeln	ihr sammelt
er/es/sie **sammelt**		sie sammeln

When the infinitive of a verb ends in **-eln,** the stem loses the **-e** in the **ich-**form.

Hamburg has long been one of the busiest seaports in Europe. Above: Hamburg in 1730. Below: The city today is a dynamic blend of the old and the new.

Wiederholung

A Erik is having a hard time getting Jürgen to do anything. Answer the questions based on the following dialogue.

ERIK	Wir gehen heute abend zu Inge. Kommst du auch?
JÜRGEN	Ach nein. Bei Inge ist es immer so langweilig. Da dürfen wir nicht richtig Musik machen.
ERIK	Willst du vielleicht ins Kino?
JÜRGEN	Ach nein. Filme finde ich doof.
ERIK	Was möchtest du denn?
JÜRGEN	Ich weiß es nicht. Ich habe zu nichts Lust.
ERIK	Du bist aber eine lahme Ente!

1. Wohin möchte Erik heute abend?
2. Warum geht Jürgen nicht mit?
3. Will er ins Kino? Warum (nicht)?
4. Was will er denn?
5. Warum ist Jürgen eine lahme Ente?

B Make up two-line dialogues by choosing a line from column A and an appropriate response from column B.

A	B
Keramik ist interessant.	Ich kann's ja mal versuchen.
Du brauchst ein Hobby.	Ja, und wie!
Ich sammle alte Autos.	Meinst du?
Möchtest du fotografieren lernen?	Ich weiß es nicht.
	Vielleicht. Ich bin nicht sicher.
Benno ist Radioamateur, nicht?	Nein, eigentlich nicht.
[Wanderst] du gern?	Das kann sein.
	Ist das nicht furchtbar teuer?
	Nein, das ist zu langweilig.

C You and Jürgen have plans for tomorrow. Form sentences using the cues provided.

1. Jürgen / müssen / aufstehen / morgen / um sechs
2. er / wollen / fahren / nach Hamburg
3. ihr / dürfen / mitkommen / auch / ?
4. wir / können / einkaufen / da
5. Jürgen / möchten / kaufen / bei Schumann / eine Platte
6. die Platten / sollen / sein / da / sehr billig
7. du / wollen / kaufen / auch / eine Platte / ?

D Complete the second line of each two-line exchange by choosing an appropriate flavoring word. Give an English equivalent of each exchange.

1. Ich wohne nicht in der Gartenstraße.
   Wo wohnst du ____? (denn, doch)
2. Fährst du nach Bergdorf?
   Ja, komm ____ mit! (denn, doch)
3. Der Anzug da kostet nur 100 Mark.
   Das ist ____ billig. (mal, ja)
4. Petra sammelt alte Ansichtskarten.
   Das ist ____ interessant! (ja, denn)
5. Ist das Buch interessant?
   Ja. Lies es doch ____. (mal, ja)
6. Der Rock hier ist zu klein.
   Welche Größe trägst du ____? (mal, denn)

E Thomas is in charge of a surprise party at his house this evening. Change the phrases in italics to the plural and restate his remarks.

1. Wo ist *das Geschenk?*
2. Hat Peter *den Bierdeckel?*
3. Ich brauche nun *die Schallplatte.*
4. Wer hat *die Cassette?*
5. Mach bitte *die Tür* auf.
6. Gib mir bitte *das Poster* da.
7. Hört ihr nicht *das Auto?*
8. Jetzt könnt ihr *die Tür* wieder zumachen.

F The following sentences contain some unfamiliar words that are either cognates or compounds of familiar words. Give the meaning of each italicized word.

1. Hast du die *Kinokarten* gekauft?
2. Weißt du, wann die *Abendvorstellung* beginnt?
3. Karl spielt gern Fußball, Basketball und Hockey. Er ist wirklich ein *Sportfreund.*
4. Eishockey spielen wir im *Wintersportzentrum.*
5. Volker braucht ein deutsch-englisches *Wörterbuch.*
6. Zum Geburtstag bekommt ein *Baby* viele *Spielsachen.*

G Answer the following questions. Then ask your teacher the same questions.

1. Hast du ein Hobby?
2. Sammelst du etwas?
3. Liest du gern?
4. Welches Buch liest du jetzt?
5. Gehst du gern spazieren?
6. Treibst du gern Sport?
7. Fotografierst du gern?

Kulturlesestück

Sammelfreuden

Viele Menschen° sammeln etwas: Briefmarken, Bierdeckel, Bücher, Ansichtskarten, Schallplatten, Poster. Auch als° Gemeinschaft° sammeln die Menschen: Museen° findet man° in vielen Städten.

⁵ Viele Deutsche gehen am Sonntag ins Museum, denn dann kostet es nichts. Sie sehen da Sammlungen° von Autos und Maschinen, von Bildern° und Postern, von Briefmarken, Büchern, Keramik und Möbeln°. Es gibt auch
¹⁰ besondere° Museen, zum Beispiel das Gutenberg-Museum in Mainz, das Grimm-Museum in Kassel, ein Ledermuseum° in Offenbach, ein Uhrenmuseum in Furtwangen, ein Fahrradmuseum° in Neckarsulm und sogar ein Brotmuseum° in Ulm.

people

as
society / museums
one

collections
pictures
furniture
special

leather museum

bicycle museum
bread museum

A Choose the phrase that best completes each statement, based on the reading.

1. Die Gemeinschaft sammelt Sachen in . . .
   a. Möbeln
   b. Geschäften
   c. Bildern
   d. Museen
2. Man findet Museen in vielen . . .
   a. Städten
   b. Kassen
   c. Sammlungen
   d. Theatern
3. Am Sonntag sind viele Menschen im Museum, denn . . .
   a. die Karten sind am Sonntag sehr billig
   b. sie brauchen keine Karten zu kaufen
   c. am Samstag müssen sie arbeiten
   d. die Museen machen nur am Sonntag auf

B Below are lists of items, grouped so that two of them have something in common and might therefore be found in the same museum. Indicate which item does not belong in each group.

1. Briefmarken, Ansichtskarten, Autos
2. Möbel, Plattenspieler, Radios
3. Bilder, Brot, Poster
4. Autos, Schlagzeug, Fahrräder
5. Kleider, Anzüge, Bierdeckel
6. Uhren, Geigen, Gitarren

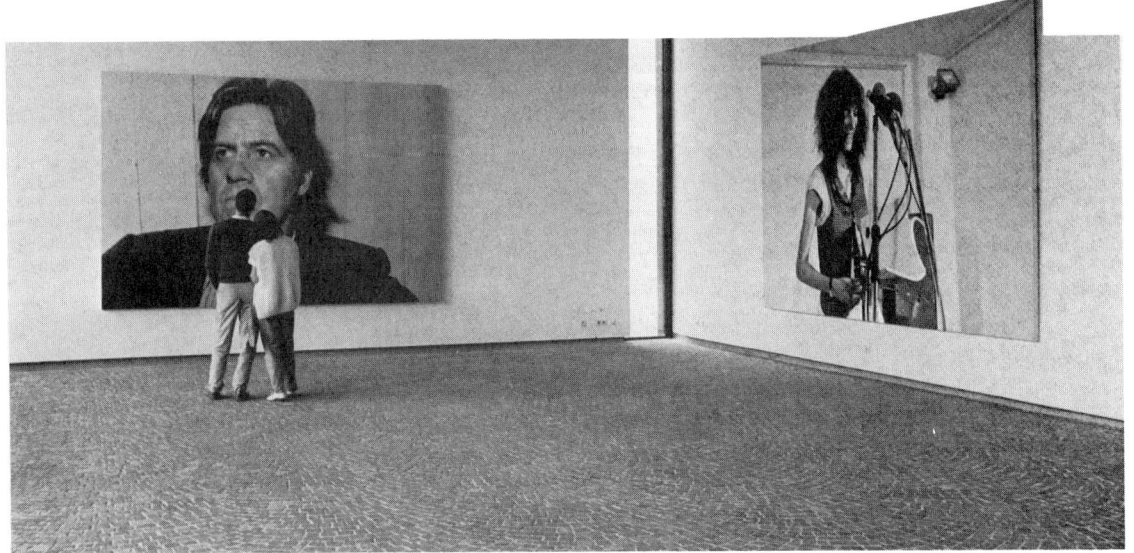

Vokabeln

SUBSTANTIVE

die Ansichtskarte, -n   picture postcard
das Auto, -s   car
der Bierdeckel, -   coaster *(used under a glass or mug)*
die Briefmarke, -n   postage stamp
das Café, -s   café
die Cassette, -n   cassette
der Cassetten-Recorder, -   cassette recorder
die Disco, -s   disco, discothèque
das Fenster, -   window
der Fernseher, -   television set
das Geschäft, -e   store
das (Geburtstags)geschenk, -e   (birthday) present
die Keramik   ceramics, pottery
die Langeweile   boredom
das Licht   light
die Platte, -n   record
der Plattenspieler, -   record player; turntable
das (*also* **der**) **Poster, -**   poster
das Radio, -s   radio
der Radioamateur, -e   "ham" radio operator
die Schallplatte, -n   record
die Stadt, ̈e   city
die Stereoanlage, -n   stereo system
die Tür, -en   door

VERBEN

an·machen   to switch on (the light)
auf·machen   to open
auf·stehen   to get up
aus·machen   to turn off (the light)
ein·kaufen   to shop; ~ **gehen** to go shopping
fahren (ä)   to drive

VERBEN

fern·sehen (ie)   to watch TV
fotografieren   to photograph
lesen (ie)   to read
mit·kommen   to come along
reparieren   to repair
sagen   to say, to tell
sammeln   to collect
sehen (ie)   to see, to watch, to look
vor·haben   to plan
verstehen   to understand
wissen (weiß)   to know
zu·machen   to shut

ANDERE WÖRTER

also   well
doch   *flavoring word (see p. 161)*
eigentlich   really, actually
etwas   something
gerade   exactly, precisely; just
immer   always
kompliziert   complicated
nun   now
wohin   where (to)
wertvoll   valuable

BESONDERE AUSDRÜCKE

eine lahme Ente   a dull, boring person
er hat zu nichts Lust   he doesn't feel like doing anything
ich habe Langeweile   I am bored
das stimmt   that's right

Kapitel 9

Ich habe zu Hause geholfen

Ich habe mein Zimmer aufgeräumt

Karin and Norbert found different ways to occupy their time over the weekend.

NORBERT   Was hast du am Wochenende gemacht?
KARIN   Ich habe geschlafen.
NORBERT   Mensch! Das ist doch nicht dein Ernst!
KARIN   Doch! Ehrenwort! Am Sonntag habe ich dann ein Flugzeugmodell gebastelt. Und was hast du gemacht?
NORBERT   Ich habe gearbeitet — wie immer.
KARIN   Was heißt das — du hast gearbeitet?
NORBERT   Ich muß zu Hause helfen. Ich habe mein Zimmer aufgeräumt und das Auto gewaschen.
KARIN   Das nennst du arbeiten?
NORBERT   Also, es ist wenigstens mehr als schlafen.

Fragen

1. Was hat Karin am Wochenende gemacht?
2. Was hat sie gebastelt?
3. Wer hat gearbeitet?
4. Welches Zimmer hat Norbert aufgeräumt?
5. Was hat Norbert sonst noch gemacht?

Du hast das Wort

A. A classmate asks you what you've done recently. How would you respond?

Was hast du	am Wochenende	gemacht?
	gestern°	

Ich habe	Hausaufgaben gemacht.
	[Tennis] gespielt.
	viel gearbeitet.
	[mein Zimmer] aufgeräumt.
	das Auto gewaschen.
	viel geschlafen.

B. You claim to have done certain things. When a friend expresses doubt or surprise, insist in your own words that what you say is true.

Ich habe am Wochenende [zwölf] Stunden geschlafen.
Ich habe gestern [zwei] Bücher gelesen.
Ich habe letzte° Woche [zehn] Platten gekauft.

Mensch! Das ist doch nicht dein Ernst!
Wirklich?
Das ist schwer zu glauben.

Ich habe eine Torte gebacken

Paul feels he spent a constructive weekend, but Sabine seems to disagree.

SABINE Was hast du am Wochenende gemacht?
PAUL Nicht viel. Ich habe für meine Mutter eine Torte gebacken. Sie hat meine Großeltern zum Kaffee eingeladen.
SABINE Sehr interessant!
PAUL Sei nicht so sarkastisch! Du hast doch gefragt.
SABINE Hat die Torte wenigstens geschmeckt?
PAUL Ich weiß es nicht. Ich habe Gerda abgeholt, und wir haben einen Spaziergang gemacht. Wir haben dann bei Gerdas Eltern Kaffee getrunken.

Fragen

1. Was hat Paul gebacken?
2. Warum hat er die Torte gebacken?
3. Hat die Torte geschmeckt?
4. Was haben Gerda und Paul gemacht?
5. Wo haben sie Kaffee getrunken?

Du hast das Wort

Give a short account of what you did this weekend.

Am Freitag nachmittag habe ich [Tennis gespielt].
Am Abend habe ich [ferngesehen].
Am Samstag ...

Arbeitsplan fürs Wochenende

Herr und Frau Gerdes haben vier Kinder. Alle müssen zu Hause helfen. Jedes Wochenende macht Frau Gerdes einen Arbeitsplan. Hier ist der Plan für letztes Wochenende.

	Freitag	Samstag	Sonntag
Werner	Badezimmer putzen	Geschirr spülen Garage aufräumen	Tisch decken
Gudrun	Tisch decken Mülleimer raustragen	abtrocknen Staub saugen	Geschirr spülen
Hilde	abtrocknen	Auto waschen Tisch decken	Frühstück machen
Erik	Geschirr spülen	einkaufen	abtrocknen

Fragen

1. Wer hat am Freitag Geschirr gespült?
2. Wer hat abgetrocknet?
3. Wer hat den Mülleimer rausgetragen?
4. Wann hat Werner das Badezimmer geputzt?
5. Wer hat fürs Wochenende eingekauft?
6. Wann hat Hilde den Tisch gedeckt?
7. Wann hat Gudrun abgetrocknet?
8. Wer hat am Sonntag Frühstück gemacht? den Tisch gedeckt?

Du hast das Wort

Ask a classmate who must do various family chores next weekend and when.

Wer muß fürs Wochenende einkaufen?
Wer muß spülen?
Wer muß ...

Wortschatzerweiterung

Doch as positive response

NORBERT	Das ist doch nicht dein Ernst!	You're not serious, are you?
KARIN	**Doch!**	Of course I am!
CAROLA	Gehst du denn nicht ins Kino?	Aren't you going to the movies?
OTTO	**Doch.**	Why, sure I am.

In Chapter 8 you learned that **doch** can function as a flavoring word. **Doch** may also be used as a one-word positive response to a negative statement or question. With **doch,** the speaker contradicts an assumption contained in a previous statement or question.

A Helga is making a number of wrong suppositions. Correct her, using *doch*.

▪ Gehst du nicht einkaufen?   *Doch. Ich gehe einkaufen.*

1. Gehst du nicht in die Stadt?
2. Kaufst du keine Platten?
3. Arbeitest du heute nicht?
4. Du gehst also heute nicht spazieren.
5. Du meinst das nicht.

B Say that you've done everything you're supposed to do.

▪ Hast du das Badezimmer geputzt?   *Ja, das habe ich geputzt.*

▪ Hast du den Tisch nicht gedeckt?   *Doch, den habe ich gedeckt.*

1. Hast du die Garage nicht aufgeräumt?
2. Hast du das Auto gewaschen?
3. Hast du die Torte gebacken?
4. Hast du deine Hausaufgaben nicht gemacht?

German cleaning products

Was hast du zu Hause gemacht?

Ich habe die Möbel abgestaubt.

Ich habe den Tisch abgeräumt.

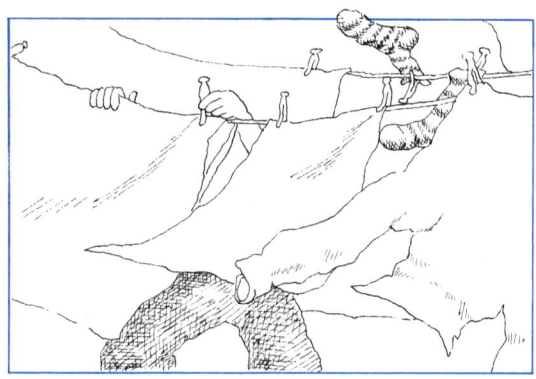
Ich habe Wäsche gewaschen.

Ich habe den Hund und die Katze gefüttert.

Ich habe Gartenarbeit gemacht.

Ich habe Kaffee gekocht.

C Confirm the fact that you've already done your chores for the day.

■▬ Hast du schon die Möbel abgestaubt?   *Ja, die habe ich schon abgestaubt.*

1. Hast du schon die Torte gebacken?
2. Hast du schon den Müll rausgetragen?
3. Hast du schon den Hund gefüttert?
4. Hast du schon die Gartenarbeit gemacht?

Du hast das Wort State three chores that you or various members of your family did this past weekend.

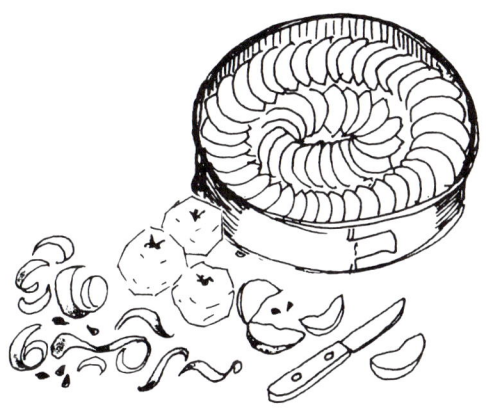

A German **Torte** has several layers, often with a cream filling. Another favorite pastry in German-speaking countries is the **Kuchen**, which consists of a single layer and sometimes has a fruit topping. The recipe below is for an **Apfelkuchen**.

Zutaten	Ingredients
150 Gramm Butter	1⅓ sticks butter
125 Gramm Zucker	½ cup sugar
1 Ei	1 egg
Eine abgeriebene Zitronenschale	grated peel of 1 lemon
150 Gramm Mehl	¾ cup flour
1 Teelöffel Backpulver	1 teaspoon baking powder
2-3 große Äpfel, geschält und in Streifen geschnitten	2-3 large apples, peeled and sliced in thin wedges

Butter und Zucker schaumig rühren, dann das Ei und die Zitronenschale dazu rühren. Mehl und Backpulver langsam hinzufügen. Eine Form mit Butter einfetten und mit Mehl bestreuen, dann den Teig in die Form füllen. (Wenn nötig, die Hände mit Mehl bestreuen, damit der Teig nicht an den Händen kleben bleibt.) Die Apfelstreifen vorsichtig in den Teig stecken und etwas Zitronensaft darüber träufeln. Backzeit: Ungefähr 45 Minuten bei mittlerer Hitze (bis der Teig schön hellbraun ist).

Combine butter and sugar and beat until creamy, then stir in egg and grated lemon peel. Sift together flour and baking powder and add gradually to mixture. Grease and flour a spring-form pan and press dough into the pan. (Add flour as necessary to keep dough from sticking to hands.) Arrange apple slices in concentric circles on the crust and sprinkle with a few drops of lemon juice. Bake at 350°F for about 45 minutes or until crust is golden brown.

Aussprache

- [ts] ganz, Platz, geht's, zehn, zu
- [z] sein, sehr, Bluse, gesund
- [s] es, essen, weiß

The letter **z** is pronounced [ts]. Before a vowel the letter **s** represents the sound [z]. In most other positions **s** represents the sound [s]. The letters **ss** and **ß** are both pronounced [s].

A Practice the sound [ts] in final position and initial position.

Tanz, schwarz, Schweiz   zehn, Zimmer, zu

B Practice the following words horizontally.

[z]	[s]	[ts]
reisen	reißen	reizen
Kurse	Kurs	kurz
heiser	heißer	Heizer
Felsen	Fels	Filz

C Practice the sounds [ts], [z], and [s]. Read the sentences aloud.

1. Sie kommen um zwölf in die Klasse.
2. Gisela kauft eine Bluse und eine Hose.
3. Franz und Inge gehen zweimal die Woche tanzen.

Wenn die Katze aus dem Haus ist, tanzen die Mäuse.

Übungen

Conversational past with auxiliary **haben**

German has several past tenses. One of them is the *conversational past,* which is commonly used in conversation to refer to past actions or states.

ich **habe** es gehört		wir **haben** es gehört
du **hast** es gehört	Sie **haben** es gehört	ihr **habt** es gehört
er/sie **hat** es gehört		sie **haben** es gehört

The conversational past is made up of an auxiliary verb and a past participle. Most verbs use **haben** as the auxiliary. The participle is in last position.

A Konrad is eager to pass on a bit of gossip to you and to various friends. Explain to him that you have already heard it.

▪ Und du? *Ich habe es schon gehört.*

1. Und Frau Weiß?
2. Und Herr Lange?
3. Und Jens und Inge?
4. Und Erika?
5. Und dein Bruder?
6. Und unsere Freunde?
7. Und ihr?
8. Und du?

Past participles of weak verbs

INFINITIVE	PAST PARTICIPLE	CONVERSATIONAL PAST
machen	ge+mach+t	Ingrid hat ihre Aufgaben nicht **gemacht**.
arbeiten	ge+arbeit+et	Sie hat schwer **gearbeitet**.

German verbs may be classified as weak or strong according to the way in which they form their past tenses.

The past participle of a weak verb is formed by adding **-t** to the unchanged stem. The **-t** expands to **-et** in verbs like **arbeiten.** In the past participle, most weak verbs also have the prefix **ge-**.

Erik hat die Wäsche gewaschen. Hilde hängt sie auf.

B Ilse asks whether you did certain things yesterday. Tell her you did.

▪ Habt ihr gestern Musik gehört? *Ja, wir haben Musik gehört.*

1. Habt ihr Platten gespielt?
2. Habt ihr auch getanzt?
3. Habt ihr Vokabeln gelernt?
4. Habt ihr gearbeitet?
5. Habt ihr Geschirr gespült?
6. Habt ihr Staub gesaugt?

C You've been very industrious. Say you've already done your chores.

▪ Machst du jetzt die Gartenarbeit? *Nein, die Gartenarbeit habe ich schon gemacht.*

1. Putzt du jetzt das Badezimmer?
2. Spülst du jetzt Geschirr?
3. Deckst du jetzt den Tisch?
4. Machst du jetzt Frühstück?
5. Fütterst du jetzt den Hund?

D The following people are as busy today as they were yesterday. Tell what they did.

▪ Ich putze Fenster. *Ich habe gestern Fenster geputzt.*

1. Ich spüle Geschirr.
2. Frank bastelt Flugzeugmodelle.
3. Thomas kocht Kaffee.
4. Ingrid und Sabine machen Mathe.
5. Gisela und Jan lernen Vokabeln.
6. Du arbeitest wirklich viel.
7. Du spielst Tennis.
8. Erik saugt Staub.

Past participles of strong verbs

INFINITIVE	PAST PARTICIPLE	CONVERSATIONAL PAST
geben	ge+geb+en	Ich habe Erika ein Radio **gegeben**.
lesen	ge+les+en	Ich habe gestern ein Buch **gelesen**.
sehen	ge+seh+en	Ich habe Ilse nicht **gesehen**.

The past participle of a strong verb is formed by adding **-en** to the stem. The past participles of most strong verbs have the prefix **ge-**.

E Hans-Dieter asks about your visit with some old friends. Satisfy his curiosity.

■ Was habt ihr Gisela gegeben? *Ja, wir haben Gisela das*
    Das Poster? *Poster gegeben.*

1. Was habt ihr Frank gegeben? Eine Platte?
2. Was habt ihr gelesen? Thomas' Buch?
3. Wann habt ihr sein Buch gelesen? Letzte Woche?
4. Wo habt ihr Erik gesehen? Im Jugendzentrum?
5. Wo habt ihr die *Hot Dogs* gesehen? In München?

INFINITIVE	PAST PARTICIPLE	CONVERSATIONAL PAST
backen	ge+back+en	Ich habe eine Torte **gebacken**.
schlafen	ge+schlaf+en	Ich habe gut **geschlafen**.
tragen	ge+trag+en	Ich habe eine Jacke **getragen**.
waschen	ge+wasch+en	Ich habe mein Auto **gewaschen**.

F Restate in the conversational past.

■ Wäscht Frank das Auto? *Hat Frank das Auto*
    gewaschen?

■ Nein, Martina wäscht es. *Nein, Martina hat es*
    gewaschen.

1. Bäckt Ingrid die Torte?
   Nein, Thomas bäckt sie.
2. Schläfst du gut?
   Ja, ich schlafe gut.
3. Trägst du Jeans ins Konzert?
   Ja, und Udo trägt auch Jeans.
4. Wann wäschst du die Wäsche?
   Ich wasche sie am Samstag.

INFINITIVE	PAST PARTICIPLE	CONVERSATIONAL PAST
helfen	ge+holf+en	Ich habe zu Hause geholfen.
nehmen	ge+nomm+en	Ich habe das Heft genommen.
schreiben	ge+schrieb+en	Ich habe Erika geschrieben.
trinken	ge+trunk+en	Ich habe Kaffee getrunken.

Many strong verbs change their stem vowel (and occasionally consonants) in the formation of the past participle.

G Sabine wants to know who did the following things. Confirm her guesses.

■ Wer hat Rudi geschrieben? Eva?   *Ja, Eva hat Rudi geschrieben.*

1. Wer hat Heike geschrieben? Udo?
2. Wer hat zu Hause geholfen? Stefan?
3. Wer hat Dieter geholfen? Ingrid?
4. Wer hat den Pulli genommen? Gerda?
5. Wer hat die Mappe genommen? Ulf?
6. Wer hat schon Kaffee getrunken? Mutter?
7. Wer hat noch nichts getrunken? Vater?

H You still haven't received answers to your questions. Ask them again in the present tense.

■ Warum hast du Beate die Briefmarken gegeben?   *Warum gibst du Beate die Briefmarken?*

1. Warum hat Jan Gisela seinen Cassetten-Recorder gegeben?
2. Was habt ihr in Englisch gelesen?
3. Wo hast du Tanja gesehen?
4. Warum hat Stefan soviel geschlafen?
5. Wer hat die Wäsche gewaschen?
6. Warum hast du keine Torte gebacken?
7. Warum hast du meinen Bleistift genommen?
8. Wer hat Meike geholfen?
9. Welche Jacke hast du getragen?

Du hast das Wort Ask various classmates what they did over the weekend.

Was hast du am Wochenende gemacht?
Hast du dein Zimmer aufgeräumt?
Hast du geschlafen?
Hast du etwas gebastelt?
Hast du gearbeitet? Wo?
Hast du das Auto gewaschen?

I Restate in the conversational past.

■· Wir sehen unsere Großeltern am Samstag.   *Wir haben unsere Großeltern am Samstag gesehen.*

■· Wir trinken um vier Kaffee.   *Wir haben um vier Kaffee getrunken.*

1. Hilft Gerd zu Hause?
   Ja, er wäscht die Wäsche.
2. Bäckt Frank die Torte?
   Nein, er schläft am Samstag bis elf.
3. Gibst du Gerda das Buch?
   Ja, sie liest es am Wochenende.

Past participles of separable-prefix verbs

INFINITIVE	PAST PARTICIPLE	CONVERSATIONAL PAST
abstauben	ab+ge+staubt	Kirstin hat die Möbel **abgestaubt**.
einladen	ein+ge+laden	Ihre Mutter hat Schmidts **eingeladen**.
fernsehen	fern+ge+sehen	Abends haben sie **ferngesehen**.

The prefix **ge-** of the past participle comes between the separable prefix and the stem of the participle.

J Ute is a hard worker. Identify her as the one who did all the chores.

■· Wer hat das Zimmer aufgeräumt?   *Ute hat das Zimmer aufgeräumt.*

1. Wer hat abgetrocknet?
2. Wer hat die Fenster aufgemacht?
3. Wer hat die Möbel abgestaubt?
4. Wer hat den Tisch abgeräumt?
5. Wer hat eingekauft?

K Your mother is checking whether you've done your chores yet. Inform her that you'll do them later.

■· Hast du das Zimmer aufgeräumt?   *Nein, das räume ich später auf.*

1. Hast du die Garage aufgeräumt?
2. Hast du die Möbel abgestaubt?
3. Hast du die Fenster aufgemacht?
4. Hast du den Tisch abgeräumt?
5. Hast du das Geschirr abgetrocknet?
6. Hast du den Mülleimer rausgetragen?

L   Restate the following exchanges in the conversational past.

- ▪ Kaufst du heute ein? *Hast du heute eingekauft?*
- ▪ Ja, ich kaufe bei Karstadt ein. *Ja, ich habe bei Karstadt eingekauft.*

1. Kaufst du nur bei Karstadt ein?
   Nein, ich kaufe auch bei Hertie ein.
2. Wann macht Karstadt auf?
   Heute machen sie schon um neun auf.
3. Macht Karstadt um fünf zu?
   Nein, sie machen erst um halb sieben zu.
4. Siehst du Samstag nachmittag fern?
   Ja, und ich sehe auch am Abend fern.
5. Wann räumst du die Garage auf?
   Ich räume sie gar nicht auf.

Grammatische Übersicht

Conversational past   (A-L)

Hast du schon Mathe **gemacht**?   *Have you done your math?*
Nein, **ich habe** Tennis **gespielt**.   *No, I played tennis.*

There are several past tenses in German. The conversational past, as the name implies, is common in conversation. It is used in many situations that require the simple past tense in English.

Auxiliary **haben**

ich habe Detlev gefragt	Sie haben Ingrid gefragt	wir haben Stefan gefragt
du hast Petra gefragt		ihr habt Silke gefragt
er hat Marta gefragt		sie haben Benno gefragt

The conversational past is made up of an auxiliary verb and a past participle. **Haben** is used as the auxiliary of most verbs. The past participle is in last position.

Ich habe gestern **nicht** gearbeitet.

Nicht often comes directly before the past participle.

Past participles of weak verbs

INFINITIVE	PAST PARTICIPLE	CONVERSATIONAL PAST
kaufen	ge+kauf+t	Erik hat eine Platte gekauft.
kosten	ge+kost+et	Wieviel hat sie gekostet?

German verbs may be classified as weak or strong according to the way they form their past tenses. A weak verb is a verb with a stem that remains unchanged in the past-tense forms. The past participle of a weak verb is formed by adding the ending **-t** or **-et** to the infinitive stem. Most past participles have the prefix **ge-**.

Past participles of strong verbs

INFINITIVE	PAST PARTICIPLE	CONVERSATIONAL PAST
schreiben	ge+schrieb+en	Ich habe eine Karte geschrieben.
nehmen	ge+nomm+en	Hast du die Karte genommen?
sehen	ge+seh+en	Nein, ich habe sie nicht gesehen.

A strong verb is a verb that changes its stem vowel (and occasionally consonants) in at least one of the past tenses. The past participle of a strong verb is formed by adding **-en** to the stem. Most strong verbs also add the prefix **ge-** in the past participle. Since there is no way to guess how or even if the stem vowel changes from infinitive to past participle, you should memorize the past participles of strong verbs.

For a list of the strong verbs used in this book, with their past participles, see the Appendix. Past participles of strong verbs are noted in the vocabularies as follows: **schreiben (geschrieben)**.

Past participles of separable-prefix verbs

INFINITIVE	PAST PARTICIPLE	CONVERSATIONAL PAST
aufräumen	auf+ge+räumt	Hast du das Zimmer aufgeräumt?
einladen	ein+ge+laden	Wir haben Schmidts eingeladen.

The prefix **ge-** of the past participle comes between the separable prefix and the stem of the participle.

Wiederholung

A Create captions that describe the activity in each picture.

B Restate the following exchanges in the conversational past.

1. Hilft Bruno zu Hause?
   Ja. Er räumt die Garage auf.
2. Wann holt ihr Schmidts ab?
   Um vier. Wir trinken um halb fünf Kaffee.
3. Was machst du Samstag nachmittag?
   Ich spiele Tennis.
4. Petra bäckt eine Torte.
   Hoffentlich schmeckt sie.
5. Dieter räumt hoffentlich sein Zimmer auf.
   Leider nein. Er liest ein Buch.

C The following people recently went shopping. Say what they think of their purchases. Use a possessive adjective in each sentence.

■ Peter / Pulli / schick   *Peter findet seinen Pulli schick.*

1. Frank / Mantel / klasse
2. Hannelore / Kleid / hübsch
3. wir / Jeans / prima
4. du / Gürtel / preiswert
5. ihr / Jacken / toll
6. ich / Hemd / schick

D The following statements are all answers to questions beginning with *Wo?* or *Wohin?* Ask the questions.

1. Karsten wohnt in Hamburg.
2. Er fährt am Samstag in die Stadt.
3. Bei Karstadt kauft er einen Anzug.
4. Dann fährt er wieder nach Hause.
5. Er möchte heute abend ins Theater.

E Give orders to the people indicated.

■ Peter: Badezimmer putzen   *Putz bitte das Badezimmer!*

1. Karin: Geschirr spülen
2. Norbert: abtrocknen
3. Werner und Dietmar: Garage aufräumen
4. Herr Schwarz: die Wäsche waschen
5. Frau Schwarz: Tisch decken
6. Sabine: Kaffee kochen
7. Inge: Katze füttern

F Several kinds of words can come at the end of a German sentence. Complete each of the following sentences with an appropriate word, according to the sense.

ab	auf	**fahren**	**gefragt**	**gekauft**
	gefüttert	**mit**	**spülen**	

1. Hat Gabi schon den Hund ____?
2. Muß sie noch das Geschirr ____?
3. Möchte sie morgen nach Frankfurt ____?
4. Ja. Sie steht früh ____.
5. Kommt ihr Freund Peter ____?
6. Hat er ein Auto ____?
7. Wann holt er Gabi ____?
8. Ich habe sie nicht ____.

Kapitel 9

G Complete the response in each conversational exchange with *Ja, Nein,* or *Doch,* as appropriate.

1. Hast du ein Hobby?
   ____, ich sammle Bierdeckel.
2. Kauft ihr heute ein?
   ____, wir bleiben zu Hause.
3. Fährt Detlev heute nicht mit?
   ____, er kommt mit.
4. Können Sie mein Auto reparieren?
   ____, ich habe leider keine Zeit.
5. Herr Siemens wohnt nicht in der Gartenstraße.
   ____, er wohnt da.
6. Spielst du oft Fußball?
   ____, es macht viel Spaß!

H Your German guest wants to know what your American friends are saying. Interpret the following conversational exchanges for your guest.

1. What did you do yesterday?
   Gerda and I took a walk.
2. Didn't you work?
   Not much. I washed our car.
3. When did you pick Gerda up?
   I picked Gerda up at four.
4. Did you invite Gerda for coffee?
   No, we had coffee with Gerda's parents.

Child-labor laws (covering anyone under the age of 14) prohibit young Germans from working at many of the part-time jobs that might be common for their American counterparts. Students between the ages of 15 and 18 who are enrolled in apprenticeship programs earn a small amount of money as they learn a trade. Students in college preparatory schools must depend on a regular allowance (**Taschengeld**) from their parents and on occasional jobs which are fairly difficult to obtain. Summer jobs require a minimum of four weeks' commitment and tend to be low-paid. They are not very popular because the summer vacation is only six weeks long and not enough time is left for the family vacation after four or five weeks of work.

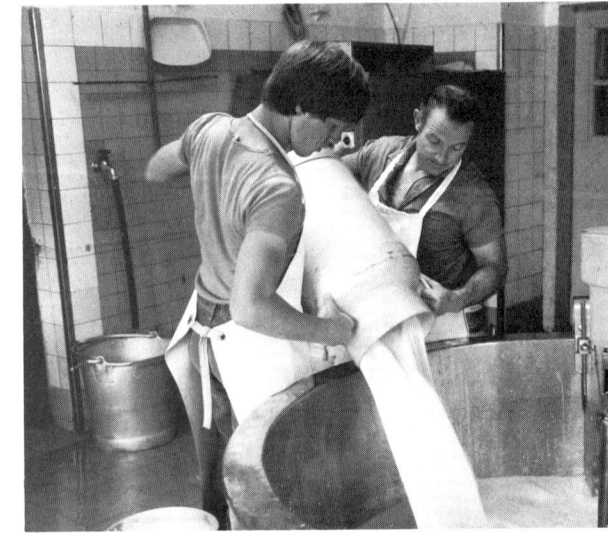

Kulturlesestück

Taschengeld und Jobs

Taschengeld° ist oft ein Problem für deutsche Schüler. Viele bekommen Taschengeld von den Eltern. Und in vielen Familien bekommen sie auch Geld für gute Zeugnisse°. Und zum Geburtstag und zu Weihnachten°. Aber das ist natürlich oft nicht genug° für Kino und Konzert, für Cassetten und Schallplatten, für Klassenfahrten° und Sport.

Viele Schüler wollen also etwas Geld verdienen°. In Deutschland ist das aber nicht so leicht. Babysitterjobs gibt es schon, aber nicht sehr oft. Ein paar Schüler können Nachhilfestunden° geben. In den Supermärkten gibt es Jobs, aber diese Jobs sind nicht leicht zu bekommen. Zeitungsjobs° gibt es auch, aber nicht für Schüler. In Deutschland kommen die Zeitungen am Morgen. Am Morgen haben die Schüler natürlich keine Zeit. So bleibt für sie die Reklame°: Sie können Reklame austragen°.

pocket money

grades
Christmas
enough

class trips

earn

tutoring sessions

newspaper jobs

advertisements
distribute

A Below is a list of statements about teen-agers, jobs, and spending money. Indicate which statements seem more characteristic of German-speaking countries, which of the United States, which of both.

1. Taschengeld ist oft ein Problem für Teenager.
2. Barbara hat jede Woche einen Babysitterjob.
3. Viele Schüler arbeiten in den Supermärkten.
4. Paula kann keinen Babysitterjob finden. Ihre Freundinnen auch nicht.
5. Thomas arbeitet abends und am Wochenende im Supermarkt.
6. Paul macht jede Woche Gartenarbeit. So bekommt er Geld von seinen Eltern. Wenn er extra Geld braucht, räumt er die Garage auf, oder er putzt die Fenster.
7. Claudia kauft zwei neue Schallplatten. Sie bekommt das Geld von ihren Eltern, denn sie hat ein sehr gutes Zeugnis.
8. Jens kann keine Zeitungen austragen. Er muß am Morgen in die Schule.
9. Zum Geburtstag hat Inge Geld bekommen. Jetzt kann sie das kaufen, was sie haben will.
10. Erik trägt am Dienstag und am Freitag Reklame aus.

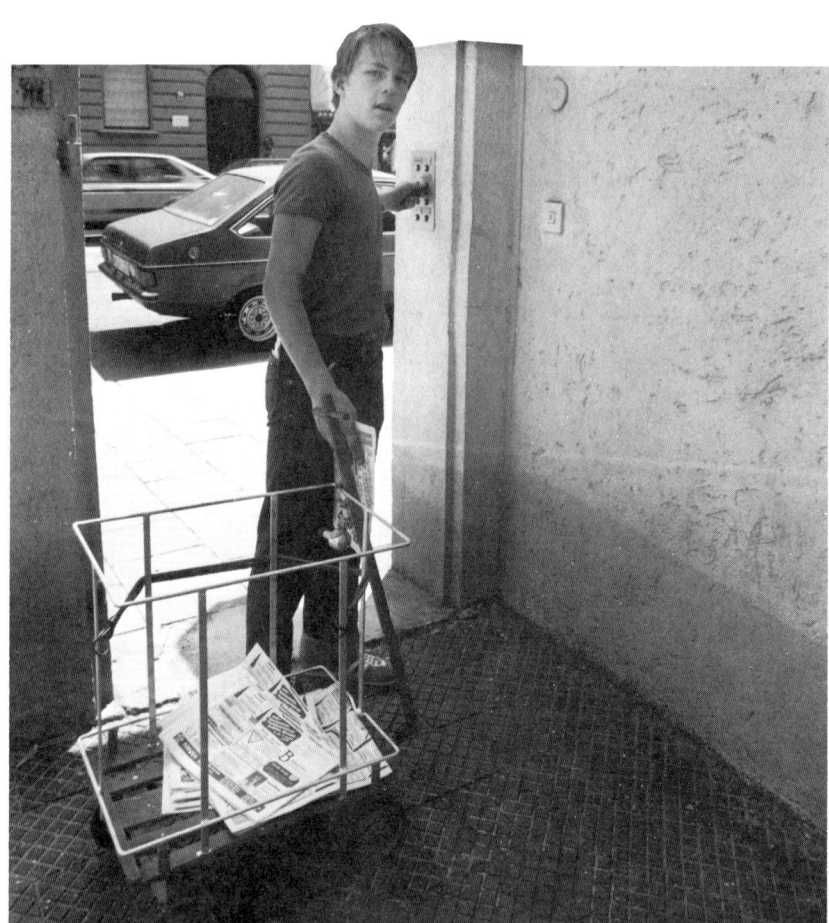

Vokabeln

SUBSTANTIVE

die Arbeit, -en work
das Badezimmer, - bathroom
der Eimer, - pail
die Eltern (pl.) parents
das Flugzeugmodell, -e model airplane
das Frühstück breakfast
die Garage, -n garage
die Gartenarbeit gardening, yard work
das Geschirr dishes
die Großeltern (pl.) grandparents
das Haus, ̈-er house
der Hund, -e dog
der Kaffee coffee
die Katze, -n cat
die Möbel (pl.) furniture
der Müll garbage
der Spaziergang, ̈-e walk, stroll; **einen ~ machen** to go for a walk
der Staub dust
der Tisch, -e table
die Torte, -n fancy layer cake
die Wäsche laundry
das Zimmer, - room

VERBEN

ab·holen to call for, to pick up
ab·räumen to clear, to remove
ab·stauben to dust
ab·trocknen to dry up, to wipe dry
auf·räumen to put in order
backen (ä; gebacken) to bake
basteln to tinker (with), to work at a hobby
decken to set (the table)
ein·laden (ä; eingeladen) to invite
füttern to feed
helfen (i; geholfen) to help

VERBEN

nennen (genannt) to name, to call
putzen to clean
raus·tragen (ä; rausgetragen) to carry out
schlafen (ä; geschlafen) to sleep
schmecken to taste (good)
spülen to wash dishes
Staub saugen to vacuum
trinken (getrunken) to drink
waschen (ä; gewaschen) to wash

ANDERE WÖRTER

alle all, everyone
als than
fürs = für das for the
gestern yesterday
jeder each, everyone
letzt last
sarkastisch sarcastic
wenigstens at least
wie (immer) as (always)

BESONDERE AUSDRÜCKE

was heißt das? what do you mean?
das ist doch nicht dein Ernst! you can't be serious!
doch! yes (in answer to a question containing a negative word)
Ehrenwort! honest! on my honor!
Kaffee trinken to drink coffee (with breakfast or with afternoon pastries)
zum Kaffee einladen to invite for coffee and cake
fürs Wochenende for the weekend

Most young people in German-speaking countries are interested in a sport of some kind. Physical education is compulsory in all schools, both elementary and secondary. In spite of this, however, there is no stress on school teams.

A person who wishes to participate in competitive sports can join a sports club (**Sportverein**). In the **BRD** there are 40,000 such clubs, and more than 1 out of every 4 Germans is a member. Many teen-agers enjoy playing in youth soccer leagues sponsored by their local **Sportverein.** Soccer is by far the most popular sport; next in order are gymnastics, tennis, marksmanship, track-and-field, handball, swimming, table tennis, horseback riding, and skiing.

Wer hat gewonnen?

Jan is on the Bergdorf soccer team. He tells Gisela the outcome of yesterday's game against Oberndorf.

GISELA	Was hast du gestern gemacht?
JAN	Wir haben Fußball gespielt.
GISELA	Gegen wen?
JAN	Gegen Oberndorf.
GISELA	Habt ihr gewonnen?
JAN	Nein, wir haben zwei zu drei verloren.
GISELA	Ach, Mensch. Das tut mir leid. Aber zwei zu drei gegen Oberndorf ist ja nicht so schlecht.
JAN	Das stimmt. Oberndorf ist gut.
GISELA	Na, vielleicht spielen wir nächstes Mal wenigstens unentschieden.

Fragen

1. Gegen wen hat Bergdorf gespielt?
2. Wer hat gewonnen? Wie hoch° haben sie gewonnen?
3. Wie spielt Bergdorf vielleicht nächstes Mal?

Du hast das Wort

Ask which team won a particular game and ask about the score.

Wer hat das [Fußball]spiel gewonnen?
Wie hoch haben sie/wir gewonnen?
Wie hoch haben sie/wir verloren?

Ich lade dich ein

Ingrid is reluctant to go to a party to which she wasn't invited.

INGRID   Was hast du heute abend vor?
DIETER   Ich gehe auf eine Party. Was machst du denn?
INGRID   Eigentlich nichts.
DIETER   Nichts? Das ist ja prima. Dann komm doch mit!
INGRID   Wohin? Auf die Party?
DIETER   Natürlich.
INGRID   Du gibst doch nicht die Party!
DIETER   Nein. Gerd. Aber ich kann dich einladen.
INGRID   Ach Quatsch! Das geht doch nicht.
DIETER   Doch. Natürlich geht das. Du kennst ihn doch gut, nicht?
INGRID   Ja . . . Also schön. Wann geht's denn los?
DIETER   Ich glaube, um acht. Ich rufe dich noch an.
INGRID   O.K. Tschüß. Bis später.

Fragen

1. Was hat Dieter heute abend vor?
2. Was hat Ingrid vor?
3. Wer gibt die Party? Dieter?
4. Warum darf Ingrid mitkommen?
5. Wann geht die Party eigentlich los?
6. Wen ruft Dieter an? Wann?

Du hast das Wort

A. A friend asks what you have planned for this evening. How would you respond?

Was hast du heute abend vor?   Ich gehe | auf eine Party.
                                         | in die Disco.
                                         | ins Kino.
                                         | ins Jugendzentrum.
Ich sehe fern.
Ich höre Musik.
Ich will [Briefe schreiben].

B. React to a classmate's announcement that he/she is giving a party.

Ich gebe am [Samstag abend]   Prima!
   eine Party.   Schön!
                                Toll!
                                Wann geht's los?
                                Wirklich?
                                Schade, ich habe schon
                                   Pläne für [Samstag].

C. Suppose you find out that a friend of yours hasn't been invited to a party. How would you react?

Jan gibt eine Party. Er hat aber [Dieter] nicht eingeladen.

Mensch! Das geht doch nicht.
Was!? Warum denn nicht?
Was ist denn los?
Wirklich?
Na und°?
Natürlich nicht.
Das ist ja prima.

Sag! Your teacher will ask you to repeat a bit of information to another classmate. Note that in requests of this kind, the verb comes at the end of the sentence.

■ Sag [Kai], daß du auf eine Party gehst!   *Ich gehe auf eine Party.*

1. Sag [Ute], daß Gerd die Party gibt!
2. Sag [Kai], daß du Gerd gut kennst!
3. Sag [Ute], daß sie mitkommen kann!
4. Sag [Kai], daß die Party um acht Uhr losgeht!

German teen-agers like to spend their free time in various kinds of places. In a **Café** they can engage in quiet conversation while enjoying a soda or a cup of coffee, and sometimes a pastry. Another popular spot with a very different type of atmosphere is a **Pinte** or **Kneipe.** Beer and other alcoholic drinks are available, and usually some snacks, like sausages. There might be a pinball machine (**Spielautomat**) or a juke box (**Musikbox**) to provide entertainment. Students also like to get together in a **Diskothek.** But conversation is usually out because the music is too loud. Sometimes a disc jockey keeps people entertained with records and general chatter.

Wortschatzerweiterung

Freizeit

Im Winter gehen Ute und Bernd Schi laufen.

Bernd kann auch gut Schlittschuh laufen.

Im Frühling zelten Paul und Norbert oft. Camping macht Spaß.

Gisela und Jan machen gern Picknicks. Dann gibt's viel zu essen.

Im Sommer gehen Gisela und Jan windsurfen. Jan fällt oft ins Wasser.

Ralf und seine Freunde gehen oft segeln. Ilse segelt nicht gern.

Im Herbst gehen Karin und Uwe oft bergsteigen.

Ilse reitet gern, Ralf aber nicht.

A Answer the following questions based on the illustrations.

1. Was machen Karin und Uwe im Herbst oft?
2. Was macht Ute im Winter?
3. Wer kann gut Schlittschuh laufen?
4. Wer zeltet gern?
5. Warum machen Gisela und Jan gern Picknicks?
6. Wer geht oft windsurfen?
7. Wer kann nicht gut windsurfen?
8. Wer geht mit Ralf segeln?
9. Wer geht nicht mit Ralf segeln?
10. Was macht Ilse gern, Ralf aber nicht?

Du hast das Wort

Tell the class some of the outdoor activities you like to engage in.

Welchen Sport treibst du im Winter? im Sommer? im Frühling?
Spielst du im Winter Tennis?
Reitest du?
Gehst du Schi laufen? Schlittschuh laufen?
Gehst du windsurfen?

Suffixes -er and -er + -in

| fahren   to drive | fahr + er   = der Fahrer   driver (m.) |
| | fahr + er + in = die Fahrerin   driver (f.) |

The suffix **-er** is often added to a verb stem to form a noun that indicates the male doer of an activity. The additional suffix **-in** indicates the female doer of an activity.

| segeln | segl + er   = der Segler |
| | segl + er + in = die Seglerin |

To form a noun from a verb ending in **-eln**, the **-e** before the **l** is dropped.

| Schi laufen | der Schiläufer |
| | die Schiläuferin |

Some nouns formed from verbs show umlaut.

Kapitel 10   **205**

B Name the male and female doers of the activities related to the following verbs and verb phrases.

■ Tennis spielen   *der Tennisspieler, die Tennisspielerin*

1. schwimmen
2. arbeiten
3. Briefmarken sammeln
4. basteln
5. bergsteigen
6. reiten
7. backen (ä)
8. tanzen (ä)
9. verkaufen (ä)

Rainer ist Verkäufer.   Rainer is *a* salesman.
Sabine ist Verkäuferin.   Sabine is *a* saleswoman.

German does not use **ein** or **eine** with a noun used to identify a member of a profession or someone temporarily engaged in an activity.

C Complete each sentence with a noun derived from the verb.

1. Lutz and Anja arbeiten bei Volkswagen.
   Er ist ____. Sie ist ____.
2. Frau Krupp und Herr Anders backen viel.
   Sie ist ____, und er ist ____.
3. Herr und Frau Braun sammeln Briefmarken.
   Er ist schon vier Jahre Briefmarken ____; sie ist erst zwei Jahre Briefmarken ____.
4. Im Sommer spielen Tanja und Erik den ganzen Tag Tennis.
   Im Sommer ist Tanja nur Tennis ____, und Erik ist nur Tennis ____.

Aussprache

[R]   **R**ock, P**r**eis, wa**r**um

The German **r** can be pronounced in two different ways. Some German speakers use a tongue-trilled [r] in which the tip of the tongue vibrates against the gum ridge behind the upper front teeth, like the **rrr** that small children often make in imitation of a car or truck starting up. Most German speakers, however, use a uvular [R] in which the back of the tongue is raised toward the uvula (the little flap of skin hanging down in the back of the mouth). It may help you to pronounce the uvular [R] if you make a gargling sound before the sound [a]: **ra**. Keep the tip of your tongue down and out of the way. It plays no role in the pronunciation of the uvular German [R].

A Practice vertically in columns and then horizontally.

[R]	[R]	[R]
f**r**agt	wa**r**um	**r**agt
K**r**okodil	ba**r**ock	**R**ock
t**r**ugen	füh**r**en	**r**ufen
P**r**eis	Nie**r**en	**R**eis
b**r**ing	da**r**in	**R**ing
g**r**ünen	schü**r**en	**r**ühmen

B Practice the sound [R]. Read the sentences aloud.

1. Frau Braun trägt heute einen Rock.
2. Können Sie mein Radio reparieren, Herr Grün?
3. Frag mal Rita, warum sie nicht schreibt!

Wer anderen eine Grube gräbt, fällt selbst hinein.

Übungen

The verbs kennen and wissen

Ich **kenne** Frau Hofer. Ich **weiß,** wer Frau Hofer ist.
Ich **kenne** Rainers Haus. Ich **weiß,** wo Rainer wohnt.

Kennen means to know (to be acquainted with) a person, place, or thing. **Wissen** means to know something as a fact.

A Answer Torsten's questions in the negative.

- ▪ Weißt du, wo Jörg Schneider wohnt?   Nein, das weiß ich nicht.
- ▪ Kennst du seine Schwester?   Nein, seine Schwester kenne ich nicht.

1. Weißt du, wie alt Jörg ist?
2. Weißt du, wie Jörgs Schwester heißt?
3. Kennst du Jörgs Freundin?
4. Kennst du denn Jörg Schneider?

Du hast das Wort Ask a classmate whether he/she is acquainted with certain people, places, or things, or knows certain facts.

Kennst du [Ingrid/Thomas]?
Weißt du, wo [sie/er] wohnt?
Weißt du, wie alt [sie/er] ist?
Kennst du [meine Schwester/meinen Bruder]?
Kennst du [meine Freundin Erika/meinen Freund Thomas]?
Kennst du [Berlin]?
Kennst du die Musik von [Beethoven]?

Verbs with stem-vowel change au > äu

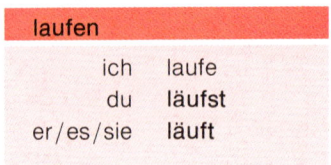

laufen	
ich	laufe
du	läufst
er/es/sie	läuft

Laufen has a stem-vowel change **au** > **äu** in the **du-** and **er/sie-**forms of the present tense.

B   Margit is trying to recruit members for a ski club. Tell her that the following people ski well.

> ▪   Peter   *Peter läuft gut Schi.*

1. Uschi
2. Gerd und Paul
3. du
4. deine Freunde
5. Silke
6. ihr

Accusative case of **wer**

NOMINATIVE	ACCUSATIVE
Wer kommt heute abend?	Wen laden wir ein?

The accusative of **wer** is **wen**.

C   Helga is chatting about various people, but you don't hear her clearly. Ask whom she is referring to.

> ▪   Ich habe Erik im Jugendzentrum gesehen.   *Wen hast du gesehen?*

1. Ich habe Christl im Kino gesehen.
2. Ich habe Dieter für heute abend eingeladen.
3. Ich habe Ingrid angerufen.
4. Ich habe die *Hot Dogs* gehört.

Accusative case of personal pronouns

mich / dich

NOMINATIVE	ACCUSATIVE
Ich verstehe Christl.	Christl versteht mich.
Du verstehst Christl.	Christl versteht dich.

D   Express surprise at your classmate's statements.

> ▪   Ich kenne dich gut.   *Wirklich? Du kennst mich gut?*

1. Ich verstehe dich.
2. Ich meine dich.
3. Ich höre dich.
4. Ich frage dich.

E Karl is feeling rejected today. Reassure him that what he says isn't true.

> Du lädst mich nicht ein.   *Doch, ich lade dich ein.*

1. Du rufst mich nicht an.
2. Du hast mich nicht gern.
3. Du kennst mich nicht gut.
4. Du fährst mich nicht nach Hause.

uns / euch

NOMINATIVE	ACCUSATIVE
Wir verstehen Frank.	Frank versteht **uns**.
Ihr versteht Frank.	Frank versteht **euch**.

F Answer the following questions in the affirmative.

> Kennt ihr uns?   *Ja, natürlich kennen wir euch.*

1. Hört ihr uns?
2. Meint ihr uns?
3. Fragt ihr uns?
4. Versteht ihr uns?
5. Braucht ihr uns?

G Petra and Erik are feeling gloomy today. Try to cheer them up.

> Ihr nehmt uns nicht mit ins Konzert.   *Doch, wir nehmen euch mit.*

1. Ihr ladet uns nicht ein.
2. Ihr habt uns nicht gern.
3. Ihr ruft uns nicht an.
4. Ihr braucht uns nicht.

ihn / es / sie

NOUN	PRONOUN
Kennst du **meinen Bruder**?	Ja, ich kenne **ihn**.
Kaufst du **den Fernseher**?	Ja, ich kaufe **ihn**.
Kennst du **das Kind**?	Ja, ich kenne **es**.
Kaufst du **das Radio**?	Ja, ich kaufe **es**.
Kennst du **meine Schwester**?	Ja, ich kenne **sie**.
Kaufst du **die Uhr**?	Ja, ich kaufe **sie**.
Kennst du **meine Freunde**?	Ja, ich kenne **sie**.
Kaufst du **die Platten**?	Ja, ich kaufe **sie**.

H Gisela is in charge of invitations to Gerd's party. Say that she intends to call the following guests later.

▪▥ Wann ruft Gisela meinen Bruder an?   *Später. Sie ruft ihn später an.*

1. Wann ruft sie Erik an?
2. Wann ruft sie meine Schwester an?
3. Wann ruft sie ihren Freund Peter an?
4. Wann ruft sie meine Freunde an?
5. Wann ruft sie Petra und Jens an?

I After an hour in the music store, Jan impatiently urges you to make up your mind. Decide that you don't want the things after all.

▪▥ Willst du nun den Cassetten-Recorder oder nicht?   *Nein, ich will ihn nicht.*

1. Willst du nun den Plattenspieler oder nicht?
2. Willst du die Stereoanlage oder nicht?
3. Willst du das Radio oder nicht?
4. Willst du die Platte oder nicht?
5. Willst du die Cassetten oder nicht?

 Teen-agers in German-speaking countries like to talk on the phone almost as much as their American counterparts. Germans usually identify themselves at once when they answer the phone. Callers also give their names before asking for the person they're trying to reach. When people end a telephone conversation, they often say **Auf Wiederhören** (literally, until we hear each other again). For example:
— Hier Ingrid Reimann!
— Tag, Ingrid! Hier Gerda. Ist Thomas zu Hause?
— Nein, er spielt heute Fußball.
— Ach ja, richtig. Ich rufe später wieder an. Auf Wiederhören, Ingrid!
— Auf Wiederhören, Gerda!

Lesen macht Spaß.

Sie

NOMINATIVE	ACCUSATIVE
Verstehen Sie **mich**?	Ja, ich verstehe **Sie**.

J Answer your teacher's questions in the affirmative.

▪▪▪ Hast du mich gehört?   *Ja, ich habe Sie gehört.*

1. Hast du mich gemeint?
2. Hast du mich gefragt?
3. Hast du mich angerufen?
4. Hast du mich zum Kaffee eingeladen?

K Angela is having difficulty with a math problem. Suggest that she ask various friends and classmates for the answer.

▪▪▪ Frank weiß es.   *Warum fragt sie ihn denn nicht?*

1. Wir wissen es.
2. Ingrid weiß es.
3. Du weißt es.
4. Heike weiß es.
5. Ihr wißt es.
6. Mein Bruder weiß es.
7. Meine Freunde wissen es.

Conversational past of inseparable-prefix verbs

INFINITIVE	PAST PARTICIPLE	CONVERSATIONAL PAST
beginnen	begonnen	Wann **hat** das Spiel **begonnen**?
bekommen	bekommen	**Hast** du noch Karten **bekommen**?
gewinnen	gewonnen	Oberndorf **hat** das Spiel **gewonnen**.
verlieren	verloren	Wir **haben** das Spiel **verloren**.
verstehen	verstanden	**Habt** ihr das **verstanden**?
versuchen	versucht	Wir **haben** alles **versucht**.

Some prefixes (including **be-, ge-, ver-**) are never separated from the verb stem.

Inseparable-prefix verbs do not add **ge-** in the past participle. Both weak and strong verbs may have inseparable prefixes.

L Werner has a few questions about yesterday's soccer game. Answer in the affirmative.

■ Hast du wirklich eine Karte bekommen? — *Ja, ich habe wirklich eine Karte bekommen.*

1. Hat Marta auch eine Karte bekommen?
2. Hat das Spiel erst um vier begonnen?
3. Hat München wirklich gewonnen?
4. Und Hamburg hat verloren?
5. Hast du das Spiel verstanden?

M Astrid and Klaus had some problems getting to the soccer game on time yesterday. Tell what happened by restating in the conversational past.

■ Astrid bekommt kein Geld von zu Hause. — *Astrid hat kein Geld von zu Hause bekommen.*

1. Astrid versucht alles.
2. Klaus bekommt Geld von zu Hause.
3. Aber sie bekommen keine guten Karten.
4. Sie versuchen alles.
5. Das Spiel beginnt um sieben.
6. Hoffentlich gewinnt Berlin.

Du hast das Wort Discuss a recent school game with your classmates.

Hast du Karten bekommen?
Wann hat das Spiel begonnen?
Wer hat gewonnen? Wer hat verloren?
Wie hoch hat sie / haben sie gewonnen / verloren?

Grammatische Übersicht

The verbs **kennen** and **wissen** (A)

Ich **kenne** Frau Braun gut.   I know Mrs. Braun well.
Ich **weiß**, wer Herr Braun ist.   I know who Mr. Braun is.

The English equivalent of both **kennen** and **wissen** is *to know*. **Kennen** means to be acquainted with a person, place, or thing. **Wissen** means to know something as a fact.

Verbs with stem-vowel change **au>äu** (B)

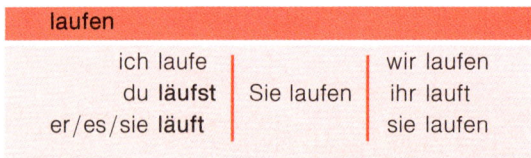

laufen		
ich laufe		wir laufen
du **läufst**	Sie laufen	ihr lauft
er/es/sie **läuft**		sie laufen

Laufen has a stem-vowel change **au>äu** in the **du-** and **er/sie-**forms of the present tense.

Accusative case of **wer** (C)

| Nominative | **Wer** hat Detlev gefragt? | *Who* asked Detlev? |
| Accusative | **Wen** hat Detlev gefragt? | *Whom* did Detlev ask? |

The accusative of **wer** is **wen**.

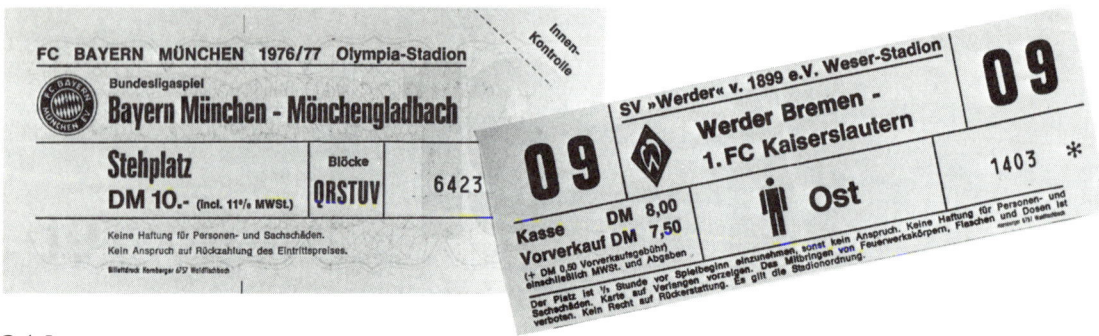

Accusative case of personal pronouns (D-K)

Ralf kennt **mich** gut.　　　　Ralf knows *me* well.
Er kennt **dich** auch, nicht?　He also knows *you*, doesn't he?

Pronouns used as direct objects are in the accusative case. Nominative and accusative forms of personal pronouns correspond as follows:

Nominative	ich	du	er	es	sie	wir	ihr	sie	Sie
Accusative	mich	dich	ihn	es	sie	uns	euch	sie	Sie

Note that **es, sie,** and **Sie** are the same in nominative and accusative.

ACCUSATIVE NOUN	ACCUSATIVE PRONOUN
Kennst du **den Mann**?	Ja, ich kenne **ihn**.
Kaufst du **den Plattenspieler**?	Ja, ich kaufe **ihn**.
Kennst du **das Kind**?	Ja, ich kenne **es**.
Kaufst du **das Radio**?	Ja, ich kaufe **es**.
Kennst du **die Frau**?	Ja, ich kenne **sie**.
Kaufst du **die Platte**?	Ja, ich kaufe **sie**.
Kennst du **die Kinder**?	Ja, ich kenne **sie**.
Kaufst du **die Platten**?	Ja, ich kaufe **sie**.

The accusative pronouns **ihn, es,** and **sie** can refer to either persons or things.

Conversational past of inseparable-prefix verbs (L-M)

INFINITIVE	PRESENT TENSE	CONVERSATIONAL PAST
beginnen	Wann **beginnt** das Spiel?	Wann **hat** das Spiel **begonnen**?
verlieren	Wir **verlieren** oft.	Wir **haben** oft **verloren**.
versuchen	Ute **versucht** alles.	Ute **hat** alles **versucht**.

The prefixes **be-, emp-, ent-, er-, ge-, ver-,** and **zer-** are never separated from the verb stem. These inseparable prefixes may occur with both weak and strong verbs. Inseparable-prefix verbs do not add the prefix **ge-** in the past participle.

In spoken German, inseparable prefixes are unstressed: **begin'nen, versu'chen.**

Chess, gymnastics, basketball, and skiing are popular activities in the German-speaking countries.

Wiederholung

A Read the excerpts from Dieter's diary and answer the questions that follow.

MONTAG

Ein prima Tag! In Englisch habe ich eine Zwei bekommen und in Deutsch eine Eins. In Mathe habe ich leider eine Vier. Aber Mathe ist schwer. Und für mich ist eine Vier eigentlich nicht schlecht.

DIENSTAG

Die *Hot Dogs* geben am Samstag abend ein Konzert. Karten habe ich aber nicht bekommen. Nichts mehr da. Alles ausverkauft. Ich bin wirklich sauer.

DONNERSTAG

Ich habe Jörg im Jugendzentrum gesehen. Er hat zwei Karten für die *Hot Dogs*. Erika kann nicht mitkommen, und er braucht jetzt nur noch eine Karte. Ich habe Erikas Karte gekauft. Ute gibt am Freitag eine Party. Sie hat mich eingeladen.

SAMSTAG

Eine tolle Party. Ich habe viel mit Ute getanzt. Sie tanzt wirklich gut. Und heute abend gehen wir ins Konzert. Ute hat auch eine Karte. Jörg und ich holen sie um sieben ab.

1. Was hat Dieter in Mathe bekommen?
2. Warum kann Dieter am Dienstag keine Karten bekommen?
3. Wen hat er im Jugendzentrum gesehen?
4. Warum braucht Jörg nur eine Karte?
5. Wer hat Dieter eingeladen?
6. Wer geht mit Dieter ins Konzert?
7. Wann holen Jörg und Dieter Ute ab?

B You and Sabine are chatting about Jörg and his forthcoming party. Answer Sabine's questions in the affirmative.

■ Kennst du Jörgs Freundin Uschi?   *Natürlich kenne ich sie.*

1. Hast du Jörg gesehen?
2. Hat er dich eingeladen?
3. Darf meine Schwester auch mitkommen?
4. Kannst du uns abholen?
5. Hast du dein Auto gewaschen?

Kapitel 10

C Express the following conversational exchanges in German.

1. Christl bought a dress.
   What did it cost?
2. Last night Peter called Meike.
   What did she say?
3. You didn't see Erika this morning?
   No, I had no time.
4. Did you invite Jörg?
   Yes, but he can't come.
5. What did you do yesterday afternoon?
   We watched television.
6. We played against Oberndorf yesterday.
   Who won?

D Prepare five or six sentences about activities you like to do. You may wish to include answers to the following questions.

Treibst du gern Sport? Hast du ein Hobby? Sammelst du etwas? Läufst du gern Schi? Liest du gern? Schläfst du viel?

E Ask your teacher five questions about what he/she likes to do in various seasons. For example:

Was machen Sie gern im Winter? Treiben Sie gern Sport?

F Describe the activities in the illustration. What are the people doing? What time of year is it?

Kulturlesestück

König Fußball

Im deutschen Sport ist der Fußball König°. Man° kann sagen, daß Fußball der deutsche Nationalsport ist. Und das ist er nicht nur in Deutschland. Man kann sicher sagen, daß Fußball der beliebteste° Sport der Welt° ist.

Überall° in Deutschland kann man sehen, daß Fußball sehr beliebt ist.
5 Was spielen die Kinder auf der Straße? Fußball. Was spielen sie im Park? Fußball. Wohin gehen viele Männer, Frauen und Kinder am Samstag- oder Sonntagnachmittag? Zum Fußballplatz° oder ins Fußballstadion°. Oder sie sehen Fußball im Fernsehen. Auch kleine Dörfer° haben einen Fußballplatz, und die großen Städte haben große Stadien°.
10 In den Schulen und Universitäten gibt es auch Fußballmannschaften°, aber da spielen sie fast keine Rolle°. Die großen Fußballmannschaften und Fußballspieler kommen aus den Sportvereinen°. Und jedes Kind kennt die Namen der großen Fußballspieler. Die besten Spieler spielen in der Nationalmannschaft. Weltmeisterschaften° gibt es alle° vier Jahre.

king / one

favorite
der Welt: in the world
everywhere

soccer field
soccer stadium

villages
stadiums
soccer teams
spielen ... Rolle: are not important / sports clubs
world championships / every

Kapitel 10 **219**

Choose the word or phrase that best completes each statement, based on the reading.

1. Der beliebteste Sport der Welt ist . . .
   a. Basketball   b. Fußball   c. Segeln   d. Schilaufen
2. Im Park spielen deutsche Kinder . . .
   a. Golf   b. Baseball   c. Basketball   d. Fußball
3. Viele Deutsche sehen am . . . ein Fußballspiel.
   a. Sonntagnachmittag   b. Sonntagabend   c. Samstagmorgen
   d. Samstagabend
4. Auch kleine Dörfer haben . . .
   a. große Stadien   b. eine Universitätsfußballmannschaft
   c. einen Fußballplatz   d. viele Sportvereine
5. Die großen Fußballmannschaften kommen aus den . . .
   a. Schulen   b. Sportvereinen   c. Universitäten
   d. Dörfern
6. Die besten Spieler können alle . . . Jahre in den Weltmeisterschaften spielen.
   a. zwei   b. drei   c. vier   d. fünf

German soccer cheers:

Zicke-Zacke, Zicke-Zacke
Hoi, Hoi, Hoi!

Tempo, Tempo, Tempo!

Ha, Ho, He
Hertha BSC! (BSC-Berliner Sport-Club)

Vokabeln

SUBSTANTIVE

das Camping camping
die Freizeit leisure time
der Frühling spring
das Fußballspiel, -e soccer game
der Herbst autumn, fall
das Mal time, occasion;
  nächstes Mal next time
die Party, -s party
das Picknick, -s picnic
der Schi, -er (also **Ski**) ski
der Schlittschuh, -e ice skate
der Sommer summer
das Spiel, -e game
das Wasser water
der Winter winter

VERBEN

an·rufen (angerufen) to call, to telephone
essen (i; gegessen) to eat
fallen (ä) to fall
gewinnen (gewonnen) to win
kennen (gekannt) to know, to be acquainted with
laufen (äu) to run, to walk
los·gehen to go, to take off
reiten to ride (horseback)

VERBEN

Schlittschuh laufen (äu) to ice-skate
Schi laufen (äu) to ski
segeln to sail
verlieren (verloren) to lose
windsurfen to go wind surfing
zelten to camp

ANDERE WÖRTER

gegen (+*acc.*) against
hoch high
na well
nächst next
unentschieden undetermined; tied (*in scoring*)
wen (*acc. of* **wer**) whom

BESONDERE AUSDRÜCKE

wie hoch hat Oberndorf gewonnen? by how much did Oberndorf win?
auf eine Party gehen to go to a party
wann geht's los? when does it start?
das geht nicht that doesn't work; that won't do
Quatsch! nonsense! rubbish!
na und? so what?
bergsteigen gehen to go mountain-climbing

noch einmal

 **Eine deutsche Zeitung.** Publish a newspaper **(die Zeitung)** in German with features, interviews, and ads. The following list may give you some ideas on what kinds of articles to include:

— Calendar of school events for a month
— Interview of student or teacher about a hobby
— Interview of a foreign student, giving her/his impressions of American schools
— Sports report
— Poll of students listing chores they do at home, favorite school subjects, favorite music or band
— Ad from bookstore for books and supplies, listing prices in **Mark, Schilling,** or **Franken**

 **Junge Deutsche.** The class is divided into several groups. Using pictures from German magazines, each group prepares a display. Topics can be clothing, sports, entertainment, and teen-agers at parties, school, or home. Each group may include illustrations on all of these subjects, or single topics can be assigned: one group takes clothing, another sports, and so on.

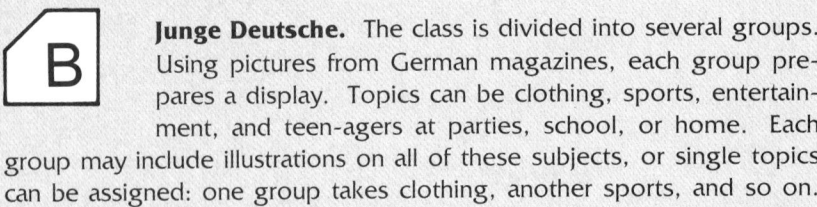 **Ein(e) Brieffreund(in).** At the end of Stage 1, one of the suggested activities was to write a short autobiography to be submitted to a panel. Use some of that information — age, appearance, family — to begin a letter to a German friend. Continue to tell about your school subjects, hobbies, interests, and activities. Describe a typical school day; tell what you and your friends like to do after school or on weekends.

If you would like to have a real German pen pal, ask your teacher for the names of some organizations that can arrange such contacts. It might be possible for your class as a whole to correspond with an English class in a high school in Austria, Germany, or Switzerland.

 **Nach der Schule.** Prepare a skit with three to four classmates. You are in a school hangout. A waiter or waitress has already taken your order, and you are involved in conversation with your friends about music, clothing, hobbies, chores, and sports.

 **Musik.** Learn the words and music to one or more German songs; records may be available from your city library, or you may ask your teacher for other sources. Have a volunteer compose music to "Pretty Baby" (page 130), and then organize a group to perform it.

 **Hier und dort.** Study the pictures on pages 73–79. Discuss the features in the photographs that seem to you more characteristic of German-speaking countries than of life in America.

 **Schicke Sachen.** With several classmates, prepare a skit in which you go shopping for clothes. You will need a salesperson, and you may want to have a friend accompany you. Dialogues may include a discussion of sizes, colors, prices, and style; possible settings may concern a somewhat pushy salesperson, an indecisive customer, or an urgent phone call home to request additional spending money.

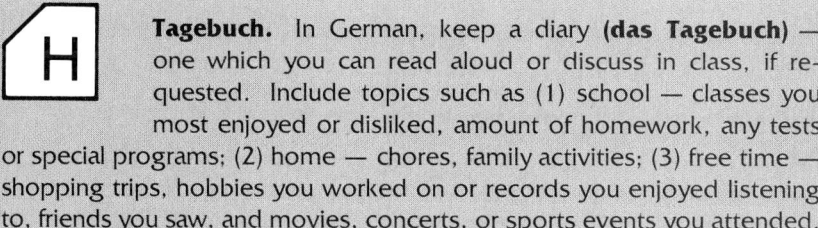 **Tagebuch.** In German, keep a diary (**das Tagebuch**) — one which you can read aloud or discuss in class, if requested. Include topics such as (1) school — classes you most enjoyed or disliked, amount of homework, any tests or special programs; (2) home — chores, family activities; (3) free time — shopping trips, hobbies you worked on or records you enjoyed listening to, friends you saw, and movies, concerts, or sports events you attended.

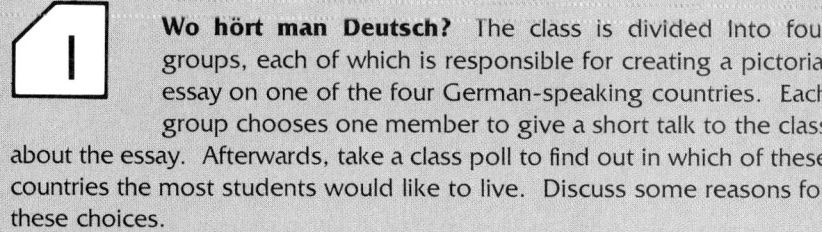 **Wo hört man Deutsch?** The class is divided into four groups, each of which is responsible for creating a pictorial essay on one of the four German-speaking countries. Each group chooses one member to give a short talk to the class about the essay. Afterwards, take a class poll to find out in which of these countries the most students would like to live. Discuss some reasons for these choices.

You may wish to present these talks to other language classes and invite them to tell you about the countries they are studying.

noch einmal **223**

Ein Stadtbesuch. Rothenburg is almost everyone's favorite medieval town, though Heidelberg, on the Neckar, is also popular. If you prefer the country, Wengen is just one of many villages in the Swiss Alps.

Sehenswürdigkeiten. Everyone likes castles. Some, like Neuschwanstein, have dramatic settings; others, like Linderhof, have lovely formal gardens. Costumed attendants or museum displays can make castle interiors fascinating, too. At the Hofburg in Vienna the annual Kaiserball includes an elegant meal.

Guten Appetit! Cafés are wonderful places to meet friends; if the setting allows a panoramic view of Salzburg, so much the better. Fruits and vegetables can be bought in open-air markets, often, as in Bonn, set up in a large square.

Kapitel 11
Bäcker, Metzger, Supermarkt

Einkaufen in Deutschland

Barbara Braun besucht ihren Brieffreund in Nürnberg. Sie schreibt einen Brief an ihre Deutschklasse.

Nürnberg, den 3. März

Liebe Klasse!

    Ich habe hier schon viel gesehen und gelernt. Meine Gastfamilie°, Herr und Frau Kraft, Ingrid und Michael, ist sehr nett. Letzte Woche bin ich dreimal° mit Frau Kraft einkaufen gegangen. Die Supermärkte sind hier fast so wie zu Hause. Nur darf man das Obst und Gemüse hier nicht anfassen°. Das habe ich natürlich falsch gemacht. Ich habe die Tomaten angefaßt. Da hat die Verkäuferin gesagt: „Einen Moment, bitte! Ich gebe Ihnen° die Tomaten. Die Tomaten kann doch schließlich° nicht jeder anfassen." — „Entschuldigung! Das habe ich nicht gewußt."

    Wir haben alle Sachen in einen Einkaufswagen° gepackt und bezahlt, wie in Amerika. Aber dann hat Frau Kraft alle Lebensmittel selbst eingepackt. Fast alle Kunden haben nämlich große Einkaufstaschen. Große Papiertüten gibt es nicht. Und für Plastiktüten° muß man bezahlen.

    Das Fleisch, das Brot und den Kuchen fürs Wochenende hat Frau Kraft aber nicht im Supermarkt gekauft. Fleisch, Wurst und Schinken haben wir beim Metzger gekauft und den Kuchen und das Brot beim Bäcker. Frau Kraft hat da „ihren" Metzger und „ihren" Bäcker. Beim Bäcker und beim Metzger sagen alle Kunden immer schön „Grüß Gott" und „Auf Wiederschauen". Und die Verkäufer antworten jedes Mal. Wie oft sagen sie wohl jeden Tag „Auf Wiederschauen"?

    Am Samstag sind wir dann noch zum Markt gegangen und haben dort eingekauft. Wir waren schon früh dort, denn dann ist noch alles frisch. Und es ist noch viel da. Aber auch hier darf man Obst und Gemüse nicht anfassen.

    Das ist alles für heute. Bald mehr!

Herzliche Grüße

Barbara

° host family
° three times
° handle, touch
° to you / after all
° shopping cart
° plastic bags

Fragen

1. Wie oft ist Barbara letzte Woche einkaufen gegangen?
2. Ist sie allein° gegangen?
3. Was hat Barbara falsch gemacht?
4. Wer hat die Lebensmittel eingepackt?
5. Warum hat Frau Kraft keine Plastiktüte genommen?
6. Was hat Frau Kraft beim Metzger gekauft? Und beim Bäcker?
7. Was sagen die Verkäufer jeden Tag sehr oft?
8. Warum ist Frau Kraft am Samstag schon früh zum Markt gegangen?

Du hast das Wort

Barbara apologized for touching the vegetables in the supermarket. How would you apologize if a classmate told you you had broken something?

Du hast [meine Platte] kaputtgemacht.

Entschuldigung.
Habe ich das gemacht?
  Ach, Entschuldigung.
Entschuldigung. Das
  habe ich nicht gewußt.
Das tut mir leid.

Sag!

1. Sag [Kai], daß du einkaufen gehst!
2. Sag [Ute], daß du Tomaten brauchst!
3. Sag [Kai], daß du Wurst beim Metzger kaufst!
4. Sag [Ute], daß du Kuchen beim Bäcker kaufst!
5. Sag [Kai], daß du alles in die Einkaufstasche packst!
6. Sag [Ute], daß du keine Plastiktüte kaufen willst!

Although there are many supermarkets in German-speaking countries, many people still prefer to do their food shopping in small grocery stores or specialty stores like the bakery, the butcher shop, and so on. The small stores are sometimes called **Tante-Emma-Läden,** similar to "Mom-and-Pop stores" in the United States. Customers like the convenience of these neighborhood stores, and they enjoy the personal attention they receive from the storekeepers. The customers and salespeople often know each other by name, and they exchange friendly greetings and farewells in the course of their business.

Wurst and **Würstchen** are very popular in German-speaking countries. Almost every town, and certainly every region, has one or more sausage specialties of its own. **Würstchen** are among the foods most commonly sold at snackbars, where they are served on an unbuttered roll or with a piece of bread, often with a dab of mustard **(Senf)**.

The snackbars are called by many different names, such as **Imbißstube, Kaltes Buffet,** and **Bier Würstl,** and they can be found almost everywhere — in the marketplace, in a railroad station, or in a shopping area. Besides many varieties of **Würstchen,** popular snacks include ham, cheese, or fish sandwiches, french fries, and pizza.

Beim Metzger

Frau Kraft kauft bei ihrem Metzger ein.

HERR LANGE	Grüß Gott, Frau Kraft! Was darf es sein?
FRAU KRAFT	Wieviel kosten die Schweinskoteletts?
HERR LANGE	7 Mark 50 das Pfund.
FRAU KRAFT	Ich brauche fünf Stück.
HERR LANGE	Gern. Sonst noch was?
FRAU KRAFT	Ich hätte gern zehn Wiener Würstchen.
HERR LANGE	So. Haben Sie noch einen Wunsch?
FRAU KRAFT	Nein. Das ist alles für heute.
HERR LANGE	Danke ... So, bitte schön. Das macht zusammen 24 Mark 50.
	* * *
	So, Sie bekommen 50 Pfennig zurück.
FRAU KRAFT	Danke schön.
HERR LANGE	Bitte. Auf Wiedersehen, Frau Kraft.
FRAU KRAFT	Auf Wiedersehen, Herr Lange.

Fragen

1. Wieviel kosten die Schweinskoteletts?
2. Wieviel Koteletts braucht Frau Kraft?
3. Was kauft Frau Kraft noch?
4. Wieviel kostet alles zusammen?
5. Wieviel bekommt Frau Kraft zurück?

Wortschatzerweiterung

Was gibt's heute auf dem Markt?

1. der Apfel, ⸚
2. die Banane, –n
3. die Orange, –n
4. die Erdbeere, –n
5. die Kartoffel, –n
6. der Spinat
7. die Erbse, –n
8. die Karotte, –n
9. der Saft
10. die Milch
11. das Ei, –er
12. die Butter
13. der Käse

A The illustration above shows part of an open-air market. Ask a classmate what he/she would like to buy.

Was möchtest du kaufen?

B Ask a classmate for her/his opinion of the food prices.

Wie findest du [die Kartoffeln] — teuer oder billig?

C How good is your memory? Start with a simple statement about buying food and pass it on. Your neighbor repeats it and adds one more item. The next person repeats the entire statement and adds another item.

STUDENT 1: Ich gehe in den Supermarkt und kaufe Brot.
STUDENT 2: Ich gehe in den Supermarkt und kaufe Brot und Kaffee.
STUDENT 3: Ich gehe in den Supermarkt und kaufe Brot, Kaffee und . . .

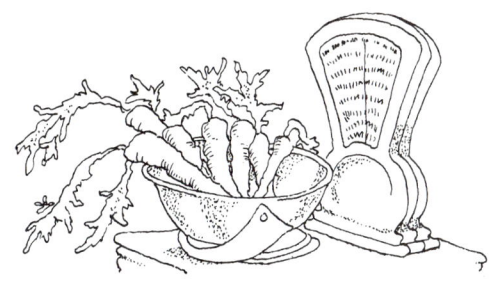

In German-speaking countries, the metric system is used to measure volume and weight. The basic measure of volume is the **Liter (l),** and the basic measures of weight are the **Gramm (g)** and the **Kilogramm (kg).** German speakers also use the older term **Pfund (Pfd.)** for half a **Kilogramm,** or 500 **Gramm.** A **Pfund** is equivalent to 1.1 American pounds.

Units of measurement and quantity

Ich möchte vier **Kilo** Kartoffeln.	I'd like four *kilos* of potatoes.
Ich nehme fünf **Pfund** Orangen.	I'll take five *pounds* of oranges.
Er kauft zwei **Liter** Milch.	He's buying two *liters* of milk.
Sie trinkt jeden Tag vier **Glas** Wasser.	She drinks four *glasses* of water every day.
Er kauft zwei **Flaschen** Saft.	He's buying two *bottles* of juice.

In German, **der-**nouns and **das-**nouns expressing measure, weight, or number are in the singular. **Die-**nouns, for example **Flasche,** are in the plural.

D Have a classmate take the part of a clerk. Tell her/him how much you want to buy.

▪▫ Wieviel Kilo Orangen möchten Sie? Drei? — *Ja, ich nehme drei Kilo Orangen.*

1. Wieviel Gramm Butter möchten Sie? Hundert?
2. Wieviel Pfund Äpfel möchten Sie? Fünf?
3. Wieviel Kilo Kartoffeln möchten Sie? Zehn?
4. Wieviel Stück Kuchen möchten Sie? Zwei?
5. Wieviel Stück Torte möchten Sie? Vier?
6. Wieviel Flaschen Saft möchten Sie? Drei?
7. Wieviel Gramm Käse möchten Sie? Fünfhundert?

Du hast das Wort Compare your eating and drinking habits with your classmates'.

Wieviel Glas Milch trinkst du jeden Tag?
Wieviel Liter Milch kauft deine Familie jede Woche?
 Wieviel Liter Saft?
Wieviel Stück Brot ißt du jeden Tag?
Wieviel Eier ißt du jede Woche?
Wieviel Gramm Käse ißt du jede Woche?
Wieviel Obst ißt du jede Woche?

Aussprache

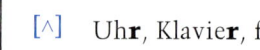 [ʌ]   Uh**r**, Klavie**r**, fäh**r**t

When the German **r** is not followed by a vowel, it tends to be pronounced like the final sound in British English *here* (hee-uh), *there* (thay-uh). The symbol [ʌ] represents this **uh** sound. In German, the sound [ʌ] occurs in the unstressed final position.

A   Practice the following words horizontally in pairs.

[R]	[ʌ]
Tie**r**e	Tie**r**
Paa**r**e	Paa**r**
Uh**r**en	Uh**r**
Tü**r**en	Tü**r**
fah**r**en	fäh**r**t
fah**r**e	fah**r**
Klavie**r**e	Klavie**r**
schwe**r**e	schwe**r**

B   Practice the sounds [ʌ] and [R]. Read the sentences aloud.

1. Warum brauchen wir soviel Papier?
2. Birgit sammelt gern Bierdeckel.
3. Jörg, darf ich die Tür hier aufmachen?
4. Hannelore spielt wirklich gut Klavier.

Glücklich ist, wer vergißt, was nicht mehr zu ändern ist.

Übungen

Conversational past with auxiliary **sein**

Erika **ist** spät nach Hause **gekommen**. Erika came home late.
Sie **ist** erst um acht **aufgestanden**. She didn't get up until eight.

Ich **bin** gestern in die Stadt **gefahren**. I went into town yesterday.

Some verbs require **sein** as an auxiliary in the conversational past. These verbs have no direct object and denote a change in location (for example, **kommen**) or a change in condition (for example, **aufstehen**).

ich bin gefahren		wir sind gefahren
du bist gefahren	Sie sind gefahren	ihr seid gefahren
er/sie ist gefahren		sie sind gefahren

A You're talking about vacations. Tell your friends who went on vacation alone, and then ask where various other people went.

■ Gretl ist allein gefahren. (Jürgen und Paul) *Jürgen und Paul sind allein gefahren.*

1. ich
2. die Jungen
3. Erika
4. wir

■ Wohin ist Regina gefahren? (Udo) *Wohin ist Udo gefahren?*

5. du
6. ihr
7. deine Freundin Inge
8. Richard

Kapitel 11

INFINITIVE	PAST PARTICIPLE	CONVERSATIONAL PAST
aufstehen	(ist) aufgestanden	Sie **sind** spät **aufgestanden**.
fahren	(ist) gefahren	Sie **sind** in die Stadt **gefahren**.
gehen	(ist) gegangen	Sie **sind** ins Kino **gegangen**.
kommen	(ist) gekommen	Sie **sind** um acht **gekommen**.
laufen	(ist) gelaufen	Sie **sind** nach Hause **gelaufen**.
wandern	(ist) gewandert	Sie **sind** durch die Stadt **gewandert**.

B You and your friends are talking about leisure activities. Restate the following exchanges in the conversational past.

■ Wandert ihr im Sommer viel?   *Seid ihr im Sommer viel gewandert?*
Ja, wir wandern ziemlich viel.   *Ja, wir sind ziemlich viel gewandert.*

1. Wohin fährst du?
   Ich fahre in die Stadt.
2. Wir gehen ins Kino.
   Gehen eure Freunde mit?
3. Lauft ihr jeden Tag?
   Nein, wir laufen nur am Samstag.
4. Wann kommst du nach Hause?
   Ich komme erst um acht.
5. Gehst du im Winter Schi laufen?
   Ja, ich gehe ziemlich oft Schi laufen.
6. Stehst du spät auf?
   Nein, ich stehe um sieben auf.
7. Kommt dein Bruder mit?
   Nein, er geht ins Theater.

Du hast das Wort

Ask a classmate the following questions. He/she will answer and then ask you the same question.

■ Wann bist du heute morgen aufgestanden?   *Um sieben. Und wann bist du aufgestanden?*
Um [acht].

Wann bist du in die Schule gegangen?
Bist du gefahren oder gelaufen?
Wann bist du in die Stadt gefahren?
⁺Wo bist du einkaufen gegangen?
⁺Wann bist du nach Hause gekommen?
Wohin bist du am Wochenende gegangen?
⁺Wann bist du am Samstag aufgestanden?

Im Supermarkt muß man die Lebensmittel selbst einpacken.

Narrative past of **sein**

ich **war** müde	I *was* tired
du **warst** müde	you *were* tired
er/sie **war** müde	he/she *was* tired
wir **waren** müde	we *were* tired
ihr **wart** müde	you *were* tired
sie **waren** müde	they *were* tired
Sie **waren** müde	you *were* tired

Although **sein** does have a conversational past, the most commonly used past-tense forms are **war, warst,** and so on. These forms are called the *narrative past.*

C   Restate the following conversational exchanges in the narrative past.

■III   Wie ist das Fußballspiel?   *Wie war das Fußballspiel?*
       Es ist langweilig.   *Es war langweilig.*

1. Wo bist du Samstag abend?
   Ich bin im Jugendzentrum, wie immer.
2. Wo seid ihr am Sonntag?
   Wir sind zu Hause.
3. Wie ist das Konzert?
   Es ist klasse.
4. Warum sind die Jungen am Wochenende zu Hause?
   Sie sind doch nicht zu Hause.

Special **der**-nouns in the accusative singular

NOMINATIVE	ACCUSATIVE
Wie heißt **der Junge** da?	Kennst du **den Jungen**?
Wie heißt **der Herr** da?	Kennst du **den Herrn**?

A few **der**-nouns add **-n** in the accusative singular.

D Jörg is telling you about various people. Inquire about some other people you're curious about.

■ Ich habe Frau Braun eingeladen. (Herr Braun)   *Hast du auch Herrn Braun eingeladen?*

1. Ich habe Frau Wagner angerufen. (Herr Wagner)
2. Ich habe Frau Lenz gesehen. (Herr Lenz)
3. Ich kenne das Mädchen dort. (der Junge)
4. Ich finde das Mädchen doof. (der Junge)
5. Ich kenne die Kundin dort. (der Kunde)
6. Ich finde Herrn Klein nett. (der Kunde)

Prepositions with the accusative case

durch	through	Gabi geht **durch** das Geschäft.
für	for	Gabi kauft ein Buch **für** ihren Vater.
gegen	against	Sie hat nichts **gegen** ihren Freund.
ohne	without	Frank macht die Hausaufgaben **ohne** mich.
um	around	Er geht **um** das Haus.

The prepositions **durch, für, gegen, ohne,** and **um** are always followed by the accusative case.

E Gerd suggests going through various buildings to get out of the pedestrian zone by a shortcut. Insist that it won't work.

■ Versuchen wir mal das Café! — *Man kann doch nicht durch das Café gehen.*

1. Versuchen wir mal den Supermarkt!
2. Versuchen wir mal das Lebensmittelgeschäft!
3. Versuchen wir mal das Musikgeschäft!
4. Versuchen wir mal das Jugendzentrum!
5. Versuchen wir mal die Bäckerei!

F You're showing Sabine all the presents you've bought. Specify whom they're for.

■ Ist die Bluse für deine Mutter oder deine Schwester? — *Für [meine Mutter].*

1. Ist der Pulli für deinen Vater oder deinen Bruder?
2. Ist das Buch für Herrn Lenz oder Frau Lenz?
3. Ist die Platte für deine Freundin oder deinen Freund?
4. Ist der Kuli für deinen Bruder oder deine Schwester?

G Frau Lerner doesn't like any of the people she deals with. Try to find out what she has against each of them.

■ Frau Lerner hat ihren Apotheker nicht gern. — *Was hat sie denn gegen ihren Apotheker?*

1. Sie hat auch ihren Bäcker nicht gern.
2. Auch ihren Metzger hat sie nicht gern.
3. Ihren Elektriker findet sie schlecht.
4. Sie findet auch ihren Friseur schlecht.
5. Sie hat ihren Arzt nicht gern.

H You and Gerd want to go on a picnic but your friends have to work. Suggest going without the individuals mentioned.

■ Jürgen muß arbeiten. *Dann gehen wir ohne ihn.*

1. Bruno muß arbeiten.
2. Heidi muß arbeiten.
3. Ich muß arbeiten.
4. Lore und Jutta müssen arbeiten.
5. Frank und Udo müssen arbeiten.

I Reassure Jutta that you have nothing against the people who will be at her party.

■ Hast du etwas gegen Franz? *Nein, ich habe nichts gegen ihn.*

1. Hast du etwas gegen Marianne?
2. Hast du etwas gegen Herrn Lenz?
3. Hast du etwas gegen mich?
4. Hast du etwas gegen uns?
5. Hast du etwas gegen Stefan und Thomas?

J Substitute the cued words for the italicized words in the following sentences. Make any necessary changes.

■ Ursel geht durch *das Geschäft.* (der Supermarkt) *Ursel geht durch den Supermarkt.*

1. Walter geht durch *das Haus.* (die Stadt)
2. Volker will nichts gegen *seine Freundin* sagen. (sein Freund)
3. Ingrid hat etwas gegen *ihren Bruder.* (ihre Schwester)
4. Trudi kauft den Pulli für *ihre Mutter.* (ihr Vater)
5. Sie kauft die Platte für *ihre Freundin.* (ihr Freund)
6. Christl kommt ohne *ihre Schwester.* (ihr Bruder)
7. Ich möchte einmal ohne *meinen Bruder* zelten gehen. (meine Eltern)
8. Arbeitest du für *deine Mutter?* (dein Vater)

Du hast das Wort Tell your classmates what you would like to buy as a birthday present for some of your friends and relatives.

■ dein Vater *Für meinen Vater möchte ich [ein Buch] kaufen.*

deine Mutter
dein Bruder [Volker]
deine Schwester [Margit]
dein Freund [Ralf]
deine Freundin [Ilse]

Frau Kraft kauft ihr Gemüse auf dem Markt.

Accusative prepositional contractions

Frank geht **durchs** Geschäft.
Ute kauft etwas **fürs** Haus.
Ingrid geht **ums** Haus.

durch das > **durchs**
für das > **fürs**
um das > **ums**

The prepositions **durch, für,** and **um** often contract with the definite article **das** to form **durchs, fürs,** and **ums.**

K Restate, using contractions.

■)) Eva ist durch das Haus gegangen.   *Eva ist durchs Haus gegangen.*

1. Hugo ist durch das Geschäft gegangen.
2. Petra hat das Geld für das Radio bekommen.
3. Hast du die Karten für das Konzert gekauft?
4. Hast du schon den Arbeitsplan für das Wochenende gemacht?
5. Michael hat einen Spaziergang um das Haus gemacht.

Du hast das Wort

Ask a classmate about her/his plans for the weekend.

Was hast du fürs Wochenende vor?
Gehst du ins Kino?
Hast du Geld fürs Kino?

Grammatische Übersicht

Conversational past with auxiliary **sein** (A-B)

ich **bin gekommen**		wir **sind gekommen**
du **bist gekommen**	Sie **sind gekommen**	ihr **seid gekommen**
er/sie **ist gekommen**		sie **sind gekommen**

Wir **sind** spät **gekommen.**   We came late.
Gabi **ist** spät **aufgestanden.**   Gabi got up late.

Some verbs require **sein** instead of **haben** as an auxiliary in the conversational past. Verbs that require **sein** must meet two conditions:

1. They must be intransitive verbs (verbs without a direct object).
2. They must indicate a change of location (as in **kommen**) or a change of condition (as in **aufstehen**).

In the vocabularies of this book, verbs that require **sein** are indicated as follows: **kommen (ist gekommen).** The following verbs require **sein** as an auxiliary in the conversational past.

INFINITIVE	PAST PARTICIPLE		INFINITIVE	PAST PARTICIPLE
aufstehen	(ist) aufgestanden		laufen	(ist) gelaufen
fahren	(ist) gefahren		reiten	(ist) geritten
fallen	(ist) gefallen		schwimmen	(ist) geschwommen
gehen	(ist) gegangen		segeln	(ist) gesegelt
kommen	(ist) gekommen		wandern	(ist) gewandert

Narrative past of **sein** (C)

ich **war**		wir **waren**
du **warst**	Sie **waren**	ihr **wart**
er/es/sie **war**		sie **waren**

Wo **warst** du gestern?   Where *were* you yesterday?

The most commonly used past-tense forms of **sein** are **war, warst,** and so on. These forms are called *narrative past*. **Sein** also has a conversational past, which you will learn in *German Today, Two.*

Special **der**-nouns in the accusative singular (D)

> Wie heißt **der Junge**?   Meinst du **den Jungen** da?
> Wie heißt **der Kunde**?   Meinst du **den Kunden** da?
> **Herr Lenz** ist mein Freund.   Ich kenne **Herrn Lenz** nicht.

Most nouns have the same form in the nominative and the accusative. A few **der**-nouns, including **Junge, Kunde,** and **Herr,** add **-n** in the accusative singular. Note that the **-n** must be added even when **Herr** is used as a title.

In the vocabularies of this book, special **der**-nouns will be followed by two endings: **der Herr, -n, -en.** The first ending is the accusative singular; the second ending is the nominative plural.

Prepositions with the accusative case (E-J)

durch	Tanja geht **durch** die Stadt.	Tanja is going *through* the city.
für	**Für** wen kauft sie die Platte?	*For* whom is she buying the record?
gegen	Sie hat nichts **gegen** den Jungen.	She has nothing *against* the boy.
ohne	Sie beginnt **ohne** Herrn Bauer.	She's beginning *without* Mr. Bauer.
um	Sie geht **um** das Haus.	She's going *around* the house.

Accusative prepositional contractions (K)

> Erika geht **durchs** Zimmer.   durch das > **durchs**
> Jörg kauft ein Geschenk **fürs** Kind.   für das > **fürs**
> Torsten geht **ums** Haus.   um das > **ums**

The prepositions **durch, für,** and **um** may contract with the definite article **das.**

In dieser Bäckerei bekommt man auch frischen Kaffee.

Die Bäckerei an der Lahnbrücke
Heinz Kugel
Brückenstraße 13 · Ruf 74 23
Bietet Ihnen täglich Ofenfrisch eine große Auswahl an:
Brot - Brötchen - Feinbackwaren und Konditoreierzeugnisse.
Für Ihre Familienfeste, Partys und ähnliches beraten wir Sie gerne.

Wählen Sie Ihren Lieblingskaffee im *Tchibo* Frisch-Depot
Mittwochs:
Laugenbrezel
»echt schwäbisch«

Wiederholung

A Your grandmother wants to know who's done various tasks. Confirm her guesses.

■ Wer hat den Bäcker angerufen? Du? — *Ja, ich habe ihn angerufen.*

1. Wer hat den Metzger angerufen? Du?
2. Wer hat das Haus aufgeräumt? Ihr?
3. Wer hat die Möbel abgestaubt? Karin?
4. Wer hat das Geschirr abgetrocknet? Karl und Erik?
5. Wer hat die Fenster aufgemacht? Du?
6. Wer hat die Wurst eingepackt? Deine Mutter?

B Read the following statements about various foods and quantities of foods. Correct the statements that aren't logical.

■ Ich möchte zwei Meter Bananen. — *Ich möchte zwei Pfund Bananen.*

1. Ich möchte zwei Liter Würstchen bitte.
2. Sind die Tomaten frisch?
3. Fleisch und Schinken kaufe ich immer beim Bäcker.
4. Ich brauche auch fünf Stück Milch bitte.
5. Kartoffeln kosten eine Mark das Gramm.
6. Im Supermarkt darf man das Obst nicht anfassen.
7. Butter kostet 6 Mark 50 das Kilometer.
8. Ich trinke jeden Tag zwei Glas Milch.

C Everyone has chores to do today. Form complete sentences in the present tense, using the cues provided.

1. Andrea / müssen / spülen / Geschirr
2. ich / sollen / decken / Tisch
3. Werner / aufräumen / Garage
4. du / füttern / Katze
5. wir / abstauben / Möbel
6. Werner / backen / Kuchen
7. ich / müssen / raustragen / Mülleimer

D List at least five things you sometimes do after school or in the evening. You may wish to include some of the following activities.

Hausaufgaben machen   einkaufen gehen   zu Hause helfen
tanzen gehen   ins Konzert gehen   fernsehen

E What are the following people and animals doing? Write a sentence related to each picture, using the preposition given.

■ um

Sie laufen um die Frau herum.

1. ohne

2. für

3. gegen

4. durch

Kapitel 11

Kulturlesestück

Der Markt

Viele Deutsche gehen nicht nur einmal° in der Woche einkaufen. Sie gehen zweimal oder öfter°, denn sie wollen frisches Obst und Gemüse haben.

5 Sie kaufen ihr Obst und Gemüse oft auf dem Markt. Hier kann man es direkt von den Bauern° kaufen. Der Markt ist oft im Zentrum einer° Stadt, auf dem Marktplatz° vor dem Rathaus°. Die Verkäufer haben ihre
10 Waren unter° großen Schirmen°. Diese Schirme haben viele Farben — rot, blau oder grün. So sieht der Markt schön bunt° aus.

In großen Städten ist jeden Tag Markt, in kleinen Städten ein- oder zweimal in der
15 Woche. Man findet oft auch Brot, Käse und Eier, Fleisch und Wurst und Fisch° da. Und Blumen°. Viele Blumen. Einige° Städte haben sogar° einen besonderen° Blumenmarkt.

one time

more often

farmers
of a / market place
town hall
under / umbrellas

colorful

fish
flowers / some
even / special

A Choose the phrase that best completes each sentence, based on the reading.

1. Viele Deutsche gehen zweimal oder öfter in der Woche einkaufen, denn . . .
   a. sie wollen nicht soviel tragen.
   b. sie wollen immer alles frisch haben.
   c. sie haben kein Auto.
   d. man kann Gemüse nur von den Bauern kaufen.
2. Die Deutschen kaufen gern auf dem Markt, denn . . .
   a. im Supermarkt ist alles frisch.
   b. in kleinen Geschäften ist alles billig.
   c. die Bauern haben alles frisch.
   d. man muß nicht so weit gehen.
3. Auf dem Markt sieht man viele bunte . . .
   a. Bauern
   b. Verkäufer
   c. Rathäuser
   d. Schirme
4. In . . . ist jeden Tag Markt.
   a. großen Städten
   b. kleinen Städten
   c. allen Städten
   d. keiner Stadt

B Which of the following would generally be available at an open-air market in a German-speaking country?

Möbel, Äpfel, Kartoffeln, Cassetten, Fernseher, Käse, Eier, Wurst, Briefmarken, Blumen, Flugzeugmodelle, Fisch, Gemüse, Brot

Whenever possible, Germans prefer food without preservatives, untouched by insecticides, and grown without chemical fertilizers. They do not decorate their cakes and cookies with bright, artificial colorings the way Americans sometimes do. Given this preference for naturalness, it is not surprising to find that there are many health food stores **(Reformhäuser)** in the German-speaking countries.

Naturalness is prized in other products as well. Advertisements proclaim soaps with natural oils, hair-care products made with herbs, and clothing made of natural fibers.

Germans stand by their concern for naturalness even in sickness. People often seek relief from their illnesses in one of the many spas in the German-speaking countries. Depending on their location, the spas might feature mineral waters for drinking or bathing, mud baths, herbal medicines, or just good clean air.

Vokabeln

SUBSTANTIVE

der Apfel, ⸚ apple
der Bäcker, –/die Bäckerin, –nen baker
die Banane, –n banana
das Brot, –e (loaf of) bread
die Butter butter
das Ei, –er egg
die Einkaufstasche, –n shopping bag
die Erbse, –n pea
die Erdbeere, –n strawberry
die Flasche, –n bottle
das Fleisch meat
das Gemüse, – vegetable
das Glas, ⸚er glass
das Gramm gram
die Karotte, –n carrot
die Kartoffel, –n potato
der Käse cheese
das Kilo(gramm) kilogram
der Kuchen, – cake
der Kunde, –n, –n/die Kundin, –nen customer
die Lebensmittel (pl.) food, groceries
der Liter, – liter
der Markt, ⸚e market
der Metzger, –/die Metzgerin, –nen butcher
die Milch milk
das Obst fruit
die Orange, –n orange
der Pfennig, –e (abbr. **Pf**) German coin
das Pfund, –e (abbr. **Pfd.**) pound
der Saft, ⸚e juice
der Schinken ham
das Schweinskotelett, –s pork chop
der Spinat spinach
das Stück, –e piece
der Supermarkt, ⸚e supermarket
die Tomate, –n tomato
die Tüte, –n bag
der Wunsch, ⸚e wish, desire
die Wurst, ⸚e sausage, cold cuts
das Würstchen, – frankfurter

VERBEN

besuchen to visit
bezahlen to pay
ein·packen to pack
packen to pack
war (past tense of **sein**) was

ANDERE WÖRTER

allein alone
denn (conjunction) for, because
dort there
durch (+ acc.) through
fast almost
frisch fresh
früh early
man (indef. pronoun) one, you, they, people
nämlich namely, you know
nett nice
ohne (+ acc.) without
selbst oneself, myself, etc.
so . . . wie as . . . as
wohl indeed, probably
zurück back
zusammen together

BESONDERE AUSDRÜCKE

einen Moment just a moment
Entschuldigung excuse me, sorry
Grüß Gott hello
auf Wiederschauen good-by
was darf es sein? what would you like?
ich hätte gern . . . I would like . . .
sonst noch was? anything else?
das macht zusammen 10 Mark that comes to 10 Marks
auf dem Markt at the open-air market

Kapitel 12
Guten Appetit!

Essen bei Familie Wolf

Was gibt's zum Frühstück?

Familie Wolf frühstückt um sieben. Zum Frühstück gibt es Brot und Brötchen mit Butter und Marmelade, manchmal auch ein Ei, Käse oder Wurst. Der Vater und die Mutter trinken Kaffee, und Gabi trinkt Schokolade oder Milch.

Fragen
1. Wann frühstücken Wolfs?
2. Was essen und trinken Wolfs zum Frühstück?
3. Was ißt und trinkst du zum Frühstück? Eier? Corn-flakes? Brot? Toast? mit Butter und Marmelade? Saft? Milch? Kaffee?

Was gibt's zum Mittagessen?

Um ein Uhr ißt Familie Wolf zu Mittag. Zum Mittagessen gibt es Suppe, dann Fisch oder Fleisch mit Kartoffeln und Gemüse und manchmal auch Salat. Zum Essen trinken sie gewöhnlich nichts. Nur am Sonntag trinken Herr und Frau Wolf vielleicht ein Glas Wein, und Gabi trinkt Saft. Als Nachtisch gibt es vielleicht Orangen oder Bananen oder einen Pudding.

Fragen
1. Wann essen Wolfs zu Mittag?
2. Was essen Wolfs zu Mittag?
3. Was ißt du mittags°? Thunfisch? Schinkenbrote°? Wurst? Würstchen? Salat? Suppe? Pommes frites°? Chips? Pizza?
4. Was trinkst du zum Mittagessen?

Was gibt's zum Abendessen?

Um sieben ißt die Familie zu Abend. Zum Abendessen gibt es Brot mit Wurst und Käse. Der Vater und die Mutter trinken oft ein Glas Bier oder eine Tasse Tee. Gabi trinkt kein Bier, sondern Limonade oder eine Cola. Wasser trinken sie nicht, denn es schmeckt nicht so gut wie Cola oder Tee.

Fragen
1. Wann essen Wolfs zu Abend?
2. Was essen Wolfs zu Abend?
3. Was ißt du abends? Steak? Rindsbraten? Schweinskoteletts? Huhn? Fisch? Würstchen? Kartoffeln? Gemüse? Nachtisch?
4. Was trinkst du zum Abendessen?

One of Gabi Wolf's chores is to set the table before each meal: fork **(die Gabel)** on the left of the plate, knife **(das Messer)** on the right, and spoon **(der Löffel)** above the plate. When people in German-speaking countries eat, they keep the fork in the left hand and the knife in the right, using both utensils at once. Germans keep their left hand on the table instead of in their lap, as Americans do.

Before beginning to eat, the head of the household may say **Guten Appetit** or **Mahlzeit**, short for **Gesegnete Mahlzeit** ("wishing everyone a good meal"). The rest of the family often responds with **Danke gleichfalls** (same to you).

Im Restaurant

Familie Wolf ißt auch gern mal im Restaurant.

OBER	Guten Tag! Möchten Sie etwas trinken?
FRAU WOLF	Ach ja. Ich habe so einen Durst. Ein Mineralwasser bitte.
HERR WOLF	Ich trinke auch ein Wasser.
OBER	Zwei Wasser.
GABI	Ich möchte eine Cola bitte.
OBER	Danke.
HERR WOLF	Und die Speisekarte bitte.

Der Ober bringt die Getränke.

OBER	Möchten Sie jetzt bestellen?
FRAU WOLF	Ja bitte. Ist der Rindsbraten zart?
OBER	Oh ja. Den kann ich empfehlen.
FRAU WOLF	Also, dreimal Rindsbraten mit Kartoffelpüree und Salat.
GABI	Ich will kein Kartoffelpüree.
FRAU WOLF	Hast du denn keinen Hunger?
GABI	Doch. Aber ich esse lieber Pommes frites.
FRAU WOLF	Wie du willst.
	* * *
OBER	So, hat's geschmeckt?
FRAU WOLF	Ja. Der Braten war ausgezeichnet.
HERR WOLF	Ich möchte gern zahlen.
OBER	Bitte sehr. Das macht zusammen 43 Mark und 50 Pfennig.
HERR WOLF	Machen Sie es 45.
OBER	Vielen Dank.

Fragen

1. Ißt Familie Wolf immer zu Hause? Wo essen sie auch gern?
2. Warum bestellt Frau Wolf ein Mineralwasser?
3. Was trinkt Gabi?
4. Wer bringt die Speisekarte?
5. Was empfiehlt der Ober?
6. Was bestellt Frau Wolf?
7. Warum will Gabi kein Kartoffelpüree?
8. Wie hat der Braten geschmeckt?
9. Wer bezahlt?

Du hast das Wort

A. Ask a classmate whether he/she likes to eat certain foods.

Ißt du gern	Kartoffelpüree? Fisch? Gemüse?

Ja, sehr gern.
Ja, [Kartoffelpüree] schmeckt gut.
Ich esse es, aber nicht gern.
Nein, [Kartoffelpüree] esse ich nicht gern.
Nein, [Kartoffelpüree] mag ich nicht.

B. Take a poll of your classmates on their preferences for foods and beverages.

Was ißt du lieber — Kartoffelpüree oder Pommes frites?
　　　　　　　　　　Eier oder Corn-flakes?
　　　　　　　　　　Fleisch oder Fisch?
　　　　　　　　　　Orangen oder Bananen?
　　　　　　　　　　Wurst oder Käse?

Was trinkst du lieber — Cola oder Kaffee?
　　　　　　　　　　　Saft oder Milch?
　　　　　　　　　　　Tee oder Wasser?

Most restaurants in German-speaking countries post the menu outside so that customers may decide whether they wish to or can afford to eat there. The price includes a value-added tax (**Mehrwertsteuer**) and a service charge (**Bedienung**) of 15%. To ask for the bill one can say **Zahlen bitte!** or **Ich möchte gern zahlen.** The waiter or waitress will total the bill and make change right at the table. Although no extra tip is usually left, the customer often rounds off the bill to the next appropriate figure.

Wortschatzerweiterung

Speisekarte

Suppen

Hühnersuppe	DM 2,50
Gemüsesuppe	DM 3,00
Tagessuppe	DM 2,00

Fleisch und Fisch

Filetsteak	DM 13,00
Rindsbraten	DM 10,50
Schweinskotelett	DM 9,50
Wiener Schnitzel	DM 10,50
Schinkenbrot	DM 6,50
Würstchen	DM 3,00
Fisch	DM 9,00
Hering	DM 3,50

Gemüse und Salate

Erbsen	DM 2,00
Karotten	DM 2,00
Spinat	DM 2,00
Pommes frites	DM 1,50
Kartoffelpüree	DM 1,50
Salat	DM 3,00
Tomatensalat	DM 3,50
Wurstsalat	DM 5,00

Zum Nachtisch

Eis	DM 3,50
Pudding	DM 2,00
Apfelkuchen	DM 2,00
Erdbeertorte	DM 2,50
Käse	DM 3,50
Obst	DM 3,00

Getränke

Kaffee	DM 1,80
Tee	DM 1,80
Schokolade	DM 1,80
Apfelsaft	DM 2,50
Cola	DM 2,30
Limonade	DM 2,00
Milch	DM 1,50
Mineralwasser	DM 2,00
Bier	DM 2,30
Wein	DM 4,30

A You have been given 18 German marks (DM 18,00) to spend on a restaurant meal. The restaurant you have chosen offers the items shown on the menu above. What will you eat? Begin with *Ich nehme...* and list the items you wish to order.

B Create a skit with a partner. One of you takes the role of a waiter or waitress. The other orders dinner or a snack from the menu.

A **Frühstück** ordered in a restaurant or hotel usually consists of a hot beverage, an assortment of rolls and breads, butter, and jam or jelly. This is what is referred to in the United States as a "continental breakfast." When people in German-speaking countries have eggs for breakfast, they generally have soft-boiled eggs **(weichgekochte Eier)**. Scrambled eggs **(Rührei)** and fried eggs **(Spiegeleier)** are eaten more for supper.

Pancakes are generally not a breakfast food in German-speaking countries. German **Pfannkuchen** are thinner and lighter than American pancakes, more like French **crêpes.** They are often filled with applesauce or jam and then rolled up and dusted with sugar.

Kleine Kochschule

der Löffel	spoon	**der Teig**	dough
der Teelöffel	teaspoon	**bestreichen**	to spread
der Eßlöffel	tablespoon	**bestreuen**	to sprinkle
die Prise	pinch	**erhitzen**	to heat
die Pfanne	pan	**gießen**	to pour
der Topf	pot	**schneiden**	to cut
die Schüssel	bowl	**verrühren**	to stir, to beat
die Zutaten	ingredients		

The list above includes some of the more common German terms used in cooking. It should help you read the following recipe for **Pfannkuchen**.

Zutaten

375 Gramm Mehl°   flour
3 Eier
1 Prise Salz°   salt
¾ Liter Milch
Butter oder Margarine
150 Gramm Marmelade
Puderzucker° zum Bestreuen   confectioner's sugar

Mehl, Eier, Milch und Salz zu einem dünnen, glatten° Teig verrühren. In einer Pfanne etwas Butter oder Margarine erhitzen, den Boden° dünn mit Teig ausgießen und die Pfannkuchen auf beiden Seiten° goldgelb backen.

    Dies so lange wiederholen°, bis der Teig aufgebraucht° ist. Jeden Pfannkuchen mit Marmelade bestreichen, einrollen° und mit Zucker bestreuen.

smooth
bottom
sides
repeat/used up
roll up

Aussprache

[ə] bitt**e**, b**e**stimmt
[ən] spiel**en**, geh**en**
[ər] Spiel**er**, bitt**er**, V**er**käuf**er**

The [ə] sound occurs in unstressed **-en** and **-e** endings and is similar to English *e* in *boxes, pocket*.

The [ər] sound occurs when the sequence **er** stands at the end of a word, before a consonant, or in an unstressed prefix. The **-r** is not pronounced as an [R], but sounds much like the final *-a* in English *sofa*.

A Practice the following words horizontally.

[ən]	[ə]	[ər]
bitt**en**	bitt**e**	bitt**er**
denk**en**	denk**e**	Denk**er**
fahr**en**	fahr**e**	Fahr**er**
fehl**en**	fehl**e**	Fehl**er**
leid**en**	leid**e**	leid**er**
nenn**en**	nenn**e**	Nenn**er**

B Practice the sounds [ə], [ən], and [ər]. Read the sentences aloud.

1. Wo haben Sie diese Platten gekauft, Frau Leber?
2. Unser Cassetten-Recorder ist wieder kaputt.
3. Die Hose ist nicht teuer, aber ich kann sie nicht kaufen.

Morgen, morgen, nur nicht heute, sagen alle faulen Leute.

Übungen

Dieser-words in the nominative and accusative

dieser

NOMINATIVE	
Der Dieser	Fernseher ist preiswert.
Das Dieses	Radio ist preiswert.
Die Diese	Stereoanlage ist preiswert.
Die Diese	Cassetten sind preiswert.

ACCUSATIVE		
Kaufst du	den diesen	Fernseher?
Kaufst du	das dieses	Radio?
Kaufst du	die diese	Stereoanlage?
Kaufst du	die diese	Cassetten?

Dieser follows the same pattern of endings in the nominative and accusative as the definite article.

A You and Martina are shopping for clothes. Compare the prices of the articles she asks about with the ones you're looking at.

▪ Ist die Jacke da teuer?   *Ja, aber diese Jacke hier ist nicht teuer.*

1. Ist die Hose da teuer?
2. Ist der Gürtel da teuer?
3. Ist der Pulli da teuer?
4. Ist das Hemd da teuer?
5. Ist das Kleid da teuer?
6. Sind die Schuhe da teuer?
7. Sind die Jeans da teuer?

B You work in a market where customers often ask about the quality of various foods. Recommend all the food items mentioned.

▪ Ist dieser Salat frisch?   *Ja, ich kann diesen Salat empfehlen.*

1. Ist diese Wurst gut?
2. Ist dieser Käse gut?
3. Ist dieser Schinken frisch?
4. Ist dieses Brot frisch?
5. Sind diese Brötchen frisch?
6. Sind diese Tomaten gut?

welcher/jeder

| Welcher Fernseher
Welches Radio
Welche Stereoanlage | ist teuer? |

| Jeder Fernseher
Jedes Radio
Jede Stereoanlage | ist teuer. |

Welcher and **jeder** have the same endings as **dieser**. **Jeder** is used in the singular only.

C Matthias has a habit of making vague statements. Ask him to clarify what he's talking about.

▪ Ich habe das Buch zweimal gelesen.   *Welches Buch?*

1. Ich habe das Poster nicht gekauft.
2. Ich habe den Kugelschreiber leider verloren.
3. Ich habe den Pulli gestern getragen.
4. Ich habe die Platte schon gehört.
5. Ich habe das Spiel natürlich gewonnen.
6. Ich habe die Schuhe nicht gekauft.
7. Ich habe die Uhr selbst bezahlt.

D Your hobby is collecting things. When a friend questions whether you actually like certain items, say that in your opinion every item has its merits.

▪ Findest du diese Uhr schön?   *Ja, für mich ist jede Uhr schön.*

1. Findest du diese Ansichtskarte interessant?
2. Findest du diesen Bierdeckel interessant?
3. Findest du diese Briefmarke schön?
4. Findest du dieses Poster schön?
5. Findest du diese Platte gut?

mancher/solcher

Manche Bücher sind zu teuer.   *Some books are too expensive.*
Solche Bücher kaufe ich nicht.   *I wouldn't buy such books.*

Solcher and **mancher** have the same endings as **dieser,** but they are used almost exclusively in the plural.

E The clerk at the market offers you less-than-perfect fruits and vegetables. State emphatically that you wouldn't buy such produce.

▪ Möchten Sie diese Kartoffeln?   *Nein, solche Kartoffeln kaufe ich nicht.*

1. Möchten Sie diese Erdbeeren?
2. Möchten Sie diese Orangen?
3. Möchten Sie diese Äpfel?
4. Möchten Sie diese Tomaten?
5. Möchten Sie diese Erbsen?

F It's easy to make generalizations. Say that each of the following statements is true of many things and people.

▪ Das Mädchen trägt Jeans.   *Manche Mädchen tragen Jeans.*

1. Die Frau kauft im Supermarkt ein.
2. Der Junge kocht gern.
3. Das Geschäft ist teuer.
4. Das Haus ist klein.
5. Die Platte ist schlecht.
6. Die Party ist langweilig.

Time expressions in the accusative case

Wann kommt Karl-Heinz?   **Diesen** Sommer.
Wie oft spielt er Tennis?   **Jeden** Samstag.
Wie lange arbeitet er im Geschäft?   **Einen** Monat.

Time expressions that answer the questions **wann?, wie oft?,** and **wie lange?** are in the accusative case. Such expressions indicate a definite time or period of time.

G Confirm the answers to the following questions.

▪ Wie oft kommt Michael? Jeden Abend?   *Ja, er kommt jeden Abend.*

1. Wie oft schreibt Frau Weiß? Jede Woche?
2. Wie oft geht Herr Neumeier einkaufen? Jeden Tag?
3. Wie lange arbeitet Erika schon? Einen Monat?
4. Wann gehen wir spazieren? Diesen Samstag?
5. Wie oft kommen Ingrids Freunde? Jedes Jahr?
6. Wann gehst du tanzen? Jedes Wochenende?

Du hast das Wort

A. Ask your classmates the following questions about their routine activities.

▪️ Arbeitest du jeden Abend?   Ja, jeden Abend. / Nein, nicht jeden Abend. Ich arbeite [nur am Montagabend].

Frühstückst du jeden Morgen?
Gehst du jeden Tag tanzen?
Trägst du jeden Tag Jeans?
Gehst du jede Woche einkaufen?
Siehst du jeden Abend fern?
Treibst du jeden Nachmittag Sport?

B. Ask your teacher the following questions.

▪️ Frag, ob er/sie jeden   Treiben Sie jeden
     Samstag Sport treibt!   Samstag Sport?

Frag, ob er/sie jeden Abend arbeitet!
Frag, ob er/sie jeden Morgen frühstückt!
Frag, ob er/sie jede Woche einkaufen geht!
Frag, ob er/sie jeden Abend fernsieht!

Present tense to express duration of time

Wie lange **lernst** du **schon** Deutsch?   How long *have* you *been studying* German?
Erik **arbeitet schon** zwei Monate im Supermarkt.   Erik *has been working* for two months in the supermarket.

To express action that started in the past and extends into the present, German uses the present tense plus a time indication, usually accompanied by **schon.**

H   Gerd wants to know how long various people have been doing certain things. Confirm his guesses.

▪️ Wie lange arbeitest du schon im Supermarkt? Zwei Wochen?   Ja, ich arbeite schon zwei Wochen im Supermarkt.

1. Wie lange lernst du schon Deutsch? Sechs Monate?
2. Wie lange wohnt Beate schon in München? Zwei Jahre?
3. Wie lange sammelt Dirk schon Bierdeckel? Ein Jahr?
4. Wie lange sammelt Heike schon Briefmarken? Drei Jahre?
5. Wie lange arbeitet Rudi schon im Musikgeschäft? Einen Monat?

Coordinating conjunctions: **aber, denn, oder, sondern, und**

Uwe trinkt Kaffee, **aber** ich trinke lieber Milch.
Ich trinke morgens Milch, **denn** ich mag keinen Kaffee.

Coordinating conjunctions are used to connect two independent clauses. They do not affect word order of subject and verb.

I Explain to your teacher that the following persons did not do their homework last night for the reasons given.

■ Ingrid hat Tennis gespielt.   *Ingrid hat die Aufgaben nicht gemacht, denn sie hat Tennis gespielt.*

1. Jan hat keine Zeit gehabt.
2. Dieter ist ins Kino gegangen.
3. Gisela hat Musik gehört.
4. Erik hat Platten gespielt.
5. Astrid hat gearbeitet.
6. Gabi ist tanzen gegangen.
7. Ich war auf einer Party.

J State your plans for several days next week by combining each pair of sentences with *und*.

■ Samstag gehen wir einkaufen. Dann gehen wir ins Kino.   *Samstag gehen wir einkaufen, und dann gehen wir ins Kino.*

1. Sonntag wandern wir. Dann trinken wir Kaffee.
2. Montag abend mache ich Mathe. Dann sehe ich fern.
3. Mittwoch arbeite ich im Supermarkt. Dann gehe ich tanzen.
4. Donnerstag spielen wir Tennis. Dann machen wir Hausaufgaben.
5. Freitag gehe ich einkaufen. Dann mache ich Abendessen.

K Sabine often changes her mind so you're never quite sure what she's going to do. Inquire about her plans.

■ Arbeitest du? Gehst du jetzt schwimmen?   *Arbeitest du, oder gehst du jetzt schwimmen?*

1. Kommst du mit? Hast du keine Zeit?
2. Möchtest du jetzt essen? Hast du keinen Hunger?
3. Trinkst du jetzt eine Cola? Hast du keinen Durst?
4. Gehst du auf den Markt? Kaufst du im Supermarkt ein?
5. Spielst du jetzt Volleyball? Machst du Hausaufgaben?
6. Rufst du Volker an? Besuchst du ihn?

aber and sondern

Wir möchten heute abend fernsehen, **aber** unser Fernseher ist kaputt.
We'd like to watch TV this evening, but *our TV set is broken.*

Wir sehen heute abend nicht fern, **sondern** gehen ins Kino.
We aren't going to watch TV this evening, instead *we're going to the movies.*

Aber as a coordinating conjunction is equivalent to *but, nevertheless*. It may be used after either a positive or a negative clause. **Sondern** is a coordinating conjunction that is equivalent to *but, instead, on the contrary*. It is used after a negative clause only, and then only if the second clause contradicts the first clause. Otherwise **aber** is used.

L Combine each pair of sentences with *aber*.

▪ Frau Meier geht jeden Tag einkaufen. Sie kauft nicht viel.   *Frau Meier geht jeden Tag einkaufen, aber sie kauft nicht viel.*

1. Ich möchte einkaufen gehen. Die Geschäfte sind zu.
2. Ich möchte ins Kino. Ich habe kein Geld.
3. Die *Hot Dogs* spielen diesen Samstag. Ich möchte sie nicht hören.

M Complete the sentences with *sondern* or *aber*, as appropriate.

1. Erikas Zimmer ist nicht groß, ____ sehr klein.
2. Ihr Zimmer ist klein, ____ schön.
3. Erika arbeitet heute abend nicht, ____ geht ins Konzert.
4. Sie hat viele Hausaufgaben, ____ sie macht sie nicht.
5. Die Schuhe sind nicht teuer, ____ sehr billig.
6. Die Schuhe sind nicht teuer, ____ ich kaufe sie nicht.

Kapitel 12 **265**

Was gibt's zum Essen?

Grammatische Übersicht

Dieser-words in the nominative and accusative (A–F)

	NOMINATIVE	ACCUSATIVE
der Pulli	Dieser Pulli ist toll.	Inge kauft diesen Pulli.
das Hemd	Dieses Hemd ist toll.	Erik kauft dieses Hemd.
die Jacke	Diese Jacke ist toll.	Jan kauft diese Jacke.
die Schuhe	Diese Schuhe sind toll.	Anna kauft diese Schuhe.

Dieser, jeder, welcher, solcher, and **mancher** (called **dieser-**words) follow the same pattern of endings in the nominative and accusative as the definite articles **der, das,** and **die.**

Meanings and uses of **dieser**-words

dieser	this; these *(plural)*
jeder	each, every *(used in the singular only)*
mancher	many a, several *(used mainly in the plural)*
solcher	such *(used mainly in the plural)*
welcher	which?

Time expressions in the accusative case (G)

Wann kommt Katrin wieder? Sie kommt **dieses Jahr** wieder.
Wie oft spielt Jan Tennis? Er spielt **jeden Tag** Tennis.
Wie lange bleibt Beate? Sie kann nur **einen Tag** bleiben.

Time expressions that indicate a definite time (answering the questions **wann?, wie oft?**) or a period of time (answering the question **wie lange?**) are in the accusative case.

Present tense to express duration of time (H)

Nun **sind** wir **schon drei Wochen** in Deutschland.
Ingrid **arbeitet schon ein Jahr** im Supermarkt.

Now we've been in Germany for three weeks.
Ingrid has been working in the supermarket for a year.

To express action that started in the past and extends into the present, German uses the present tense plus a time indication, usually accompanied by **schon.** To express the same concept, English uses such forms as *have been, has been . . . -ing.*

Independent clauses

INDEPENDENT CLAUSE	COORDINATING CONJUNCTION	INDEPENDENT CLAUSE
Wir möchten einkaufen gehen,	aber	wir haben kein Geld.
Ich kaufe die Jacke nicht,	denn	sie ist zu teuer.

An independent clause can make sense standing alone. When used as parts of sentences, two independent clauses may be connected with each other by coordinating conjunctions.

Coordinating conjunctions (I-M)

> Ich habe Hunger, **aber** das Essen ist noch nicht fertig.
> Wir können im Restaurant essen, **denn** ich habe heute Geld.
> Nimmst du den Fisch, **oder** magst du keinen Fisch?
> Er geht nicht ins Restaurant, **sondern** ins Café.
> Du nimmst ein Eis, **und** ich bestelle den Pudding.

Five common coordinating conjunctions are **aber, denn, oder, sondern,** and **und.** Coordinating conjunctions do not affect the word order of subject and verb. The conjunctions are generally preceded by a comma.

Ich schreibe Ute einen Brief **oder besuche** sie nächste Woche.	*I'll write* Ute a letter *or visit* her next week.
Sie arbeiten bis sieben **und gehen** dann ins Kino.	*They'll work* until seven *and* then go to the movies.

Oder and **und** are not preceded by a comma when the subject in both independent clauses is the same. The subject is not repeated in the second clause.

aber and sondern

Ich möchte im Restaurant essen, **aber** ich habe kein Geld.	I'd like to eat in a restaurant, *but* I don't have any money.
Wir gehen heute nicht ins Restaurant, **sondern** essen zu Hause.	We're not going to a restaurant today; *instead* we'll eat at home.

Aber as a coordinating conjunction is equivalent to *but, however, nevertheless*. It may be used after either a positive or a negative clause. **Sondern** is a coordinating conjunction that expresses a contrast or contradiction. It is equivalent to *but, instead, on the contrary*. **Sondern** is used after a negative clause only. When the subject is the same in both clauses, it is not repeated:

> **Wir gehen** nicht ins Restaurant, sondern **essen** zu Hause.

 ...und nach dem Essen

Wiederholung

A Answer the following questions, based on your personal experience or preferences. Then ask your teacher the same questions.

1. Ißt du lieber zu Hause oder im Restaurant?
2. Wie heißt dein Lieblingsrestaurant?
3. Ist es da teuer oder billig?
4. Wie oft ißt du dort?
5. Was bestellst du gewöhnlich?
6. Welchen Nachtisch bestellst du gern?

B Ilse is talking to her friends about a dinner she had last night at a restaurant. Express their conversational exchanges in German.

1. Did you eat in a restaurant yesterday?
   Yes. Sabine and Ralf also went along.
2. Why didn't you invite me?
   We called you up. You weren't home.
3. Did you order the roast beef?
   Yes. The waiter recommended it.
4. Did it taste good?
   Yes. It was very tender.
5. What did Ralf eat?
   He had the ham.
6. How much did you pay?
   Nothing. We didn't have any money.
7. And why did you come home so late?
   We washed the dishes.

C Ask the questions that the following sentences answer. Use the following interrogatives:

**Wann?   Wen?   Wer?   Was?   Wie?   Wo?   Wohin?
Wie oft?   Wie lange?**

1. Detlev sammelt *alte Ansichtskarten*.
2. Benno findet Ansichtskarten *langweilig*.
3. Kurt segelt *jeden Samstag*.
4. Martina geht oft *ins Jugendzentrum*.
5. Ute arbeitet schon *ein Jahr* im Supermarkt.
6. Gerd kauft seine Briefmarken *in Hamburg*.
7. *Petra* hat kein Hobby.
8. Lothar ruft *seine Freunde* oft an.
9. Frank sieht *abends* fern.

D Begin each sentence with the word or phrase in italics, and make the necessary changes in word order.

1. Peter spielt *jeden Tag* Tennis.
2. Er sieht *abends* fern.
3. Er hat *gestern* Gartenarbeit gemacht.
4. Seine Schwester Petra hat *heute morgen* das Auto gewaschen.
5. Sie fahren *am Wochenende* nach Bremen.
6. Sie kommen *Sonntag abend* wieder nach Hause.

E Replace each word in italics with the appropriate antonym.

**einfach   frisch   hübsch   kaputt
langweilig   leicht   verloren**

1. Unser Fernseher ist wieder *repariert*.
2. Wir haben das Fußballspiel *gewonnen*.
3. Dieses Hobby ist wirklich *interessant*.
4. Unsere Matheaufgabe ist heute *kompliziert*, nicht?
5. Chemie finde ich aber *schwer*.
6. Ist das Brot da *alt*?
7. Die Bluse da ist wirklich *häßlich*, nicht?

F Change one German word to another by changing a single letter. Use the English cues as guidelines.

■▥ we > how   wir > wie

1. then > because
2. beautiful > already
3. then > thin
4. of course > you *(acc.)*
5. now > only
6. four > much
7. go > against
8. still > after
9. butter > mother
10. can > know

G In six to eight sentences describe a party you gave recently. You may wish to include answers to the following questions.

Wieviel Personen hast du eingeladen?
Wann hat die Party begonnen?
Was habt ihr alles gemacht?
Habt ihr getanzt? Musik gehört?
Was habt ihr gegessen und getrunken? Wie war die Party?

Kulturlesestück

Kaffeestunde

Am Sonntag trinken viele Deutsche nachmittags Kaffee. Sie trinken aber natürlich nicht nur Kaffee, sondern sie essen auch Kuchen. Manche Familien trinken fast jeden Nachmittag Kaffee, nicht nur am Sonntag.

Es ist besonders° schön, nachmittags in ein Café oder in eine Konditorei° zu gehen. Da gibt es viele Torten und Kuchen. Alles schmeckt ausgezeichnet, besonders mit Sahne°.

Oft kommen Freunde zum Kaffee zusammen. Frau Weiß lädt Familie Kuhn ein: „Können Sie am Sonntag zu uns zum Kaffee kommen? Sagen wir um halb fünf?"

Pünktlich° um halb fünf stehen° Herr und Frau Kuhn vor der Tür. Herr Kuhn hat Blumen° in der Hand. Er gibt sie Frau Weiß. Der Kaffeetisch sieht° sehr schön aus: Auf dem Tisch liegt eine schöne weiße Decke°; Tassen und Teller° sind aus Porzellan°; die Blumen sind frisch; und natürlich gibt es viel Kuchen und Sahne. Ein schöner Nachmittag.

especially
shop serving pastries and coffee
whipped cream

punctually / stand
flowers
sieht . . . aus: looks
tablecloth / plates / china

A Choose the word or phrase that best completes each statement, based on the reading.

1. ... jeden Tag Kaffee.
   a. Kein Deutscher trinkt
   b. Viele Deutsche trinken
   c. Alle Deutschen trinken
   d. Alte Deutsche trinken
2. Wenn man „zum Kaffee" kommt, bekommt man ...
   a. nur Kaffee. b. Kaffee und Kuchen. c. ein warmes Essen. d. nur Kuchen.
3. „Kaffee" trinkt man ...
   a. morgens. b. zu Mittag. c. nachmittags. d. abends.
4. ... gibt es nachmittags viele Torten und Kuchen.
   a. Auf dem Markt b. In einem Supermarkt c. In einem Geschäft d. In einer Konditorei
5. Wenn man zum Kaffee eingeladen ist, bringt man oft ...
   a. Blumen. b. Bücher. c. einen Kuchen. d. Tassen und Teller.
6. Ein Stück Torte schmeckt besonders gut mit ...
   a. Butter. b. Sahne. c. Porzellan. d. Kaffeedecken.

B Which of the following things would you expect to find when invited *zum Kaffee?*

Torte, eine weiße Kaffeedecke, Wurst, Tomaten, Teller aus Porzellan, Pudding, frische Blumen, Tee, Speisekarte, Salat, Sahne, Kaffee

When Germans eat dessert with the main noon meal, it is often pudding or fruit rather than baked goods. Cakes and pastries are eaten during the **Kaffeestunde** later in the afternoon.

Vokabeln

SUBSTANTIVE

das Abendessen supper
das Bier beer
das Brötchen, - hard roll
die Cola (*also* **das Cola**) cola drink
der Durst thirst
das Eis ice cream; ice
der Fisch, -e fish
das Getränk, -e beverage
das Huhn, ̈er chicken
der Hunger hunger
das Kartoffelpüree mashed potatoes
die Limo(nade) soft drink
die Marmelade jam
das Mineralwasser mineral water
der Mittag noon
das Mittagessen lunch
der Nachtisch dessert
der Ober, - waiter
die Pommes frites (*pl.*) french fries
der Pudding pudding
das Restaurant, -s restaurant
der Rindsbraten roast beef, pot roast
der Salat, -e (head of) lettuce; salad
das Schinkenbrot, -e ham sandwich
die Schokolade, -n chocolate, hot chocolate; bar of chocolate
die Speisekarte, -n menu
die Suppe, -n soup
die Tasse, -n cup
der Tee tea
der Wein wine

VERBEN

bestellen to order
bringen (gebracht) to bring
empfehlen (ie; empfohlen) to recommend
frühstücken to have breakfast
zahlen to pay

ANDERE WÖRTER

als as
ausgezeichnet excellent
gewöhnlich usually
mancher some, several
manchmal sometimes
mittags at noon, at lunch time
nachmittags in the afternoon
nicht nur ... sondern auch not only ... but also
sondern but (on the contrary)
zart tender, delicate

BESONDERE AUSDRÜCKE

Durst haben to be thirsty
Hunger haben to be hungry
guten Appetit! enjoy your meal
ich esse lieber ... I prefer to eat ...
zum Frühstück for breakfast
zum Mittagessen for lunch
zum Abendessen for supper
zu Abend essen to have supper
zu Mittag essen to have lunch
bitte sehr certainly
vielen Dank! thank you very much
wie lange? how long?

Kapitel 13
Über das Wetter kann man immer sprechen

Ein Quiz

Was weißt du über das Wetter in Deutschland?

Weißt du,

    wo es im Sommer wärmer ist — in Ohio oder in Deutschland?
    was wärmer ist — 60 Grad Fahrenheit oder 20 Grad Celsius?
    wo es im Winter kälter ist — in Pittsburgh oder in Bonn?
    welche Stadt nördlicher liegt — New York oder München?
    welche Stadt südlicher liegt — Chicago oder Frankfurt?
    wo es im Winter mehr schneit — in Minnesota oder in Norddeutschland?
    wo es öfter regnet — in den Smoky Mountains oder im Schwarzwald°?   Black Forest

        How did you do? Answers are printed on page 279.

In Deutschland ist das Wetter anders

Jim aus° St. Louis besucht seinen Freund Klaus in Kassel. Klaus findet es heiß — Jim findet es warm.   from

Es ist Juli. In Kassel ist das Wetter gut. Die Sonne scheint. Jim ist gerade erst drei Tage in Kassel, da sagt Klaus: „Heute ist es wirklich heiß, furchtbar heiß." Jim aber denkt: Heiß? Hier? Jetzt? Nein! Schön warm.

    In Deutschland ist das Wetter anders, denn Deutschland liegt weiter nördlich als Amerika. Bonn, die Hauptstadt der° Bundesrepublik Deutschland, liegt circa° 1300 Kilometer weiter nördlich als Washington, die amerikanische Hauptstadt. Auch beeinflußt° der Atlantische Ozean das Klima°. So ist das Wetter oft kühl im Sommer und nicht so kalt im Winter. Der Wind kommt gewöhnlich von Westen und bringt vom Atlantischen Ozean Regen mit. Es regnet also viel; und Jim lernt, daß man einen Regenschirm mitnimmt, wenn man spazierengeht.

*of the
approximately
influences
climate*

Fragen

1. Liegt St. Louis oder Kassel weiter nördlich?
2. Wie heißt die Hauptstadt der Bundesrepublik?
3. Wie heißt die Hauptstadt der USA?
4. Wie ist das Wetter in Deutschland im Sommer oft?
5. Was kommt von Westen?
6. Was bringt der Wind mit?
7. Was nimmt Jim mit, wenn er spazierengeht?

Wie ist das Wetter?

Im Frühling

STEFAN	Was meinst du? Regnet es morgen wieder?
KARIN	Wahrscheinlich.
STEFAN	Das ist wirklich dumm!
KARIN	Warum?
STEFAN	Mein Regenschirm ist kaputt.

Im Sommer

DIETER	Heute ist es schön, nicht?
INGRID	Ja, endlich ist es mal warm.
DIETER	Hoffentlich wird es nicht zu heiß.
INGRID	Lieber heiß als kalt.

Im Herbst

FRAU KRAFT	Schönes Wetter, nicht?
HERR WOLF	Ja, ich habe diese Jahreszeit besonders gern. Es ist so schön kühl.
FRAU KRAFT	Das ist gutes Wanderwetter.
HERR WOLF	Zu dumm, daß wir arbeiten müssen.

Im Winter

RALF	Der Wind ist aber ganz schön kalt heute morgen.
ILSE	Ja, es hat letzte Nacht gefroren.
RALF	Heute nachmittag soll es schneien.
ILSE	Das ist ja prima. Dann können wir rodeln gehen.

Fragen

1. Warum ist Stefan unglücklich?
2. Hat Ingrid es lieber warm oder kalt?
3. Warum findet Herr Wolf den Herbst schön?
4. Was macht Ilse gern im Winter?

Du hast das Wort

A. Ask a classmate questions about the weather.

Hast du den Winter oder den Sommer lieber? Den Frühling oder den Herbst?
Hast du es lieber kalt oder warm?
Welchen Sport treibst du im Winter? Im Sommer?
Welchen Sport treibst du im Frühling? Im Herbst?
Hast du Regen gern? Schnee°?
Wie ist das Wetter heute?
Wie war es gestern?
Wie soll es morgen sein?

B. A classmate is trying to make conversation by talking about the weather. Do you agree with, disagree with, or doubt her/his comments?

Morgen soll es wieder regnen.   Das stimmt.
Heute ist es schön.   Das finde ich auch.
Es hat letzte Nacht gefroren.   Du hast recht°.
Heute abend soll es schneien.   Das glaube ich nicht.
Jetzt regnet es schon eine Woche.   Das kann nicht stimmen.
Morgen soll es wieder [heiß] werden.   Du spinnst°.
Schönes Wetter heute, nicht?   Meinst du?
                                       Glaubst du?

Sag!

Sag [Ute], daß es morgen regnen soll!
Sag [Kai], daß es schon drei Tage regnet!
Sag [Ute], daß der Wind kalt ist!
Sag [Kai], daß es letzte Nacht gefroren hat!
Sag [Ute], daß das Wetter furchtbar ist!
Sag [Kai], daß es übermorgen schneien soll!

Although summers in Germany are usually moderate, it does get warm at times. School is in session well into July, so the classrooms may get very warm. If the temperature reaches 27°C (about 81°F) by the end of the third period, which comes about 10:30 A.M., the general practice is to declare **hitzefrei,** and to dismiss school for the rest of the day.

Wortschatzerweiterung

Das Thermometer

37°C = 98.6°F

−18°C = 0°F

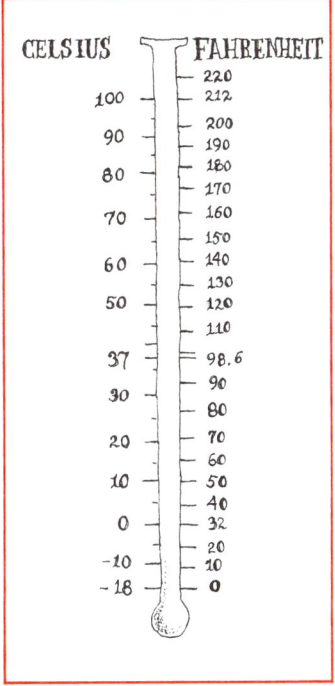

100°C = 212°F

0°C = 32°F

In German-speaking countries the Celsius thermometer is used. To find out the temperature, a German asks: **Wieviel Grad haben wir heute?** The answer may be **Es sind** [15] **Grad** or **Heute haben wir** [15] **Grad.**

A What's the temperature in degrees Celsius? *Wieviel Grad Celsius sind ...*

1. 12°F
2. 98.6°F
3. 68°F
4. 32°F
5. 212°F
6. 80°F

> **Answers to the weather-quiz:**
> 1. Ohio 2. 20 Grad Celsius 3. Pittsburgh 4. München
> 5. Chicago 6. Minnesota 7. Schwarzwald

Kapitel 13

Das Wetter und ein Bericht

Es schneit.
Die Straßen sind glatt.

Es regnet.
Die Straßen sind naß.

Es ist windig.
Es ist kalt.

Es ist bewölkt.
Es ist kühl.

Die Sonne scheint.
Es ist warm.

Es ist heiß.
Es ist trocken.

B Jim made a report of the weather in Kassel in early March for his class at home. Using his report as a model, keep your own daily record of the weather for a week, recording the temperature in degrees Celsius.

Montag	Es hat den ganzen Tag geregnet. Es war kalt; nur 6 Grad.
Dienstag	Bewölkt und kühl. Es waren 8 Grad.
Mittwoch	Die Sonne hat endlich geschienen. Es war fast warm — 12 Grad.
Donnerstag	Es war wieder kühl und windig. Es waren 10 Grad. Furchtbares Wetter.
Freitag	Es war sehr kalt. Es hat wieder geregnet. Temperatur: 7 Grad.
Samstag	Am Morgen war es noch kühl. Aber am Nachmittag hat die Sonne geschienen. Es waren 13 Grad. Abends ist es wieder kühl geworden.
Sonntag	Es war sehr schön — die Sonne war fast heiß. Es waren 18 Grad.

Aussprache

[x]   a**ch**, no**ch**, Bu**ch**, au**ch**

The sound [χ] is made in the back of the mouth, where the sound [k] is pronounced. It is produced by forcing air through a narrow opening between the back of the tongue and the back of the roof of the mouth. To produce the sound [χ], keep the tongue below the lower front teeth and, without moving the tongue or lips, make a gentle gargling noise. Do not substitute the [k] sound for the [χ] sound.

A   Practice the following words horizontally in pairs.

[k]	[x]	[k]	[x]
na**ck**t	Na**ch**t	lo**ck**en	lo**ch**en
Sa**ck**e	Sa**ch**e	Po**ck**en	po**ch**en
la**ck**en	la**ch**en	bu**k**	Bu**ch**
Do**ck**	do**ch**	Hau**k**e	hau**ch**e

The sound [χ] is represented by the letters **ch** and occurs after the vowels **a, o, u,** and **au**.

B   Practice the following words.

a**ch**, ma**ch**en, na**ch**   Bu**ch**, Ku**ch**en, versu**ch**en
n**och**, d**och**, k**och**en   au**ch**, brau**ch**en, tau**ch**en

C   Practice the sound [χ]. Read the sentences aloud.

1. Frau Meier bäckt jede Woche einen Kuchen.
2. Was machen wir noch?
3. Heute nachmittag besuchen wir Herrn Luckenbach.

Wer zuletzt lacht, lacht am besten.

Übungen

Comparison of adjectives and adverbs

Comparison of equality

Bernd ist **so alt wie** Jens.
Er arbeitet aber nicht **so viel wie** Jens.

Bernd is *as old as* Jens.
He doesn't work *as much as* Jens, however.

The construction **so ... wie** is equivalent to English *as ... as*.

A Inge comments on her friends' interest and ability in sports. Ask Inge whether theirs match hers.

▪ Ulrike spielt gut Tennis. *Spielt sie so gut wie du?*

1. Dieter schwimmt gut.
2. Anja spielt oft Volleyball.
3. Benno geht oft bergsteigen.
4. Kirstin reitet viel.
5. Jörg segelt viel.

Comparison of inequality

Base form	klein	Ute ist klein.	Ute is *small*.
Comparative	kleiner	Ute ist kleiner als Petra.	Ute is *smaller than* Petra.

The comparative of an adjective or adverb is formed by adding **-er** to the base form. The word **als** is equivalent to *than*.

B You are shopping for clothing with Gerda. Compare the articles she points out with the ones you see.

▪ Der Pulli da ist schön. *Ja, aber der Pulli hier ist noch schöner.*

1. Die Bluse da ist schön.
2. Das Hemd da ist dünn.
3. Der Gürtel da ist toll.
4. Der Mantel da ist leicht.
5. Die Krawatte da ist furchtbar.
6. Die Jacke da ist billig.
7. Die Schuhe da sind schwer.
8. Die Socken da sind billig.

Base form	groß	Petra ist groß.	Petra is *tall*.
Comparative	größer	Petra ist größer als Ute.	Petra is *taller than* Ute.

Many one-syllable adjectives and adverbs show umlaut in the comparative: **älter/jünger; kürzer/länger; wärmer/kälter; größer; dümmer.**

C Michael is misinformed about a number of things. Correct him by saying that everything is the opposite of what he thinks.

■ Ulf ist älter als Katja, nicht?   *Unsinn, er ist jünger.*

1. Aber Katja ist jünger als Susanne, nicht?
2. Katja ist kleiner als Susanne, nicht?
3. Aber Katja ist kleiner als Ulf, nicht?
4. Es ist heute wärmer als gestern, nicht?
5. Aber es war gestern kälter als am Samstag, nicht?
6. Dieses Jahr ist es wärmer als letztes, nicht?

Base form	gern	gut	viel	hoch
Comparative	lieber	besser	mehr	höher

A few adjectives and adverbs are irregular in the formation of their comparatives.

D You and Klaus are discussing mutual acquaintances. Provide Klaus with more information about the people he mentions.

■ Liese spielt gern Basketball.   *Sie spielt lieber Tennis.*
— Und Tennis?

1. Ernst spielt gern Klavier. — Und Gitarre?
2. Jens reitet gut. — Und Erik?
3. Eva tanzt gut. — Und Cornelia?
4. Ingrid singt hoch. — Und Heike?
5. Dietmar arbeitet viel. — Und sein Bruder?
6. Karin liest viel. — Und ihre Schwester?

Du hast das Wort   Ask a classmate which of two things he/she prefers.

Was spielst du besser — Tennis oder Basketball?
Was machst du lieber — Schi laufen oder rodeln?
Was hörst du lieber — Geige oder Klavier?
Was trinkst du lieber — Cola oder Milch?
Wohin gehst du lieber — ins Theater oder ins Kino?
Wo ißt du lieber — zu Hause oder im Restaurant?

The verb **werden**

Present tense of **werden**

ich werde		wir werden
du **wirst**	Sie werden	ihr werdet
er/es/sie **wird**		sie werden

The verb **werden** is irregular in the **du-** and **er/sie-**forms of the present tense.

E On a picnic you and your friends have been playing games all afternoon. Say that everyone is getting tired.

▪ Erik   *Erik wird müde.*

1. Petra
2. ich
3. Christl
4. du
5. wir
6. ihr
7. Hans und Karin

Conversational past of **werden**

Ich **bin** müde **geworden.**   I've become tired.
Herr Lenz **ist** alt **geworden.**   Mr. Lenz has grown old.

Because the verb **werden** expresses a change of condition, it requires **sein** as an auxiliary in the conversational past.

F Agree with your friend that the following people have changed in the last few years.

▪ Herr Fischer ist aber alt, nicht?   *Ja, er ist wirklich alt geworden.*

1. Dieter ist aber groß, nicht?
2. Herr Schmidt ist aber dick, nicht?
3. Frau Meier ist furchtbar dünn, nicht?
4. Peter ist sehr faul, nicht?
5. Ingrid ist schön schlank, nicht?

Du hast das Wort

Ask various classmates questions about their age.

▪ Wie alt wirst du dieses Jahr?   *Ich werde [sechzehn].*

▪ Wann wirst du zwanzig?   *[1987] werde ich zwanzig.*

Strandkörbe — gegen Wind und Wetter (Kiel)

Indirect statements

| Direct statement | Petra sagt: „Jan spielt morgen Tennis." |
| Indirect statement | Petra sagt, **daß** Jan morgen Tennis **spielt**. |

An indirect statement is a dependent clause. A dependent clause is introduced by a subordinating conjunction, for example **daß**. In a dependent clause, the verb is in final position.

G Report to a mutual friend what Jens says and does.

▪ Der Pulli ist häßlich.   *Jens sagt, daß der Pulli häßlich ist.*

1. Er kauft ihn nicht.
2. Er findet die Jacke aber schön.
3. Sie kostet aber viel.
4. Sie ist zu teuer.
5. Er kauft sie auch nicht.

| Direct statement | Petra sagt: „Jan ruft uns später an." |
| Indirect statement | Petra sagt, **daß** Jan uns später **anruft**. |

In a dependent clause, the separable prefix is attached to the base form of the verb, which is in final position.

H Pass on to Carola what Ingrid and Gisela recently told you.

▪ Stehen Ingrid und Gisela immer früh auf?   *Sie sagen, daß sie immer früh aufstehen.*

1. Kommen sie heute mit?
2. Rufen sie uns später noch an?
3. Kaufen sie morgen ein?
4. Haben sie Samstag etwas vor?

Kapitel 13

Direct statement	Petra sagt: „Jan muß jetzt gehen."
Indirect statement	Petra sagt, **daß** Jan jetzt **gehen muß**.

In a dependent clause, the modal auxiliary follows the infinitive and is in final position.

I Marianne has a busy day ahead of her. Inform Jens that you think his information about Marianne's activities is correct.

■ Will sie arbeiten?   *Ja, ich glaube, daß sie arbeiten will.*

1. Muß sie zu Hause helfen?   4. Muß sie noch Mathe machen?
2. Soll sie das Essen kochen?   5. Kann sie um zehn Uhr anrufen?
3. Will sie dann fernsehen?

Direct statement	Petra sagt: „Jan hat Mathe gemacht."
Indirect statement	Petra sagt, **daß** Jan Mathe **gemacht hat**.

In a dependent clause in the conversational past, the auxiliary verb **haben** or **sein** follows the past participle and is in final position.

J Someone did a lot of work around your house last week. Tell your parents that your brother Frank claims he did it.

■ Wer hat die Garage aufgeräumt?   *Frank sagt, daß er die Garage aufgeräumt hat.*

1. Wer hat die Fenster geputzt?   3. Wer hat die Wäsche gewaschen?
2. Wer hat Staub gesaugt?   4. Wer hat die Torte gebacken?

Schikjöring — ein ungewöhnlicher Wintersport (Stuttgart)

Indirect questions

Specific questions

Direct question	**Wer ist** das Mädchen?
Indirect question	Paul möchte wissen, **wer** das Mädchen **ist**.

An indirect question is a dependent clause; therefore, the verb is in final position. In indirect *specific* questions (that is, questions introduced by an interrogative like **wer**), the interrogative functions as a subordinating conjunction.

K Günter is having a birthday party. Ask your classmates for information about the party.

▪ Wo ist die Party?   *Weißt du, wo die Party ist?*

1. Wen hat Günter eingeladen?
2. Was machen wir?
3. Was gibt es zu essen?
4. Wer soll den Kuchen backen?
5. Was soll ich mitbringen?
6. Wie alt wird Günter?

General questions

Direct question	**Kommt** Inge zur Party?
Indirect question	Günter möchte wissen, **ob** Inge zur Party **kommt**.

In indirect *general* questions (that is, questions that can be answered by **ja** or **nein**), the indirect-question clause is introduced by **ob** (*whether, if*).

L On Monday morning you run into a friend who is curious about what Petra and Rainer did over the weekend. Express your ignorance about their activities.

▪ Hat Rainer gearbeitet?   *Ich weiß nicht, ob er gearbeitet hat.*

1. Hat Petra zu Hause geholfen?
2. Sind sie schwimmen gegangen?
3. Sind Dieter und Inge mitgefahren?
4. Haben sie einen Spaziergang gemacht?
5. Sind sie zusammen tanzen gegangen?

Heute ist es aber kalt!

Grammatische Übersicht

Comparison of adjectives and adverbs (A-D)

Regular forms

Base form	leicht	easy	schön	beautiful
Comparative	leichter	easier	schöner	more beautiful

German forms the comparative of adjectives and adverbs by adding the suffix **-er** to the base form. Note that English can form the comparative either by adding **-er** to the base form or by using the modifier *more*.

Forms with umlaut

Base form	alt	groß	jung
Comparative	älter	größer	jünger

Many one-syllable adjectives and adverbs add umlaut in the comparative: **älter, dümmer, größer, jünger, kälter, kürzer, länger, wärmer.** From now on, adjectives and adverbs of this type will be listed in the vocabularies of this book as follows: **kalt (ä).**

Irregular forms

Base form	gern	gut	hoch	viel
Comparative	lieber	besser	höher	mehr

A few adjectives and adverbs are irregular in the comparative form.

so . . . wie

Bernd spielt nicht **so gut wie** Jens.   Bernd doesn't play *as well as* Jens.

The construction **so . . . wie** with the base form of the adjective or adverb is used to make comparisons of equality. It is equivalent to English *as . . . as*.

Comparative with als

Jens ist **größer als** Erik.   Jens is *taller than* Erik.
Petra tanzt **besser als** Gretl.   Petra dances *better than* Gretl.

The comparative form of the adjective or adverb with **als** is used to make comparisons of inequality. **Als** is equivalent to English *than*.

The verb werden (E-F)

Present tense

ich werde		wir werden
du **wirst**	Sie werden	ihr werdet
er/es/sie **wird**		sie werden

Werden is irregular in the **du-** and **er/sie-**forms of the present tense.

Ich **werde** müde.   I *am getting* tired.
Der Mann **wird** alt.   The man *is growing* old.
Wie alt **wirst** du?   How old *are* you *going to be*?
Was möchtest du **werden?**   What would you like *to be*?

English uses a number of different verbs to express the many ideas of **werden** in German.

Conversational past

Frank **ist** krank **geworden.**   Frank *became* ill.

Because the verb **werden** expresses a change of condition, it requires **sein** as an auxiliary in the conversational past.

Word order in dependent clauses (G-L)

INDEPENDENT CLAUSE	SUBORDINATING CONJUNCTION	DEPENDENT CLAUSE
Ute sagt,	daß	sie morgen Tennis spielt.
Sie möchte wissen,	ob	du auch spielen willst.

A dependent clause cannot stand alone as a complete sentence. It is introduced by a subordinating conjunction such as **daß** or **ob**. The conjunction is always preceded by a comma.

Verb in final position

1. In a dependent clause, the verb is in final position:
   Ingrid sagt, daß sie in die Stadt **fährt.**

2. A separable prefix is attached to the base form of the verb, which is in final position:
   Sie sagt, daß Astrid **mitfährt.**

3. A modal auxiliary follows the infinitive and is in final position:
   Sie sagt, daß sie in die Stadt **fahren müssen.**

4. In the conversational past, the auxiliary verb **haben** or **sein** follows the past participle and is in final position:
   Sie sagt, daß sie gestern nicht **gefahren sind.**

Indirect statements

Direct statement	Ingrid sagt: „Jan macht jetzt Mathe."
Indirect statement	Ingrid sagt, **daß** Jan jetzt Mathe **macht.**

Indirect statements are introduced by the subordinating conjunction **daß** *(that).*

Indirect specific questions

Direct question	Wann macht Jens Mathe?
Indirect question	Ich möchte wissen, **wann** Jens Mathe **macht**.

Indirect specific questions are introduced by the same interrogatives that are used to introduce direct specific questions.

Indirect general questions

Direct question	**Macht** Ingrid jetzt Mathe?
Indirect question	Ich weiß nicht, **ob** Ingrid jetzt Mathe **macht**.

Indirect general questions are introduced by the subordinating conjunction **ob** *(whether, if)*.

Wiederholung

A Make three sets of comparisons for each pair of sentences.

■ Ich bin 1,40 m groß. Mein Bruder ist 1,30.

Ich bin größer als mein Bruder.
Mein Bruder ist kleiner als ich.
Mein Bruder ist nicht so groß wie ich.

1. Ich bin sechzehn Jahre alt.
   Meine Schwester ist erst dreizehn.
2. Dieser Bleistift ist 17 cm lang.
   Dieser Kugelschreiber ist nur 13 cm lang.
3. Im August haben wir oft 30 Grad.
   Im Januar haben wir oft 0 Grad.
4. Gisela läuft einen Kilometer in drei Minuten.
   Jan läuft einen Kilometer in vier Minuten.

B Form sentences in the present tense, using the cues provided.

1. Trudi / helfen / viel / zu Hause
2. sie / raustragen / der Mülleimer
3. am Wochenende / sie / waschen / das Auto
4. sie / müssen / auch / machen / Gartenarbeit
5. sie / werden / einfach / nicht / müde
6. sie / tragen / gern / alte Jeans
7. ihr Vater / lesen / abends / gern
8. ihr Bruder / fernsehen / lieber

C Jörg and Sabine are discussing a typical weekend. Show that it was the same last weekend by restating their conversation in the conversational past.

1. Stehst du früh auf?
   Nein, ich schlafe bis neun.
2. Fährst du in die Stadt?
   Nein. Birgit und ich gehen windsurfen.
3. Macht das Spaß?
   Nein. Ich falle zu oft ins Wasser.
4. Wann kommt ihr nach Hause?
   Um fünf. Wir essen um sechs zu Abend.
5. Seht ihr fern?
   Nein. Wir gehen ins Kino.

D Complete each sentence with one of the following prepositions.

durch für gegen ohne um

1. Gerd geht ____ den Supermarkt.
2. Er kommt oft ____ seine Familie.
3. ____ seinen Bruder Otto kauft er 100 Gramm Schokolade.
4. Er kauft nichts ____ Trudi.
5. Hat er etwas ____ seine Schwester?
6. ____ drei Uhr kommt er wieder nach Hause.

E Choose the appropriate conjunction to connect each pair of sentences.

■ Willst du heute abend fern-sehen? (oder, aber) Willst du lieber ins Kino? *Willst du heute abend fernsehen, oder willst du lieber ins Kino?*

1. Ich kann ins Kino. (oder, denn)
   Ich habe meine Hausaufgaben schon gemacht.
2. Meine Hausaufgaben sind nicht fertig. (sondern, aber)
   Ich kann sie später machen.
3. Ich lade Paula ein. (und, sondern)
   Du kannst Heidi einladen.
4. Ich möchte nicht Heidi einladen. (aber, sondern)
   Ich möchte Ute einladen.
5. Ruf sie jetzt an! (denn, oder)
   Es wird zu spät.

F Give the individual words that make up the compounds, and supply the definite article for each noun. Then give the English equivalents of the compounds.

■ die Wintersonne   *der Winter, die Sonne (winter sun)*

1. der Sonnenschirm   3. die Windjacke   5. der Schneemann
2. der Wetterbericht   4. der Stadtplan   6. der Regenmantel

G Express the following conversation in German.

DIETER   Hi, Gisela. How are you?
GISELA   Hi, Dieter. Fine, thanks.
DIETER   Do you have anything planned for today?
GISELA   This morning I have to wash our car and clean out the garage. But this afternoon I'm free.
DIETER   Would you like to go swimming?
GISELA   Glad to. It's hot.
DIETER   I'll pick you up at two-thirty.
GISELA   Great. See you later.

Kulturlesestück

Geographie

Deutschland liegt im Zentrum Europas und hat neun Nachbarländer°: im Norden Dänemark; im Westen die Niederlande, Belgien, Luxemburg und Frankreich; im Süden die Schweiz und Österreich; und im Osten die Tschechoslowakei und Polen. Man spricht nicht nur in Deutschland Deutsch, sondern auch in Österreich und in einem Teil° der Schweiz. Seit° 1949 gibt es zwei deutsche Staaten — im Osten die Deutsche Demokratische Republik (DDR) und im Westen die Bundesrepublik Deutschland (BRD).

In Deutschland ist das Land im Norden flach°. In der Mitte gibt es die Mittelgebirge°. Im Süden liegen die Alpen, ein Hochgebirge°. Die großen Flüsse° — der Rhein, die Weser, die Elbe und die Oder — fließen° von Süden nach Norden in die Nordsee und in die Ostsee. Nur die Donau fließt von Westen nach Osten.

Im Norden sind die großen Hafenstädte°: Bremen an der Weser, Hamburg an der Elbe und Rostock an der Ostsee. In der Mitte gibt es im Westen viel Kohle°. Daher° ist an der Ruhr das deutsche Schwerindustriezentrum°. Nur ein kleiner Teil von Deutschland liegt in den Alpen. Aber Österreich und die Schweiz sind vor allem° Alpenländer. Hier findet man daher die international bekannten° Wintersportzentren wie Zermatt und St. Moritz oder Innsbruck und Kitzbühel.

Richtig oder falsch?

1. In Deutschland liegen die Berge im Norden.
2. Das Land im Süden ist flach.
3. Die Weser und die Elbe sind Flüsse.
4. Die Donau und die Oder fließen von Westen nach Osten.
5. Der Rhein fließt in die Nordsee.
6. Hamburg ist eine Hafenstadt.
7. Die Ruhr ist ein Alpenland.
8. Die deutsche Schwerindustrie liegt im Hochgebirge.
9. Kitzbühel liegt in den Alpen.

Vokabeln

SUBSTANTIVE

der Atlantische Ozean Atlantic Ocean
der Bericht, -e report
der Grad degree
die Hauptstadt, ¨-e capital city
die Jahreszeit, -en season, time of the year
der Norden north
der Osten east
der Regen rain
der Regenschirm, -e umbrella
der Schnee snow
die Sonne sun
der Süden south
die Temperatur, -en temperature
das Thermometer, - thermometer
der Westen west
das Wetter weather
der Wind wind

VERBEN

denken (gedacht) to think
frieren (gefroren) to freeze, to be very cold
liegen (gelegen) to lie, to be (situated)
mit·nehmen (i; mitgenommen) to take along
regnen to rain
rodeln (ist gerodelt) to toboggan
scheinen (geschienen) to shine
schneien to snow
sprechen (i; gesprochen) to speak
werden (wird; ist geworden) to become

ANDERE WÖRTER

amerikanisch American
anders different
besonders particularly, especially
bewölkt cloudy, overcast
da then
endlich finally
glatt slippery
heiß hot
kalt (ä) cold
kühl cool
naß wet
nördlich northern, north of
südlich southern, south of
trocken dry
über about, above, over
wahrscheinlich probably
weiter further
wenn if, when
windig windy

BESONDERE AUSDRÜCKE

du hast recht you're right
du spinnst you're crazy
lieber haben to like better, to prefer
noch [schöner] even more [beautiful]

Kapitel 14

Christa macht den Führerschein

Aus Briefen an Jochen

Christa wird bald achtzehn und darf dann den Führerschein machen. Sie schreibt oft an ihren Freund Jochen und erzählt von ihren Fortschritten.° progress

Mittwoch, den 16.° Januar   **sechzehnten:** sixteenth

... Du weißt, ich werde am Samstag 18. Dann kann ich endlich meinen Führerschein machen. Heute haben meine Eltern mich gefragt, was ich zum Geburtstag haben möchte. Vielleicht bezahlen sie ja das Geld oder wenigstens etwas Geld für die Fahrschule. ...

Samstag, den 19. Januar

... Ich bin sehr glücklich. Ich habe von meinen Eltern das Geld für die Fahrschule bekommen. Vielleicht kann ich nächste Woche den Sehtest° machen und mit dem Erste-Hilfe-Kurs° beginnen. ...   eye test / first aid course

Dienstag, den 5. Februar

... Mit dem Erste-Hilfe-Kurs bin ich fertig. Mit dem Sehtest auch. Ich bin zur Fahrschule gegangen. Am Montag beginnt der theoretische° Unterricht; meine erste Fahrstunde ist am Dienstag. ...   theoretical

Montag, den 18. Februar

... Der theoretische Unterricht ist furchtbar langweilig. Niemand macht ihn gern, aber er muß ja wohl sein. Die theoretische Prüfung soll sehr kompliziert sein. Hast Du auch gehört, daß 40%° durchfallen? ...   **Prozent:** per cent

Freitag, den 7. März

... Der Fahrlehrer ist sehr nett. (Brauchst aber nicht eifersüchtig zu werden!) Es ist nur gut, daß er auch eine Bremse hat. Ich habe zu meinen Freunden schon gesagt, sie sollen abends zwischen 6 und 7 zu Hause bleiben. Da mache ich die Straßen unsicher ...

Mittwoch, den 23. April

... Morgen ist die praktische Prüfung. Halt mir die Daumen, daß ich sie bestehe ...

Donnerstag, den 24. April

... Heute habe ich die Fahrprüfung bestanden. Endlich! Die Prüfungsfahrt° ist gut gegangen. Ich habe aber auch etwas Schwein gehabt. Nicht viele Autos auf den Straßen ...   road test

Dienstag, den 6. Mai

... Heute habe ich einen gebrauchten° VW gekauft. Was sagst Du nun?   used
Jetzt kann ich endlich an den See fahren, wenn *ich* es will. Jetzt bin ich
am Wochenende endlich unabhängig. ...

Mittwoch, den 7. Mai

... große Diskussion mit meinen Eltern: Soll ich mit dem Auto zur° Ar-   to
beit fahren? Es ist natürlich toll, mit dem Auto in die Stadt zu fahren.
Aber Zug und Straßenbahn sind billiger. Dann können wir am Wochenende mehr fahren. Ich fahre also jeden Tag mit dem Zug. Und dann mit
der Straßenbahn. Leider! ...

Richtig oder falsch?

1. In Deutschland macht man gewöhnlich erst mit achtzehn den Führerschein.
2. Christa möchte nichts zum Geburtstag.
3. Christa beginnt ihren Fahrkurs mit dem praktischen Unterricht.
4. Christa kann gut sehen.
5. Der theoretische Unterricht ist interessant.
6. Die theoretische Prüfung soll nicht schwer sein.
7. Christa fällt in der theoretischen Prüfung durch.
8. Christa bleibt abends zwischen sechs und sieben zu Hause.
9. Christa hält die Bremse mit den Daumen.
10. Das Auto macht Christa am Wochenende unabhängiger.
11. Christa will nicht mit dem Auto zur Arbeit fahren.
12. Christa fährt mit dem Zug und mit der Straßenbahn, denn es ist billiger.

Du hast das Wort

Ask a classmate about driver's education.

Wieviel kostet die Fahrschule hier?
Hast du schon einen Fahrkurs gemacht?
Hast du schon die Fahrprüfung gemacht? Hast du sie bestanden? Wieviele sind durchgefallen?
Wieviele Bremsen hat dein Auto?

Für die theoretische Prüfung muß man die Verkehrszeichen lernen.

Baustelle | Verbot für Fahrzeuge über eine bestimmte Breite | Radfahrer kreuzen | Gegenverkehr | Gefälle

The **BRD** has an extensive highway system. Superhighways **(Autobahnen)** link major cities, and numerous other roads crisscross the country. With few exceptions, there is no speed limit **(Geschwindigkeitsbegrenzung)** on the **Autobahn,** and some people tend to drive at very high speeds when traffic and weather conditions permit.

The large number of vehicles in circulation (about one car for every two people) results in numerous traffic jams **(Staus),** especially on weekends and holidays. The traffic jams on the **Autobahn** are particularly bad at the beginning and end of school vacations, despite the fact that each German state has different vacation dates in an attempt to stagger arrivals and departures.

Dein Auto, dein Traum-Auto

Manche Teenager kaufen oder bekommen ein Auto, wenn sie den Führerschein machen. Wie ist es bei dir°? Hast du ein Auto? Oder hast du vielleicht nur ein Traum-Auto? Beschreibe es!

bei dir: in your case

1. Was für ein Auto hast du? Was für ein Auto möchtest du haben?
2. Hast du das Auto gebraucht oder neu gekauft?
3. Ist das Auto groß oder klein?
4. Braucht das Auto viel Benzin? 1 Liter auf 10 Kilometer? 1° Gallone auf 20 Meilen°?

eine
20 miles to the gallon

5. Läuft es gut?
6. Reparierst du gern alte Autos? Ist das dein Hobby?
7. Fährst du gern schnell oder lieber langsam?
8. Wie schnell fährst du auf der Landstraße°? Auf der Autobahn? In der Stadt? 90 Kilometer pro Stunde? 55 Meilen pro Stunde?

highway

Du hast das Wort   Interview your classmates about their cars (real or imagined). Take brief notes, then share the information with the class.

Ist dein Auto alt oder neu?
Welche Farbe hat dein Auto?
Ist dein Auto amerikanisch?

Kapitel 14

Wortschatzerweiterung

Wie fährt man?

das Fahrrad (das Rad)

das Mofa

das Motorrad

der Bus

die Straßenbahn

die U-Bahn

der Zug

das Flugzeug

das Schiff

A Ask a classmate the following questions about transportation.

1. Hast du ein Fahrrad? Ist es neu? Alt?
2. Fährst du gern mit dem Rad?
3. Möchtest du eine lange Radtour machen? Wohin?
4. Hast du letzten Sommer eine Radtour gemacht? Wohin?
5. Hast du ein Motorrad? Ein Mofa? Ist es neu? Alt?
6. Fährst du gern mit dem Motorrad? Mit dem Mofa?
7. Bastelst du gern am Fahrrad oder am Motorrad?
8. Hat deine Stadt eine Straßenbahn?

B Ask your teacher some questions about transportation.

1. Wie fahren Sie zur Schule? Mit dem Bus? Mit dem Rad? Mit dem Mofa? Mit dem Auto?
2. Wie kann man von Österreich in die Schweiz kommen? Von Deutschland in die Schweiz?
3. Fliegen Sie gern? Wie oft sind Sie schon geflogen? Wohin?
4. Wie möchten Sie nach Europa fahren? Mit dem Schiff oder mit dem Flugzeug? Warum?

Kilometer und Meile

1 (ein) Kilometer = 0,62 Meilen
1 (eine) Meile = 1,6 Kilometer

C You are driving in Germany but have an American car showing only miles. How fast can you drive in miles per hour when you see these German signs?

▪ 50 km   *31 Meilen pro Stunde*

1. 80 km   2. 100 km   3. 20 km   4. 120 km

Although some young people in Germany have cars, most teen-agers take public transportation, use mopeds or bicycles, or walk to school and work. The minimum age for a driver's license is eighteen (though exceptions are sometimes made for sixteen-year-olds who need a car to make a living). Very few schools have driver-education courses. Taking a course in a private driving school (**Fahrschule**) and passing a test are required in order to get a license. The course in a **Fahrschule** is rather expensive, and insurance costs a great deal, two more factors that reduce the number of teen-agers who drive. But once one gets a license, it is valid for life.

Aussprache

[ç] Mi**ch**, schle**ch**t, Bü**ch**er

The sound [ç] is similar to that used by many Americans for the *h* in such words as *hue, huge, Hugh*. The sound [ç] is represented by the letters **ch** when they occur after the vowel sounds written as **e, i, ie, ü, äu, eu,** and **ö,** and after consonants.

A Practice the following words.

mi**ch**	re**ch**t	eu**ch**	man**ch**	Bü**ch**er
endli**ch**	mö**ch**te	Bräu**ch**e	dur**ch**	Tü**ch**er

B Practice the following words horizontally in pairs, to contrast [ʃ] (as in *Fisch* and *waschen*) with [ç].

[ʃ]	[ç]	[ʃ]	[ç]
Kir**sch**e	Kir**ch**e	Men**sch**	Mön**ch**
fi**sch**te	Fi**ch**te	Bü**sch**e	Bü**ch**er
fri**sch**	fre**ch**	mi**sch**	mi**ch**

C Practice the following words horizontally in pairs.

[x]	[ç]	[x]	[ç]
do**ch**	di**ch**	Bu**ch**	Bü**ch**er
Da**ch**	Dä**ch**er	Brau**ch**	Bräu**ch**e
To**ch**ter	Tö**ch**ter	Lo**ch**	Lö**ch**er

D Practice the sound [ç]. Read the sentences aloud.

1. Hoffentlich hast du nichts gegen Bücher!
2. Er spricht gut Deutsch.
3. Ich möchte ein Glas Milch, aber frisch, bitte.

Gleich und gleich gesellt sich gern.

Was ist mit dem Auto los?

Übungen

Dative case of definite articles and nouns

Singular

NOMINATIVE
Der Fernseher ist kaputt.
Das Radio spielt nicht.
Die Platte ist schlecht.

DATIVE
Was hast du mit **dem Fernseher** gemacht?
Was hast du mit **dem Radio** gemacht?
Was hast du mit **der Platte** gemacht?

The dative case is used with certain prepositions, one of which is **mit**. The definite article changes form in the dative case.

A Jörg cites the reasons for avoiding various means of transportation. Reply that you're not traveling by those means anyway.

▪ Der Bus ist zu langsam.   *Ich fahre doch nicht mit dem Bus.*

1. Die Straßenbahn fährt nach zwölf nicht mehr.
2. Die U-Bahn fährt um diese Zeit nicht.
3. Das Auto läuft nicht.
4. Das Motorrad ist kaputt.
5. Und das Fahrrad ist leider auch kaputt.

Kapitel 14   **303**

Plural

NOMINATIVE
Die **Fernseher** sind kaputt.
Die **Radios** spielen nicht.
Die **Platten** sind schlecht.

DATIVE
Was hast du mit **den Fernsehern** gemacht?
Was hast du mit **den Radios** gemacht?
Was hast du mit **den Platten** gemacht?

The dative plural form of the definite article is **den.** In the dative plural, an **-n** is added to the plural form of the noun, unless the plural already ends in **-n** or in **-s.**

B Christl says she no longer collects the following things. Ask her what she did with them.

■ Ich sammle keine Briefmarken mehr. *Was hast du denn mit den Briefmarken gemacht?*

1. Ich sammle keine Ansichtskarten mehr.
2. Ich sammle keine Poster mehr.
3. Ich sammle keine Bierdeckel mehr.
4. Ich sammle keine Schallplatten mehr.
5. Ich sammle keine Flugzeugmodelle mehr.

Dative case of **dieser**-words

Von **welchem** Fernseher sprichst du?	Von **diesem.**
Von **welchem** Radio sprichst du?	Von **diesem.**
Von **welcher** Stereoanlage sprichst du?	Von **dieser.**
Von **welchen** Platten sprichst du?	Von **diesen.**

Dieser-words (**dieser, jeder, solcher, mancher, welcher**) follow the same pattern of endings in the dative case as the definite articles. The dative case is used with the preposition **von.**

C At a party Ingrid offers you various refreshments. Thank her and tell her which ones you'd like.

■ Möchtest du etwas Käse? *Ja, bitte. Ich nehme ein Stück von diesem hier.*

1. Möchtest du etwas Wurst?
2. Willst du etwas Brot?
3. Möchtest du etwas Kuchen?
4. Willst du etwas Torte?

D Hans-Jürgen is commenting on some clothes in the men's department, but you're not paying attention. Ask him which items he means.

▪‖ Dieser Anzug ist aber teuer.   *Von welchem Anzug sprichst du?*

1. Diese Jacke ist ja toll.
2. Dieser Pulli ist wirklich klasse.
3. Diese Schuhe sind aber billig.
4. Diese Krawatte ist aber häßlich.
5. Dieser Mantel ist zu dick.
6. Diese Handschuhe sind wirklich warm.

Dative case of indefinite articles and **ein**-words

> Erika hat das von **einem** Mann im Geschäft gehört.
> Dieter hat das von **einem** Mädchen im Café gehört.
> Uwe hat das von **einer** Frau im Supermarkt gehört.
>
> Gabi hat das von **ihren** Freunden gehört.

Indefinite articles and **ein**-words (**mein, dein, sein,** and so on) follow the same pattern of endings in the dative as **dieser-**words.

E Gisela wants to find out what various people think about the new horror movie. Say that you haven't spoken to them yet.

▪‖ Was denkt dein Bruder?   *Mein Bruder? Mit meinem Bruder habe ich noch nicht gesprochen.*

1. Was denkt deine Schwester?
2. Was denkt dein Vater?
3. Was denkt deine Mutter?
4. Was denken deine Freunde?

F Silke claims people are saying the weather will change drastically tomorrow. Express surprise that they're all talking about it.

▪‖ Unser Metzger hat es gesagt.   *Wirklich? Von eurem Metzger habt ihr es gehört?*

1. Unser Bäcker hat es auch gesagt.
2. Unser Elektriker hat es auch gesagt.
3. Und unsere Friseuse hat es gesagt.
4. Unser Lehrer hat es gesagt.
5. Und unsere Ärztin hat es gesagt.

Du hast das Wort Make a series of statements to a classmate. Your classmate will tell you whether the statements make sense and correct them if they don't.

- Man schreibt mit einem Buch, nicht? *Unsinn! Man schreibt mit einem Bleistift.*
- Man spült Geschirr mit Wasser, nicht? *Ja, das stimmt.*

Man fährt mit dem Rad von hier nach Österreich, nicht?
Man bäckt eine Torte mit Eiern, nicht?
Man spricht mit dem Deutschlehrer Deutsch, nicht?
Du fährst mit der Straßenbahn zur Schule, nicht?

Dative case of special **der**-nouns

Nominative	Wie heißt der Herr da?
Accusative	Kennst du **den Herrn** da?
Dative	Willst du mit **dem Herrn** arbeiten?

Special **der**-nouns that add an **-n** or **-en** in the accusative also add **-n** or **-en** in the dative singular. The special **der**-nouns you know are **Herr, Junge, Kunde.**

G Clarify with whom you did various things, using the cues in parentheses.

- Hast du mit dem Mädchen da gearbeitet? (Junge) *Nein, mit dem Jungen da.*

1. Bist du mit der Frau da gefahren? (Herr)
2. Hast du mit dem Verkäufer da gesprochen? (Kunde)
3. Hast du mit dem Jungen da Tennis gespielt? (Herr)
4. Hast du mit dem Mädchen da gegessen? (Junge)

H Say that Gabi spoke with the persons mentioned.

- die Frau da *Gabi hat mit der Frau da gesprochen.*

1. der Herr da
2. der Junge da
3. der Friseur da
4. der Kunde da
5. die Männer da
6. die Verkäuferin da
7. die Frauen da
8. das Mädchen da

Mit dem Mofa geht's besser.

Dative case of **wer**

Nominative	**Wer** ist das?	*Who* is that?
Dative	Mit **wem** spricht Gabi?	With *whom* is Gabi speaking?

The dative form of the interrogative pronoun **wer** is **wem**.

I Ask Christl to say again with whom various friends are doing things this weekend.

▪ Erik geht mit seinem Bruder ins Kino.   *Mit wem geht er ins Kino?*

1. Andrea spielt mit ihrer Schwester Tennis.
2. Eva geht mit einer Freundin schwimmen.
3. Volker geht mit seiner Freundin einkaufen.
4. Dirk fährt mit seinen Freunden an den See.
5. Karin kommt mit Paul zur Party.
6. Ingrid fährt mit Dieter in die Stadt.

Du hast das Wort

State with whom you did various things during the last few weeks. If necessary, invent an answer.

▪ Mit wem bist du einkaufen gegangen?   *Mit meinem Vater. / Mit einer Freundin.*

Mit wem bist du ins Kino gegangen?
Mit wem bist du zum Basketballspiel gegangen?
Mit wem bist du tanzen gegangen?
Mit wem hast du Musik gehört?
Mit wem hast du ferngesehen?
Mit wem bist du auf die Party gegangen?
Mit wem bist du schwimmen gegangen?

Wie fährt man? Young people often decorate their cars with colorful stickers. Others like to build their own contraptions. Bottom left: A driving school in Munich. Bottom right: River traffic on the Rhine near Niederlahnstein.

Grammatische Übersicht

Dative case of articles and nouns (A-F)

	SINGULAR			PLURAL
Nominative	der	das	die	die
Accusative	den	das	die	die
Dative	**dem**	**dem**	**der**	**den**
	dies**em**	dies**em**	dies**er**	dies**en**
	ein**em**	ein**em**	ein**er**	—
	sein**em**	sein**em**	sein**er**	sein**en**

In addition to nominative and accusative, German has a third case called dative. It is used with certain prepositions, two of which are **mit** and **von.**

The definite article has three forms in the dative case: **dem, der,** and **den. Dieser-**words **(dieser, jeder, welcher, solcher, mancher),** the indefinite article, and **ein-**words **(kein, mein, dein, sein,** and so on) follow the same pattern of endings in the dative case as the definite article.

NOMINATIVE	DATIVE
Der Fernseher ist kaputt.	Was hast du mit **dem Fernseher** gemacht?
Das Radio spielt nicht.	Was hast du mit **dem Radio** gemacht?
Die Platte ist schlecht.	Was hast du mit **der Platte** gemacht?
Die Fernseher sind kaputt.	Was hast du mit **den Fernsehern** gemacht?
Die Radios spielen nicht.	Was hast du mit **den Radios** gemacht?
Die Platten sind schlecht.	Was hast du mit **den Platten** gemacht?

In the singular, the dative form of a noun is identical with the nominative and accusative forms.

In the plural, the dative form of a noun adds an **-n** unless the plural form of the noun already ends in **-n** or in **-s.**

The letters before the dash on a German license plate tell you where the car is registered. Single letters stand for large cities **(N** is **Nürnberg);** three letters identify the smallest townships.

Dative case of special **der**-nouns (G-H)

Nominative	der Herr	der Junge	der Kunde
Accusative	den Her**rn**	den Jung**en**	den Kund**en**
Dative	dem Her**rn**	dem Jung**en**	dem Kund**en**

Special **der**-nouns that add **-n** or **-en** in the accusative also add **-n** or **-en** in the dative singular.

Dative case of **wer** (I)

Nominative	**Wer** ist das?	*Who* is that?
Dative	Mit **wem** gehst du?	With *whom* are you going?

The dative form of the interrogative pronoun **wer** is **wem**.

Wiederholung

A Lore was quite surprised when she saw Dieter yesterday. Read the following dialogue and then relay the content of the dialogue to a friend from Lore's point of view.

LORE: Mensch, Dieter, habe ich richtig gesehen?
DIETER: Wie soll ich das wissen? Was hast du denn gesehen?
LORE: Du bist ja mit dem Rad gefahren.
DIETER: Na und?
LORE: Tu nicht so dumm! Du weißt schon, was ich meine. Wo ist denn dein Mofa?
DIETER: Kaputt.
LORE: Aha! Und jetzt bist du sauer.
DIETER: Ja, natürlich, und wie! Komm, ich fahr dich zu Großinger. Ich lade dich zu einer Cola ein.
LORE: Schön. Aber nicht mit dem Fahrrad. Ich nehme dich auf *(on)* meinem Mofa mit.

You may want to begin your narrative as follows:

Gestern habe ich Dieter gesehen. Er ist . . .

B Indicate with whom Mr. Wolf is speaking. Base your choice on the content of Mr. Wolf's statements.

Ärztin   Bäcker   Fahrlehrer   Elektriker
Metzger   Verkäuferin

■ „Haben Sie noch Brot von gestern?"   *Er spricht mit dem Bäcker.*

1. „Das Licht im Badezimmer ist kaputt. Können Sie es heute noch reparieren?"
2. „Ich möchte ein Kleid in Blau für meine Frau. Ich glaube, sie trägt Größe 40."
3. „Das habe ich wieder falsch gemacht, nicht? Autofahren ist nicht leicht zu lernen."
4. „Ich bin den ganzen Tag müde und habe keinen Appetit."
5. „Ich hätte gern ein Pfund von dem Schinken da."

C Form sentences about clothes shopping, using the cues provided.
1. ich / möchten / kaufen / jedes Hemd hier
2. warum / manche Kleider / sein / so teuer / ?
3. was / ich / sollen / machen / mit / dieser Mantel / ?
4. welcher / Rock / ich / sollen / nehmen / ?
5. du / können / bezahlen / dieser Anzug / ?
6. du / finden / solche / Schuhe / schön / ?

D Change each English word to its German equivalent by changing one or two letters.

■ milk   *Milch*

1. word
2. friend
3. water
4. thick
5. for
6. long
7. green
8. new
9. half
10. was

E Complete each of the following sentences with the appropriate form of the words in parentheses.
1. Christa und Jochen sind durch ____ gefahren. (die Stadt)
2. Du hast doch hoffentlich ____ nicht wieder verloren. (dein Führerschein)
3. Frank muß für ____ lernen. (die Fahrprüfung)
4. Er ist durchgefallen, aber er hat nichts gegen ____. (sein Fahrlehrer)
5. Mußt du für ____ viel lernen? (der Fahrkurs)
6. Petra kann nicht ohne ____ fahren, denn sie hat noch keinen Führerschein. (ihr Fahrlehrer)

F Complete the following dialogue by using words from the list below.

Karten   Kino   Lust   sicher   teuer   Vorstellung

FRANK   Hast du ____, heute abend ins Konzert zu gehen?
PAUL   Wann beginnt die ____?
FRANK   Ich bin nicht ____. Ich glaube, um halb acht.
PAUL   Was kosten die ____?
FRANK   25 Mark.
PAUL   Mensch, das ist viel zu ____. Ich gehe ins ____.

G Prepare a paragraph of from eight to ten sentences about the illustration below. You may wish to include answers to some of these questions.

1. Wie ist das Wetter heute? Scheint die Sonne? Regnet es?
2. Welche Jahreszeit ist es?
3. Wieviel Personen sind hier?
4. Wer sind sie?
5. Was tragen sie? Warum?
6. Wohin wollen sie fahren?
7. Was haben sie vor? Gehen sie Schi laufen? Zelten sie? Besuchen sie Freunde?
8. Wie lange bleiben sie?
9. Wann kommen sie zurück?

Kapitel 14   **313**

Kulturlesestück

Die Bahn

In den deutschsprachigen° Ländern gibt es viele Autos. Aber viele Leute° fahren auch noch mit der Bahn°. Die Züge sind modern, schnell und fast immer pünktlich°. Man kann alle Städte und fast alle Städtchen° mit dem Zug erreichen°. Und es gibt jeden Tag genug° Züge, so daß man nicht viele Stunden warten° muß.

Viele Leute fahren mit dem Zug zur Arbeit. Sie nehmen den Nahschnellverkehrszug°. Zwischen den großen Städten gibt es die Inter-City-Züge. Von Land zu Land fahren die TEE-Züge°. In diesen Zügen ist der Service besonders gut. Man kann gut essen, man kann telefonieren, man kann Briefe diktieren°. Natürlich sind diese Züge teuer. Billiger sind die D-Züge (Schnellzüge)° für weitere Reisen° und die Eilzüge° für kürzere Reisen. Aber auch für diese Züge sind die Karten nicht gerade billig. Trotzdem° produziert die Bahn jedes Jahr ein Defizit. Der Staat° deckt° dieses Defizit und bezahlt jedes Jahr viele Millionen, denn alle Bahnen sind staatlich°.

German-speaking / people
railroad
punctual / small towns
reach / enough
wait

local train
TEE = Trans-Europ-Express
dictate
express trains / trips / semi-fast trains
nevertheless / state / covers
owned by the state

Richtig oder falsch?

1. In den deutschsprachigen Ländern fahren viele Leute mit der Bahn, denn es gibt wenige Autos.
2. Die Züge sind fast immer pünktlich.
3. Mit dem Zug kann man alle Großstädte erreichen.
4. Leider muß man oft lange warten, denn es gibt nicht genug Züge.
5. Zur Arbeit nehmen alle Leute einen Inter-City-Zug.
6. Von der Schweiz nach Dänemark kann man mit einem TEE-Zug fahren.
7. Für lange Reisen fährt man mit dem Eilzug.
8. Es ist nicht teuer, mit dem Zug zu fahren, denn der Staat bezahlt jedes Jahr Millionen.
9. Die Bahn verliert jedes Jahr viel Geld.
10. Die Bahn in den deutschsprachigen Ländern ist privat.

The cars on most German trains consist of a long corridor on one side with doors leading into a series of compartments **(Abteile).** Each compartment has luggage racks and seats for six passengers. Most trains have two classes — first and second. Generally the first- and second-class compartments are similar, being equally comfortable. The chief advantage to traveling first class is that the compartments are often less crowded than the cheaper second-class sections.

Vokabeln

SUBSTANTIVE

die Autobahn, -en expressway
das Benzin gasoline
die Bremse, -n brake
der Bus, -se bus
die Diskussion, -en discussion, debate
das Fahrrad, ¨er bicycle
der Fahrlehrer, - driving instructor
die Fahrschule, -n driving school
die Fahrstunde, -n driving lesson
das Flugzeug, -e airplane
der Führerschein, -e driver's license
der Kurs, -e course
das Mofa, -s moped, motorbike
das Motorrad, ¨er motorcycle
die Prüfung, -en exam, test
das Rad, ¨er bicycle (*short for* **das Fahrrad**); wheel
das Schiff, -e ship
der See, -n lake
die Straßenbahn, -en streetcar
die Tour, -en tour, trip
der Traum, ¨e dream
die U-Bahn, -en subway
der Unterricht lesson, instruction
der VW (Volkswagen)
der Zug, ¨e train

VERBEN

beschreiben (beschrieben) to describe
bestehen (bestanden): die Prüfung bestehen to pass a test
durch·fallen (ä; ist durchgefallen) to fail, to flunk
erzählen to tell
fliegen (ist geflogen) to fly

ANDERE WÖRTER

auf (+ *acc. or dat.*) on
eifersüchtig jealous
langsam slowly
mit (+ *dat.*) with; by (*of vehicles*)
niemand no one
praktisch practical
pro per
schnell fast
unabhängig independent
unsicher dangerous; unsure, insecure
was für ein what kind of
zwischen (+ *acc. or dative*) between

BESONDERE AUSDRÜCKE

halt mir die Daumen cross your fingers for me (*literally:* hold your thumbs for me)
Schwein haben to be lucky
1 Liter auf 10 Kilometer 10 kilometers to the liter
an den See to the lake

Kapitel 15

Ein Stadtbesuch

Wohin gehen wir denn nun?

Kai, Lore und Dieter gehen in Frankfurt zur Schule. Fast jedes Jahr macht ihre Klasse eine Klassenfahrt. Dieses Jahr sind sie nach Bayern gefahren, nach München. Am Tag besuchen sie Museen und Kirchen; oder sie bummeln durch die Fußgängerzone, vom Rathaus zum Karlsplatz und zurück. Aber abends wollen sie keine Museen und Kirchen sehen; abends wollen sie tanzen gehen.

Jetzt stehen Kai und Lore vor ihrem Hotel.

KAI   Wollen wir hier noch lange stehen? Wohin gehen wir denn nun?
LORE   Dieter sagt, daß die Musik im *Western Club* ganz toll ist. Aber wo ist denn der *Western Club*?
KAI   Da kommt der Dieter. Frag ihn doch! Er weiß ja immer alles.
LORE   Dieter, sag mal, wo ist der *Western Club*?
DIETER   In Schwabing.
KAI   Mensch, das ist aber weit! Wie kommen wir denn nach Schwabing?
DIETER   Ihr könnt mit der U-Bahn fahren, mit der Drei oder der Sechs. Ihr könnt aber auch laufen.
KAI   Zu Fuß nach Schwabing?
DIETER   Ja, es ist nur eine halbe Stunde von hier.
LORE   Willst du nicht mitkommen?
DIETER   Ach nein.
LORE   Warum denn nicht?
DIETER   Weil ich zu müde bin.
KAI   Das kannst du doch sehen, Mensch. Er schläft ja schon fast.
LORE   Na gut, dann gehen wir also allein. Gute Nacht, Dieter, schlaf gut!

Fragen

1. Wo wohnen Kai und Lore?
2. Wie oft macht ihre Klasse eine Klassenfahrt?
3. Wo sind die Schüler dieses Jahr?
4. Was besuchen die Schüler am Tag? Wo bummeln sie?
5. Was machen sie am Abend?
6. Wo ist die Musik ganz toll?
7. Mit welcher U-Bahn können Lore und Kai fahren?
8. Warum geht Dieter nicht tanzen?

Du hast das Wort

Ask a classmate how he/she came to school today.

Wie bist du heute zur Schule gekommen?

Zu Fuß.
Mit dem Rad / Bus / Auto.
Mit der Straßenbahn / U-Bahn.
[Mein Vater] hat mich gefahren.

Du hast das Wort   Ask a classmate to locate various landmarks on the map of Munich.

1. Wieviele Museen kannst du auf dem Stadtplan finden? Wie heißen sie? Wo sind sie?
2. Wieviele Kirchen kannst du finden? Wieviele Theater? Tore°? Märkte?

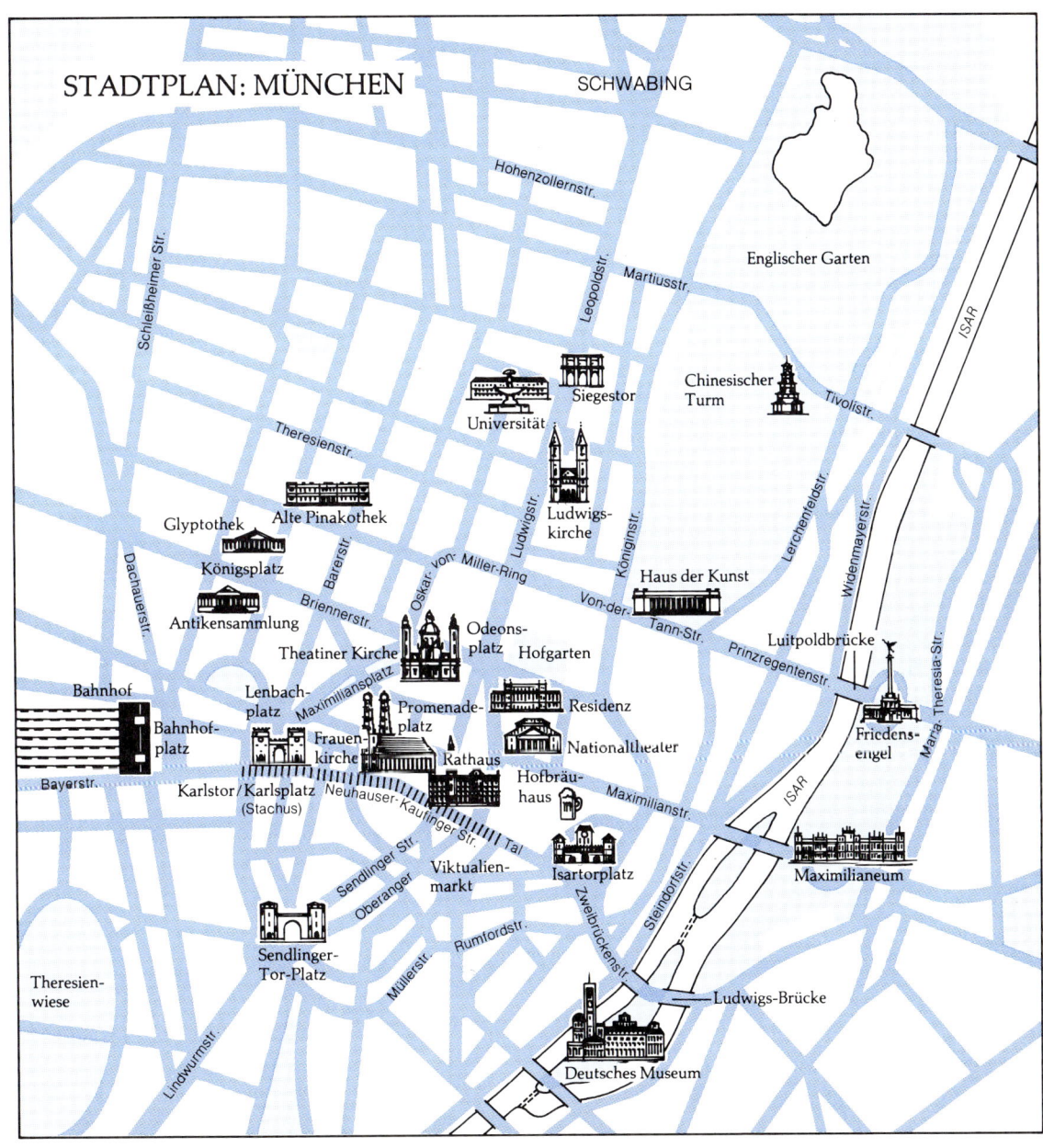

Wie kommen wir zum Western Club?

Jetzt sind Kai und Lore in Schwabing, aber sie können den Western Club nicht finden.

KAI Ich bin froh, daß wir mit der Bahn gefahren sind.
LORE Ja, aber wo ist denn nun der *Western Club*?
KAI Schau doch mal in den Stadtplan!
LORE Ich habe ihn nicht. Hast du ihn denn vergessen?
KAI So scheint's. Dann müssen wir wohl jemanden fragen. Entschuldigung! Können Sie uns sagen, wie wir zum *Western Club* kommen?
STUDENT Ja, das kann ich. Ihr geht geradeaus bis zur Ampel. Bei der Ampel geht ihr rechts. Dann wieder geradeaus, bis ihr zu einem Platz mit einem Brunnen kommt. Da geht ihr links. Dann seht ihr das Schild mit dem großen Stiefel schon.
KAI Vielen Dank!
STUDENT Bitte schön. Oh, Moment mal. Da fällt mir gerade ein – der *Western Club* hat heute zu.
LORE Nein, so ein Pech! Was machen wir denn nun?
STUDENT Geht doch zu *Alfons*. Bei *Alfons* ist auch viel los. Das ist auch ein Studentenlokal.

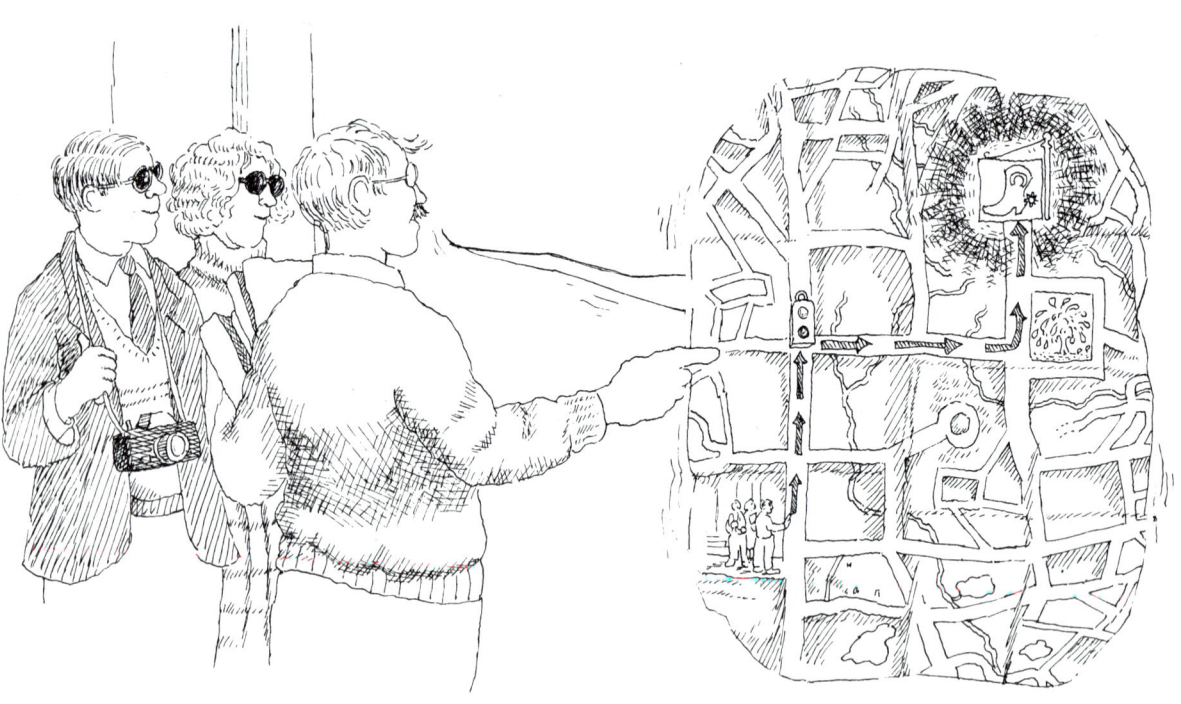

Fragen

1. Wie sind Kai und Lore nach Schwabing gekommen?
2. Wer hat den Stadtplan?
3. Wen fragen sie, wo der *Western Club* ist?
4. Was für ein Schild hat der *Western Club*?
5. Warum können Lore und Kai nicht in den *Western Club*?
6. Was für ein Lokal ist *Alfons*?

Du hast das Wort

Take the role of a native of Munich. Have a classmate take the role of a stranger who asks for directions.

Entschuldigung, wie komme ich vom Bahnhof° [zum Karlsplatz]?
Entschuldigung, ich suche° [die Marienkirche].

Gehen Sie immer geradeaus!
Gehen Sie diese Straße entlang°, bis Sie zu [einer Kirche / einem Tor] kommen!
Gehen Sie die nächste Straße [rechts]!
An der Kreuzung° biegen° Sie [links] ab!
Gehen Sie um die Ecke°!

Schwabing started as a village populated by Swabians, who came from Baden-Württemberg. They continued to speak their Swabian dialect for a while and the village remained outside the Munich city limits. Today Schwabing is a district of Munich which is often compared with the Latin Quarter in Paris. Its close proximity to the university and the Academy of Fine Arts attracts many people with artistic and intellectual interests.

Schwabing is an exciting place to live in and visit. The streets come alive in the early afternoon, and during the **Kaffeestunde** the many sidewalk cafés are filled with people. Sidewalk artists attract onlookers and young people peddle paintings, jewelry, and other handmade items.

By evening, it is often hard to make one's way through the crowded streets as local inhabitants and tourists head for the more than 300 restaurants, pubs, or wine taverns. Like Lore and Kai, young people also come to Schwabing to hear jazz or rock or to dance in the discos.

Wortschatzerweiterung

Was findet man in einer Stadt?

1. die Bank
2. die Kirche
3. das Museum
4. der Park
5. die Post
6. das Rathaus
7. die Schule
8. der Supermarkt
9. die Tankstelle
10. das Warenhaus

A You are expecting some exchange students from Austria. In order to give them some advance information, describe briefly your home town. You may wish to prepare a map to make your description clearer. Be sure to mention the size, what state it's in, the chief public buildings, and transportation.

Points of the compass

der Norden	nördlich	Norddeutschland
der Osten	östlich	Ostdeutschland
der Süden	südlich	Süddeutschland
der Westen	westlich	Westdeutschland

The four points of the compass are **der**-nouns. Adjectives related to the four points of the compass end in **-lich**. The names of the points of the compass can form noun compounds.

B Complete the statements by choosing one of the alternatives. You may wish to refer to the atlas section at the beginning of your book.

> ■ München liegt in ____. *München liegt in*
>   a. Norddeutschland *Süddeutschland.*
>   b. Süddeutschland

1. Italien liegt in ____. a. Südeuropa b. Nordeuropa.
2. Kanada liegt in ____. a. Nordamerika b. Südamerika
3. China liegt im ____. a. Westen b. Osten
4. Hamburg liegt in ____. a. Norddeutschland b. Süddeutschland
5. Schweden liegt in ____. a. Nordeuropa b. Südeuropa

Word families

die **Arbeit**	the work
arbeiten	to work
die **Arbeit**erin	the worker

Like English, German has many words that belong to "families" which are derived from a common stem.

C Give the English equivalents of the following words.

1. die Klasse, die Klassenfahrt, der Klassenlehrer, die Klassenarbeit
2. einkaufen, kaufen, der Käufer, die Verkäuferin, verkaufen, das Kaufhaus, der Einkäufer, der Kauf, der Verkauf

Kapitel 15

Some of the sights in Munich: **Nymphenburg Palace** was built in the 17th century for the Bavarian rulers. The **Karlstor** stands at one end of the pedestrian **Neuhauser-Kaufinger Straße**. At the other end is the neo-Gothic **Neues Rathaus** with its famous **Glockenspiel**.

Aussprache

[l] a**l**le, **l**ese, vie**l**, küh**l**
[ŋ] Ju**ng**e, Hu**ng**er, Sä**ng**er

To produce the German **l**, place the tip of the tongue against the upper gum ridge, as in English, but keep the tongue flat. A very tight smile helps. Many Americans use this *l*-sound in such words as *million*, *billion*, and *William*.

The combination **ng** is pronounced [ŋ], as in English *singer*. It does not contain the sound [g] as in English *finger*.

A Practice the following words vertically in columns.

[l]		[ŋ]	
a**l**le	**l**assen	Ju**ng**e	Fi**ng**er
Ju**l**i	**l**esen	Frühli**ng**	lä**ng**er
wei**l**	**L**ehrer	Vorstellu**ng**	Hu**ng**er
Fi**l**m	**B**lume	kli**ng**eln	si**ng**en
to**ll**	**F**lamme	Di**ng**e	hä**ng**en

B Practice the sounds [l] and [ŋ]. Read the sentences aloud.

1. Im Frühling werden die Tage länger.
2. Der Junge kauft eine tolle Platte.
3. Du hast das Flugzeugmodell wohl selbst gebastelt.

Aller guten Dinge sind drei.

Das Olympiagelände ist jetzt ein Park.

Übungen

Prepositions with the dative case

The prepositions **aus, außer, bei, mit, nach, seit, von,** and **zu** are always used with the dative case.

mit   with, by means of

Ingrid fährt **mit** dem Zug.   Ingrid goes *by (means of)* train.
Sie fährt **mit** ihrer Schwester.   She goes *with* her sister.

A   Erik wants to go to the Olympic Village in the northern part of Munich. Assure him that he can use any of the following means of transportation.

▪ Kann ich die Straßenbahn nehmen?   Natürlich kannst du mit der Straßenbahn fahren!

1. Kann ich den Bus nehmen?   3. Kann ich das Auto nehmen?
2. Kann ich die U-Bahn nehmen?   4. Kann ich das Rad nehmen?

bei at, with

Brigitte ist **bei** ihren Großeltern. Brigitte is *at* her grandparents'.
Kurt wohnt **bei** seinen Großeltern. Kurt lives *with* his grandparents.

B Gisela wants to know what your plans are. Tell her with whom you're going to do various things.

▪ Ißt du bei deinen Groß- *Ja, bei meinen Großeltern.*
eltern zu Mittag?

1. Trinkst du bei deiner Schwester Kaffee?
2. Siehst du bei deinem Bruder fern?
3. Spielst du bei Rudi Karten?
4. Hörst du bei Monika Musik?

Du hast das Wort Ask a classmate with whom he/she does various things.

Bei wem ißt du zu Abend?
Bei wem hörst du Musik?
Bei wem siehst du fern?

aus out of, from (= is a native of)

Udo kommt **aus** dem Haus. Udo comes *out of* the house.
Monika kommt **aus** Frank- Monika comes *from* Frankfurt.
furt.

C State that the following people have just come from the places named.

▪ Paul und Dieter / Lokal *Paul und Dieter kommen gerade aus dem Lokal.*

1 Lore und Frank / Café 4. Grete und Liese / Bank
2. Paula und Regina / 5. Ingrid und Jan / Post
Warenhaus
3. Gerd und Ilse / Restaurant

D You've met some new people at the youth hostel, and you want them to meet your friends. Introduce them as in the model.

▪ Maria / München *Das ist Maria. Sie kommt aus München.*

1. Gerhard / Frankfurt 4. Rudi / Bern
2. Anja / Hamburg 5. Helga / Berlin
3. Günter / Wien

von from

Was hörst du **von** deiner Freundin Meike?   What do you hear *from* your friend Meike?

E Jan has just heard from various reliable sources that summer vacation will start a week early. Ask him for reassurance that he really did hear the news from those sources.

▪ Mein Bruder hat es gesagt.   *Hast du das wirklich von deinem Bruder gehört?*

1. Meine Schwester hat es gesagt.
2. Mein Vater hat es gesagt.
3. Meine Lehrerin hat es gesagt.
4. Meine Großeltern haben es gesagt.

zu to

Ich gehe heute abend **zu** meinem Freund Udo.   I'm going *to* my friend Udo's this evening.

F You're visiting your pen pal in Frankfurt, and you've received many invitations from her friends and relatives. Ask her to specify the time of each invitation.

▪ Mein Freund Jochen hat uns für Dienstag eingeladen.   *Um wieviel Uhr gehen wir zu deinem Freund?*

1. Meine Freundin Christl hat uns für Donnerstag eingeladen.
2. Meine Großeltern haben uns für Samstag eingeladen.
3. Meine Schwester hat uns für Sonntag eingeladen.
4. Mein Bruder hat uns für Montag eingeladen.

nach to, after

Wir fahren **nach** München.   We're driving *to* Munich.

The preposition **nach,** used with cities and countries, is equivalent to English *to (in the direction of).*

Nach dem Essen gehen wir ins Kino.   *After* dinner we'll go to the movies.

The preposition **nach** is also equivalent to English *after.*

G Say that you're going to visit the places your friend asks about.

▪▫ Möchtest du Deutschland sehen?   *Ja. Ich fahre im Sommer nach Deutschland.*

1. Besuchst du auch Bayern?
2. Dann besuchst du sicher auch München?
3. Du möchtest dann auch Österreich sehen, nicht?
4. Und Wien?

H Ask whether the following people are really coming home after the time mentioned.

▪▫ Schmidts bleiben zwei Monate in Berlin.   *Kommen sie dann nach zwei Monaten zurück?*

1. Schneiders bleiben einen Monat in Zürich.
2. Hofers bleiben zwei Wochen in Zermatt.
3. Langes bleiben zehn Tage in Salzburg.
4. Wagners bleiben eine Woche in Kiel.

Du hast das Wort

Ask a classmate when he/she does various things.

Wann gehst du ins Kino? Nach dem Essen?
Wann spielst du Tennis? Nach der Schule?
Wann machst du Hausaufgaben? Nach der Arbeit?

Blick auf das Alte Rathaus (links unten) in München.

seit since, for

    Christl ist **seit** einem   Christl has been in Munich *for* a
      Monat in München.   month.

To express an action or condition that started in the past but is still continuing in the present, German often uses the present tense and a time phrase with **seit.**

I   Lore asks you how long certain things have been going on. Confirm her guesses as to the exact period of time.

    ■▥ Wie lange ist Gerd schon in   *Ja, seit einem Monat.*
        Hamburg? Einen Monat?

1. Wie lange ist Gabi schon in Österreich? Ein Jahr?
2. Wie lange ist Frank schon krank? Vier Wochen?
3. Wie lange hat er nichts gegessen? Drei Tage?
4. Wie lange ist dein Auto schon kaputt? Eine Woche?

außer besides, except

    Was hast du **außer** dem   What did you see *besides* the
      Museum gesehen?   museum?
    Ich habe nichts **außer** dem   I saw nothing *except* the museum.
      Museum gesehen.

J   Birgit lists the sights she and her classmates saw in Munich. Inquire what else they saw.

    ■▥ Wir haben das Rathaus gesehen.   *Was habt ihr außer dem*
                                                             Rathaus gesehen?

1. Wir haben das Hofbräuhaus gesehen.
2. Wir haben die Fußgängerzone gesehen.
3. Wir haben die Frauenkirche gesehen.
4. Wir haben die Isar gesehen.
5. Wir haben die Straßencafés gesehen.
6. Wir haben die Theater gesehen.

Dative prepositional contractions

> Unser Radio ist **beim** Elektriker.
> Ich komme gerade **vom** Elektriker.
> Gehst du jetzt **zum** Supermarkt?
> Ja, ich gehe auch **zur** Bank.

> bei dem > **beim**
> vom dem > **vom**
> zu dem > **zum**
> zu der > **zur**

The contractions **beim, vom, zum,** and **zur** are frequently used.

K Say you already have been at the places mentioned. Use the appropriate dative prepositional contractions.

■ Gehst du jetzt zum Bäcker?   *Nein, beim Bäcker war ich schon.*

1. Gehst du jetzt zum Metzger?
2. Gehst du jetzt zum Elektriker?
3. Gehst du jetzt zum Friseur?
4. Gehst du jetzt zum Arzt?

L You are lost in a strange city. Ask a police officer for directions to the following places.

■ die Post   *Können Sie mir sagen, wie ich zur Post komme?*

1. die Bank
2. das Museum
3. das Rathaus
4. der Bahnhof
5. die Fußgängerzone
6. der *Western Club*
7. das Theater

M You're thinking of accompanying Petra on her errands, but you're tired. Ask her how far it is from one place to the next.

■ Ich muß zum Bäcker und zur Apotheke.   *Wie weit ist es vom Bäcker zur Apotheke?*
■ Dann gehe ich zum Metzger.   *Wie weit ist es von der Apotheke zum Metzger?*

1. Ich muß dann zum Markt.
2. Dann gehe ich zum Warenhaus.
3. Und dann gehe ich zum Elektriker.
4. Ich gehe dann zur Post.
5. Dann muß ich noch zur Bank.

Du hast das Wort

A. Tell various classmates they need an item and ask where they would go to get it.

▩ Du brauchst [Wurst]. Wohin gehst du?   [Zum Metzger.]

Du brauchst | Brot.
            | Briefmarken.
            | Milch.
            | Geld.
            | Benzin.
            | Obst.

B. You notice that various classmates have bought certain items. Ask them where they were.

▩ Du hast [Brot] gekauft. Wo warst du?   [Beim Bäcker.]

Du hast | Gemüse | gekauft.
        | eine Torte
        | einen Mantel

Schools in the **BRD** occasionally close for a day so that teachers and students can go on an outing. On these days **(Wandertage)** the classes go hiking or visit a local place of interest — Roman ruins, an old castle, or a hill used by glider pilots, for example. The relatively short distances between historical sights make it possible to have several interesting **Wandertage** in a year.

An individual class sometimes takes a longer trip **(Klassenfahrt)**. In the winter or early spring they may go on a week-long skiing trip. Other classes may choose to visit some city in order to explore its museums, churches, and historical sights. These trips are part of the school program and expenses are kept down by subsidies from the town.

Nächstes Jahr fährt unsere Klasse nach Heidelberg.
(Alte Brücke und Schloß)

Grammatische Übersicht

Prepositions with the dative case (A-J)

aus	Udo geht **aus** dem Haus.	Udo goes *out* of the house.
	Andrea kommt **aus** Wien.	Andrea comes *from* Vienna.
außer	**Außer** meinem Freund war mein Bruder da.	*Besides* my friend, my brother was there.
	Ich esse alles gern **außer** Fisch.	I like everything *except* fish.
bei	Sonja ist **bei** ihrer Freundin.	Sonja is *with* her friend.
		Sonja is *at* her friend's.
mit	Rita spricht **mit** dem Verkäufer.	Rita is speaking *with* the salesman.
	Udo fährt **mit** dem Bus.	Udo is going *by* bus.
nach	Gabi fliegt **nach** Berlin.	Gabi is flying *to* Berlin.
	Nach dem Essen gehen wir schwimmen.	*After* dinner we're going swimming.
seit	**Seit** dem Essen habe ich Durst.	I've been thirsty *since* dinner.
	Schmidts wohnen **seit** einem Jahr in Berlin.	Schmidts have been living in Berlin *for* a year.
von	Günter kommt gerade **von** der Party.	Günter is just coming *from* the party.
	Das Geschenk ist **von** seinen Eltern.	The present is *from* his parents.
	Sprichst du **von** meinem Freund?	Are you speaking *of* my friend?
zu	Petra geht **zu** ihrer Freundin.	Petra is going *to* her friend's.
	Sie hat sie **zu** einer Party eingeladen.	She invited her *to* a party.

The prepositions **aus, außer, bei, mit, nach, seit, von,** and **zu** are always used with the dative case.

Nach, used with cities and countries, is equivalent to English *to.* In most other instances the equivalent of *to* is **zu.**

Seit + present tense is used in German to express an action or condition that started in the past but is still continuing in the present. English uses the present perfect tense with *since* or *for.*

Dative prepositional contractions (K-M)

Unser Fernseher ist **beim** Elektriker.	bei dem > **beim**
Ich komme gerade **vom** Elektriker.	von dem > **vom**
Gehst du **zum** Supermarkt?	zu dem > **zum**
Ja, und dann gehe ich **zur** Post.	zu der > **zur**

The contractions **beim, vom, zum,** and **zur** are frequently used.

Wiederholung

A Choose the place in column B that is associated with each statement in column A. Supply the definite article for each noun in column B.

A	B
1. Ich brauche Geld.	a. Bahnhof
2. Ich habe Briefmarken gekauft.	b. Bank
3. Ich möchte einen neuen Mantel kaufen.	c. Café
4. Am Sonntag machen wir immer einen schönen Spaziergang.	d. Kino
5. Orangen sind heute besonders preiswert.	e. Park
6. Frank ist leider durchgefallen.	f. Post
7. Die Vorstellung beginnt um sieben Uhr.	g. Schule
8. Möchtest du eine Cola trinken?	h. Supermarkt
9. Wir fahren mit dem Zug nach Salzburg.	i. Warenhaus

B Complete each sentence with an appropriate dative preposition.

1. Am Montag bin ich ____ meinem Bruder gefahren. Er wohnt in München.
2. Ich habe ____ meinem Bruder und seiner Frau in Schwabing gewohnt. Sie wohnen ____ einem Jahr da.
3. Mein Bruder hat nicht immer in München gewohnt. Er kommt ____ Köln, wie ich.
4. Ich bin oft ____ meinem Bruder und seiner Frau im Englischen Garten spazierengegangen.
5. ____ seinem Haus bis zum Englischen Garten ist es nicht so weit.
6. In die Stadt sind wir dann ____ der U-Bahn gefahren.
7. Am Freitag muß ich ____ Köln zurück.
8. In den fünf Tagen habe ich sehr viel ____ München gesehen.

C Make sense out of the following sentences by replacing the italicized phrase with the phrase in parentheses. Make any other necessary changes.

1. Frau Wächter geht mit *ihrer Geige* einkaufen. (ihr Mann)
2. Sie bummelt durch *den Brunnen*. (die Fußgängerzone)
3. Frau Wächter arbeitet bei *der Ampel*. (die Post)
4. Frau Wächter schreibt ihre Briefe mit *einer Flöte*. (ein Kugelschreiber)
5. Sie kauft oft Geschenke für *ihren Metzger*. (ihre Familie)
6. Sie geht nicht ohne *ihren Fernseher* in die Stadt. (ihre Einkaufstasche)
7. Frau Wächter trinkt Cola aus *einer Socke*. (ein Glas)

D Compare the following items, using the adjective or adverb in parentheses.

1. Schallplatten sind ____ als Cassetten. (billig)
2. Dieses Radio ist nicht so ____ wie dieser Cassetten-Recorder. (teuer)
3. Kostet der Cassetten-Recorder so ____ wie der Plattenspieler? (viel)
4. Dieser Plattenspieler ist viel ____ als der Plattenspieler da. (gut)
5. Der Preis im Radiogeschäft ist viel ____ als der Preis im Warenhaus. (hoch)
6. Ich spiele Platten ____ als Cassetten. (gern)

E Complete the second sentence in each pair by reporting what Kai and Lore said.

▪ Kai sagt: „Ich bin mit meiner Klasse nach München gefahren."
Kai sagt, daß er *mit seiner Klasse nach München gefahren ist.*

1. Kai sagt: „Wir haben eine Klassenfahrt gemacht."
   Kai sagt, daß sie . . .
2. Lore fragt: „Habt ihr viele Museen und Kirchen besucht?"
   Lore fragt, ob sie . . .
3. Kai sagt: „Wir sind ins Deutsche Museum gegangen."
   Kai sagt, . . .
4. Lore fragt: „Seid ihr auch durch die Fußgängerzone gebummelt?"
   Lore fragt, . . .

Viele Münchner fahren nach Garmisch-Partenkirchen zum Schifahren.

F Express the following dialogue in German.

GISELA	Do you know where the Western Club is?
SABINE	Naturally. In Schwabing.
TORSTEN	Is that far from here?
SABINE	To Schwabing? No. You can go by subway.
GISELA	Can we go on foot?
SABINE	Sure. I'll come along.
TORSTEN	Ask Anke whether she wants to come along too.
SABINE	All right. She likes to dance.

G Write two postcards from Kai and Lore telling about the highlights of their class trip to Munich. Have Kai write to his parents, while Lore writes to one of her friends. You may want to mention some of the following places and activities.

Schwabing	mit der U-Bahn fahren
Museen	bummeln
Fußgängerzone	tanzen

Munich, with its population of over 1 million, is one of the most popular cities in the BRD. Located on the Isar river, only an hour's ride from the Alps and famous lakes such as the Tegernsee, Chiemsee, and Starnberger See, Munich attracts tourists from other parts of Germany as well as from other countries. The city has many beautiful churches, impressive palaces, important museums, excellent theaters, and extensive parks. The following places are just some of the attractions.

The **Deutsches Museum** is an important museum devoted to science and technology.

The **Alte Pinakothek** contains one of the most famous art collections in the world.

The **Frauenkirche,** with its onion domes, has long been one of the symbols of Munich.

The **Hofbräuhaus** is a popular tourist attraction, offering music, beer, sausages, and atmosphere.

The **Englischer Garten,** a large park with lakes and wooded areas, is a popular place for afternoon strolls.

Kulturlesestück

Wien

Touristen in Österreich wollen oft *eine* Stadt ganz bestimmt° sehen: Wien, die Hauptstadt. Wien hat viele schöne alte Kirchen wie zum Beispiel° den Stephansdom. Und es hat schöne Schlösser°. Schloß Schönbrunn ist die frühere° Sommerresidenz der Kaiser°. Mitten° in der Stadt steht die Hofburg, die frühere Winterresidenz der Kaiser.

Wien hat berühmte° Cafés. Das Kaffeehaus *Zur blauen Flasche* soll das älteste° in der deutschsprachigen° Welt° sein. Und Wien hat Theater und Museen. Das Kunsthistorische Museum gehört° zu den besten Museen in der Welt.

Wenn man an Wien denkt, denkt man vor allem° an Musik. Viele kennen die Wiener Operetten und den „Walzerkönig"° Johann Strauß. Mozart und Beethoven haben lange in Wien gelebt°. Die Wiener Sängerknaben° geben Konzerte in Wien und in der ganzen Welt.

Touristen besuchen Wien gern. Aber auch für die Österreicher spielt Wien eine große Rolle°. Es liegt am Rand° von Österreich, ziemlich weit im Osten. Trotzdem° ist es das politische und das kulturelle Zentrum von Österreich.

definitely

for example / palaces
former / der Kaiser: of the emperors / in the middle
famous
oldest / German-speaking / world
belongs

vor allem: above all
Waltz King
lived
Boys' Choir

spielt . . . Rolle: is important / edge
nevertheless

A Match the items in column B with the information in column A.

A	B
1. eine schöne alte Kirche	a. Wien
2. der Walzerkönig	b. der Stephansdom
3. die Hauptstadt von Österreich	c. die Hofburg
4. dieses Schloß steht mitten in der Stadt	d. ein Wiener Kaffeehaus
5. viele Touristen besuchen es	e. Musik in Wien
6. Operetten	
7. liegt ziemlich weit im Osten	
8. die frühere Winterresidenz der Kaiser	
9. Mozart	
10. das politische und kulturelle Zentrum von Österreich	
11. Sängerknaben	
12. das älteste in der deutschsprachigen Welt	

Schloß Belvedere in Wien

Vokabeln

SUBSTANTIVE

die Ampel, -n traffic signal
die Bahn, -en train, railway
der Bahnhof, ⸚e train station
die Bank, -en bank
Bayern Bavaria
der Besuch, -e visit
der Brunnen, - fountain, well, spring
der Club, -s club
die Ecke, -n corner
die Fußgängerzone, -n pedestrian zone
die Kirche, -n church
die Klassenfahrt, -en class trip
die Kreuzung, -en intersection
das Lokal, -e place to eat, drink, dance; restaurant
das Museum, die Museen museum
der Park, -s park
der Platz, ⸚e square
die Post post office, mail
das Rathaus, ⸚er town hall
das Schild, -er sign
der Stadtplan, ⸚e city map
der Stiefel, - boot
der Student, -en, -en/die Studentin, -nen student (at a university)
die Tankstelle, -n service station, gas station
das Tor, -e gate
das Warenhaus, ⸚er department store

VERBEN

ab·biegen (ist abgebogen) to make a turn
bummeln (ist gebummelt) to go for a stroll, for a walk
schauen to look
stehen (gestanden) to stand
suchen to look for
vergessen (i; vergessen) to forget

ANDERE WÖRTER

allein alone
aus (+ *dat.*) out of, from
außer (+ *dat.*) besides, except for
bis zu up to
froh glad, happy
jemand someone
links (to the) left
rechts (to the) right
seit (+ *dat.*) since, for
weil (*sub. conj.*) because
zu shut, closed

BESONDERE AUSDRÜCKE

so scheint's so it seems
Moment mal just a moment
da fällt mir gerade ein it just occurs to me
es ist viel los there is a lot going on
so ein Pech what bad luck, how unfortunate
zu Fuß on foot
immer geradeaus straight ahead
die Straße entlang along (down) the street

noch einmal

A **Besuch.** Your pen pal (from the end of Stage 2) has just written that he/she will soon have the opportunity to visit you and would like to know what to expect. Write a reply in which you explain what your friend may find different in your area. You may wish to compare some or all of the following: geography, landscape, weather, food, meals, transportation to school and into town, and town landmarks such as a market, pedestrian zone, town hall, museums.

B **Guten Appetit!** As a class project, assemble a German meal. Plan a menu, with individual students or small groups volunteering to prepare the various foods. At the dinner, each student should receive a booklet in English and German containing the menu and the recipes for each dish. Be sure to set the table and to eat as a German family would.

As an extension of this activity, or as an alternative, your class may want to compile a cookbook of favorite German recipes. If there are German-speaking people in the community, members of the class could ask them for suggestions as to what to include.

C **Eine deutsche Stadt.** In groups of four to five, prepare poster displays of a city in a German-speaking country. Provide a map of the city; draw or cut out of magazines pictures of famous buildings, and label them. Select a speaker to present a brief report on the city, using the poster.

D **Ein Geschenk.** You've been spending the summer with a family in Switzerland. Now that you're about to leave, you want to get them a present to express your gratitude; but you're not sure what to buy. Choose a partner to take the role of a salesperson in a department store. Create a dialogue in which the salesperson tries to help you make a decision by asking questions about the family's tastes and interests. As the salesperson finds out more about the family, he/she can offer various suggestions. You may want to bring in props to help you perform the dialogue.

E **Im Verkehrsamt.** Because you can speak German, you have been given a job in an information center **(das Verkehrsamt)** of the city of your choice (for example, Hamburg, Berlin, Salzburg, or Basel). Your task is to assist strangers in town. Learn about the sights in these cities. Several of your classmates will then play the role of tourist. When they ask which sights you recommend and how to get there, you give them the correct information. You may want to begin by asking how long they are staying and what their particular interests are — museums, theater, shopping, and so on.

F **Deutsche in Amerika.** At the end of Stage 1, one of the suggested activities was to look briefly into the extent of German influence in your area — German city names and names in a telephone book. Now go into this question more deeply. Are there any stores or shops near you owned or managed by native speakers of German? Members of local government? Teachers or others employed in an educational capacity, such as in a museum or in an institute on German culture? Perhaps there is a town or a historic sight with a German name you can investigate. If possible, you may want to conduct interviews or prepare a description.

G **Ein Spiel.** The class is divided into two teams. Each team has 15 minutes to compile a list of questions that elicit information from Chapters 10–15. The questions may concern either the introductory reading material in each chapter, or the **Kulturlesestücke.** For example, a question from Chapter 14 might be, "Mit wieviel Jahren darf man in Deutschland Auto fahren?" Members of both teams take turns asking the questions of members of the opposing team. The team with the most correct answers wins.

H **Kleines Theater.** The class is divided into pairs or small groups. Each group or set of partners makes up a skit consisting solely of dialogue lines from Chapters 1–15. Try to invent comical situations or funny sequences of lines. A variation of this activity would be to have the class as a whole make up a dialogue, with students adding lines spontaneously.

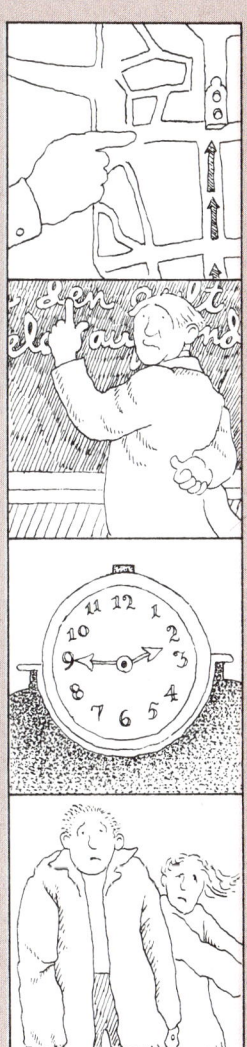

 **Ein Problem.** Create a skit in which you must solve a problem. In it, be sure to include expressions of apology, agreement, or disagreement. Use one of the following situations, or invent one of your own.

1. You've planned to spend an evening at a disco, then discover that it is closed. Find out where you can go instead.
2. After you have eaten a meal in a restaurant, you discover that you have no money to pay the bill.
3. You are in a German supermarket with an American friend who knows no German and isn't familiar with German customs. When your friend does something wrong — such as touching the vegetables, or not packing the groceries — you must apologize and explain to the clerks.

 **Ein Kreuzworträtsel.** In small groups, prepare a crossword puzzle (**das Kreuzworträtsel**), using a single set of words: vocabulary relating to weather, transportation, buildings, food, shopping, and so on. When the puzzles are finished, each group exchanges its puzzle for that of another and tries to solve it.

 **Deutsche Touristen.** You've just been approached by some German tourists who want to know what there is to see in your town. Tell them about some of the major points of interest, and direct them how to get there.

One of the tourists would like to know what is being performed at the local theater or concert hall. Tell her what's playing and explain how to get tickets.

 **Wo möchtest du sein?** Look at the photographs on pages 225–231. In which place would you most like to be? Which person would you most like to meet? Would you choose a situation in which you feel at home and comfortable, or one which is new and different? In German, discuss your answers and the reasons for them. Then pretend that you are actually in one of the situations shown, and make up and enact a suitable dialogue. As necessary, select several classmates to work with you.

Reference section

German first names

The following list includes some of the most popular German names. It is not a complete list of first names.

girls

Andrea	Isabelle	Alex	Karl-Heinz
Angelika	Jutta	Andreas	Karsten
Anja	Karin	Anton	Klaus
Anke	Katja	Axel	Konrad
Anne	Katrin	Benjamin	Kurt
Anneliese	Kirstin	Benno	Lars
Astrid	Liese	Bernd	Lothar
Barbara	Lore	Bernhard	Lutz
Beate	Lotte	Bruno	Manfred
Bettina	Luise	Christian	Mark
Birgit	Margit	Christoph	Markus
Brigitte	Maria	Detlev	Martin
Carola	Marianne	Dieter	Matthias
Christa	Marita	Dietmar	Michael
Christl	Marta	Dirk	Norbert
Christine	Martina	Erik	Otto
Claudia	Meike	Ernst	Paul
Cordula	Monika	Frank	Peter
Cornelia	Nicole	Fritz	Rainer
Erika	Paula	Georg	Ralf
Elke	Petra	Gerd	Robert
Ellen	Regina	Gerhard	Rudi
Erna	Renate	Günter	Rüdiger
Eva	Rita	Gustav	Stefan
Gabi	Sabine	Hans	Thomas
Gabriele	Silke	Hans-Dieter	Torsten
Gerda	Sonja	Hans-Jürgen	Udo
Gisela	Stephanie	Heinz	Ulf
Gitte	Sylvia	Heinz-Dieter	Ulrich
Gretchen	Susanne	Helmut	Urs
Grete	Tanja	Herbert	Uwe
Gudrun	Trudi	Hugo	Volker
Hannelore	Ulrike	Jan	Walter
Heidi	Ursel	Jens	Werner
Heike	Ursula	Jochen	Willi
Helga	Ute	Johann	Wim
Hilde	Veronika	Jörg	Wolf
Ilse		Jürgen	
Inge		Kai	
Ingrid		Karl	

The girls/boys split: columns 1–2 are girls, columns 3–4 are boys.

appendix **347**

English equivalents of dialogues

Below you will find English equivalents of the dialogues in this book. Because the English dialogues are not literal translations they sometimes contain words that do not have exact equivalents in the German text. Don't let this bother you. Two languages often express the same idea in different ways.

chapter 1   Hi! How are you?

What's your name?

UTE BRAUN	What's your name?
UTE SCHMIDT	Ute.
UTE BRAUN	Amazing! My name is Ute, too.

How are you?

INGRID	Hi, Gisela. How are you?
GISELA	Fine, thanks.
INGRID	Hi, Dieter. How are you?
DIETER	Bad.
INGRID	Well, what's the matter?
DIETER	I'm tired.

Are you satisfied?

VOLKER	Well, Monika, are you satisfied?
MONIKA	Yes, very much. You too?
VOLKER	No, I'm really unhappy.
MONIKA	I'm sorry.

Why is Volker so cross?

FRANK	How's Volker?
MONIKA	Bad.
FRANK	Is he sick again?
MONIKA	Nonsense! He's just lazy.

chapter 2   How old are you?

Young or old?

HEIKE	How old is Michael?
DIRK	Sixteen.
HEIKE	And you?
DIRK	Sixteen too. We're both sixteen.
HEIKE	Are you both *really* sixteen?
DIRK	Of course. Why?
HEIKE	You're so young.
DIRK	Well, how old are *you*?
HEIKE	Already seventeen.
DIRK	That really is very old!

When is your birthday?	PETRA	My birthday's in March. Yours too, isn't it?
	DIRK	No.
	PETRA	Well, when is your birthday?
	DIRK	In April.
	PETRA	Oh. Isn't Gerd's birthday in April, too?
	DIRK	No, it's not until May.
	PETRA	Oh yes, that's right.

chapter 3   This afternoon

Where do you live?	ERIK	Are you going home now?
	SABINE	Yes.
	ERIK	Where do you live?
	SABINE	On Garden Street.
	ERIK	Is that far from here?
	SABINE	No, just ten minutes.

What are you going to do?	JAN	Are you staying home this afternoon?
	GISELA	Yes, of course.
	JAN	What are you going to do?
	GISELA	Homework. What else?

chapter 5   Do you need new clothes?

That's too expensive	ASTRID	How expensive is that dress over there?
	GISELA	20 marks, and that's too expensive.
	ASTRID	What do you mean by that?
	GISELA	I think it's ugly.
	ERIK	Those jeans are really terrific.
	ASTRID	You think so? How much do they cost?
	ERIK	50 marks.
	ASTRID	50 marks! That's a bargain. Are you going to buy them?
	ERIK	Yes.

What size do you wear?	ASTRID	Here's a coat in brown. Nice, isn't it?
	ERIK	Yes, terrific. It's also nice and warm.
	ASTRID	Does it fit?
	ERIK	Unfortunately not. It's too big.
	ASTRID	What size do you wear?
	ERIK	Size 40.
	ASTRID	Here's your size.
	ERIK	But that's not a coat. That's a jacket.
	ASTRID	Oh yes. Too bad.

chapter 6 The school day

In the classroom

GISELA	What do we have at nine? Chemistry?
DIETER	No, we don't have chemistry today. We have math.
GISELA	Oh, great!
DIETER	You think math is great?
GISELA	Yes, I think math is interesting. Math's my favorite subject.

During recess

KARIN	Have you finished your homework assignments yet?
NORBERT	Which one? The math assignment?
KARIN	No, the chemistry assignment.
NORBERT	That I'll do tonight. What are you doing this afternoon?
KARIN	I'm doing biology.
NORBERT	Oh, man! We have homework in biology, too?
KARIN	Of course.

What time is it?

DIETER	What time is it?
SABINE	It's five after ten.
DIETER	Oh no! I'm going to be late again!
SABINE	That's not so bad. You're good in chemistry after all.

chapter 7 Do you want to go to the concert?

Concert at the youth center

INGRID	Hey, Dieter, the *Hot Dogs* are playing tonight.
DIETER	Boy, that's dumb. I can't go tonight, unfortunately.
INGRID	And tomorrow night?
DIETER	Tomorrow night will be all right. Do you think we can still get tickets?
INGRID	Well, we can give it a try.

At the box office

INGRID	Do you still have tickets for tomorrow night?
MAN	I'm sorry. There's nothing left for tomorrow night. I do have a couple of tickets for the day after tomorrow.
INGRID	*(To Dieter)* What do you think?
DIETER	I can make it. But don't you have to work then?
INGRID	Yes, I do. But I can certainly get time off. I just have to hear the *Hot Dogs*.
DIETER	OK, that's settled.

chapter 8 What are your plans?

Picture postcards are interesting

THOMAS	Say, just why do you collect picture postcards?
PETRA	I don't know. It's fun.
THOMAS	Really? I don't understand that.
PETRA	It's very simple. Old postcards are interesting and valuable as well.

Thomas needs a hobby	GERD	That Thomas is really a bore.
	PETRA	Yes, he's always tired. And he always thinks everything is boring.
	GERD	He never feels like doing anything, either.
	PETRA	What he needs is a hobby.
	GERD	Maybe ham radio operator.
	PETRA	Or ceramics.
What are you planning to do today?	ASTRID	Hey, Klaus, what are you going to do this afternoon?
	KLAUS	We're going to Hamburg.
	ASTRID	Are you going shopping?
	KLAUS	Yes, we're going to buy Gerd's birthday present.
	ASTRID	Where?
	KLAUS	I don't know yet. At Karstadt's maybe.
Why don't you come along?	ASTRID	Are you coming along this afternoon?
	ERIK	Where to?
	ASTRID	Downtown. To *Musikhaus Schumann*.
	ERIK	Today, on Saturday?
	ASTRID	Yes, today is "long Saturday," you know.
	ERIK	Oh yes, that's right. The stores won't close until five. What do you want at Schumann's?
	ASTRID	To buy the new record by Katja Peters. All right, do you want to come along now or not?
	ERIK	I really don't have time.
	ASTRID	Oh, come on!
	ERIK	Well, OK.

chapter 9   I helped around the house

I straightened up my room	NORBERT	What did you do over the weekend?
	KARIN	I slept.
	NORBERT	Oh, come on! You can't be serious!
	KARIN	Yes. I am! Honest! Then on Sunday I built a model airplane. And what did you do?
	NORBERT	I worked — as usual.
	KARIN	What do you mean you worked?
	NORBERT	I have to help at home. I straightened up my room and washed the car.
	KARIN	You call that working?
	NORBERT	Well, at least it's more than sleeping.
I baked a layer cake	SABINE	What did you do last weekend?
	PAUL	Not much. I baked a cake for my mother. She invited my grandparents over for coffee and cake.
	SABINE	How interesting!
	PAUL	Don't be so sarcastic! You did ask, you know.
	SABINE	Did the cake at least taste good?
	PAUL	I don't know. I picked up Gerda and we took a walk. Then we had coffee and cake with Gerda's parents.

chapter 10   Sports and leisure time

Who won?

	GISELA	What did you do yesterday?
	JAN	We played soccer.
	GISELA	Against whom?
	JAN	Oberndorf.
	GISELA	Did you win?
	JAN	No, we lost two to three.
	GISELA	Oh man, I'm really sorry. But two to three against Oberndorf isn't really so bad.
	JAN	That's true. Oberndorf is good.
	GISELA	Well, maybe next time we can at least play a tie game.

I'm inviting you

	INGRID	What do you have planned for tonight?
	DIETER	I'm going to a party. What are you going to do?
	INGRID	Nothing, actually.
	DIETER	Nothing? That's great. Then you can come along.
	INGRID	Where? To the party?
	DIETER	Of course.
	INGRID	But you're not giving the party.
	DIETER	No, Gerd is. But I can invite you.
	INGRID	Don't be silly. You can't do that.
	DIETER	Sure I can. You know him pretty well, don't you?
	INGRID	Yes . . . Well, all right. When does it start?
	DIETER	At eight, I think. I'll call you.
	INGRID	OK. So long. See you later.

chapter 11   Baker, butcher, supermarket

At the butcher shop

	MR. LANGE	Hello, Mrs. Kraft. May I help you?
	MRS. KRAFT	How much are the pork chops?
	MR. LANGE	7 marks 50 a pound.
	MRS. KRAFT	I'll need five chops.
	MR. LANGE	Fine. Anything else?
	MRS. KRAFT	I would like ten frankfurters.
	MR. LANGE	There you are. Would you like something else?
	MRS. KRAFT	No. That's all for today.
	MR. LANGE	Thank you . . . So, here you are. That will be 29 marks 50 all together.
		* * *
		Here you go. You get 50 pfennigs back.
	MRS. KRAFT	Thank you very much.
	MR. LANGE	You're welcome. Good-by, Mrs. Kraft.
	MRS. KRAFT	Good-by, Mr. Lange.

chapter 12   Enjoy your meal!

At the restaurant

	WAITER	Good day, would you care for something to drink?
	MRS. WOLF	Oh yes. I am so thirsty. One mineral water, please.
	MR. WOLF	I'll have a mineral water too.
	WAITER	Two mineral waters.
	GABI	I'd like a cola, please.
	WAITER	Thank you.
	MR. WOLF	And the menu, please.
	WAITER	Would you like to order now?
	MRS. WOLF	Yes, please. Is the roast beef tender?
	WAITER	Oh yes. I can recommend it.
	MRS. WOLF	Well then, three roast beef dinners with mashed potatoes and salad.
	GABI	I don't want any mashed potatoes.
	MRS. WOLF	Aren't you hungry?
	GABI	Yes, I am, but I'd rather eat French fries.
	MRS. WOLF	Whatever you want.
		* * *
	WAITER	Well now, did you enjoy your meal?
	MRS. WOLF	Yes. The roast was excellent.
	MR. WOLF	I'd like the check, please.
	WAITER	Very well. All together it comes to 43 marks and 50 pfennigs.
	MR. WOLF	Make it 45.
	WAITER	Thank you very much.

chapter 13   You can always talk about the weather

How's the weather?

In the spring

	STEFAN	What do you think? Is it going to rain tomorrow?
	KARIN	Probably.
	STEFAN	That is really dumb!
	KARIN	Why?
	STEFAN	My umbrella is broken.

In the summer

	DIETER	Nice today, isn't it?
	INGRID	Yes, it's finally getting warm.
	DIETER	I hope it won't get too hot.
	INGRID	I'd rather have it hot than cold.

In the fall

	MRS. KRAFT	Beautiful weather, isn't it?
	MR. WOLF	Yes, I really like this season. It's so nice and cool.
	MRS. KRAFT	This is good hiking weather.
	MR. WOLF	Too bad that we have to work.

In the winter

	RALF	The wind is rather cold this morning.
	ILSE	Yes, there was a frost last night.
	RALF	This afternoon it's supposed to snow.
	ILSE	That's great. Then we can go sledding.

chapter 15 A city visit

Where shall we go now?

KAI   Are we going to stand here forever? Where are we going to go now?
LORE   Dieter says that the music at the Western Club is terrific. But where in the world is the Western Club?
KAI   Here comes Dieter now. Why don't you ask him. He always knows everything.
LORE   Dieter, tell us, where is the Western Club?
DIETER   In Schwabing.
KAI   Boy, that's a long way from here. How are we going to get to Schwabing?
DIETER   You can go by subway — take the 3 or the 6. You can also walk.
KAI   To Schwabing on foot?
DIETER   Yes, it's only about a half an hour from here.
LORE   Don't you want to come along?
DIETER   No.
LORE   Why not?
DIETER   Because I'm too tired.
KAI   You can see that, man. He's almost asleep already.
LORE   Well OK, then we'll just go alone. Good night, Dieter. Sleep well (pleasant dreams).

How do we get to the Western Club?

KAI   I'm glad that we took the subway.
LORE   Yes, but now where is the Western Club?
KAI   Why don't you look at the map!
LORE   I haven't got it. Did you forget it?
KAI   So it seems. Then we'll just have to ask someone. Excuse me. Can you tell us how we can get to the Western Club?
STUDENT   Yes, I can. You go straight ahead to the traffic light. Turn right at the light. Then go straight ahead again until you come to a square with a fountain. There you turn left. Then you'll see the sign with the big boot.
KAI   Thanks a lot.
STUDENT   Don't mention it. Oh, wait a minute. It just occurred to me — the Western Club is closed today.
LORE   No, what rotten luck. What are we going to do now?
STUDENT   Why don't you go to Alfons. At Alfons there's always something going on. It's also a student hangout.

Grammatical summaries

Pronouns

personal pronouns

	SINGULAR				PLURAL				FORMAL
Nominative	ich	du	er	es	sie	wir	ihr	sie	Sie
Accusative	mich	dich	ihn	es	sie	uns	euch	sie	Sie
Dative	mir	dir	ihm	ihm	ihr	uns	euch	ihnen	Ihnen

interrogative pronouns

Nominative	wer	was
Accusative	wen	was
Dative	wem	

demonstrative pronouns

	SINGULAR			PLURAL
Nominative	der	das	die	die
Accusative	den	das	die	die
Dative	dem	dem	der	denen

Words that introduce nouns

definite article

	SINGULAR			PLURAL
Nominative	der	das	die	die
Accusative	den	das	die	die
Dative	dem	dem	der	den

dieser-words

	SINGULAR			PLURAL
Nominative	dieser	dieses	diese	diese
Accusative	diesen	dieses	diese	diese
Dative	diesem	diesem	dieser	diesen

The **dieser**-words are: **dieser, jeder, mancher, solcher,** and **welcher.**

appendix

indefinite article and **ein**-words

	SINGULAR			PLURAL
Nominative	ein	ein	eine	keine
Accusative	einen	ein	eine	keine
Dative	einem	einem	einer	keinen

The **ein**-words are **kein** and the possessive adjectives:

mein	my	**unser**	our
dein	your (*fam.sg.*)	**euer**	your (*fam.pl.*)
sein	his, its	**ihr**	their
ihr	her, its	**Ihr**	your (*formal*)

Noun plurals

		SINGULAR	PLURAL
Pattern 1	no change in plural	das Mädchen	die Mädchen
	plural adds umlaut	der Bruder	die Brüder
Pattern 2	plural adds **-e**	der Freund	die Freunde
	plural adds **-e** and umlaut	der Rock	die Röcke
Pattern 3	plural adds **-er**	das Kind	die Kinder
	plural adds **-er** and umlaut	der Mann	die Männer
Pattern 4	plural adds **-n**	die Familie	die Familien
	plural adds **-en**	die Frau	die Frauen
	plural adds **-nen**	die Schülerin	die Schülerinnen
Pattern 5	plural adds **-s**	der Pulli	die Pullis

Special **der**-nouns

	SINGULAR	PLURAL
Nominative	der Herr	die Herren
Accusative	den Herrn	die Herren
Dative	dem Herrn	den Herren

The special **der**-nouns include **der Junge, der Kunde,** and **der Student.**

Comparison of irregular adjectives and adverbs

Base form	gern	gut	viel	hoch
Comparative	lieber	besser	mehr	höher

Prepositions

WITH ACCUSATIVE	CONTRACTIONS
durch	durch das > durchs
für	für das > fürs
gegen	um das > ums
ohne	
um	

WITH DATIVE	CONTRACTIONS
aus	bei dem > beim
außer	von dem > vom
bei	zu dem > zum
mit	zu der > zur
nach	
seit	
von	
zu	

Numbers

- 0 = null
- 1 = eins
- 2 = zwei
- 3 = drei
- 4 = vier
- 5 = fünf
- 6 = sechs
- 7 = sieben
- 8 = acht
- 9 = neun
- 10 = zehn
- 11 = elf
- 12 = zwölf
- 13 = dreizehn
- 14 = vierzehn
- 15 = fünfzehn
- 16 = sechzehn
- 17 = siebzehn
- 18 = achtzehn
- 19 = neunzehn
- 20 = zwanzig
- 21 = einundzwanzig
- 22 = zweiundzwanzig
- 23 = dreiundzwanzig
- 24 = vierundzwanzig
- 25 = fünfundzwanzig
- 26 = sechsundzwanzig
- 27 = siebenundzwanzig
- 28 = achtundzwanzig
- 29 = neunundzwanzig
- 30 = dreißig
- 40 = vierzig
- 50 = fünfzig
- 60 = sechzig
- 70 = siebzig
- 80 = achtzig
- 90 = neunzig
- 100 = hundert
- 101 = hunderteins
- 102 = hundertzwei
- 121 = hunderteinundzwanzig
- 500 = fünfhundert
- 1.000 = tausend

Verbs

regular verbs

Infinitive	kommen	finden[1]	tanzen[2]
Present	ich komme	finde	tanze
	du kommst	findest	tanzt
	er/sie kommt	findet	tanzt
	wir kommen	finden	tanzen
	ihr kommt	findet	tanzt
	sie kommen	finden	tanzen
	Sie kommen	finden	tanzen
Imperatives	komm!	finde!	tanz!
	kommt!	findet!	tanzt!
	kommen Sie!	finden Sie!	tanzen Sie!
Conversational past	ich bin gekommen	habe gefunden	habe getanzt

1. A verb with stem ending in **-d** or **-t** has an **-e** before the **-st** and **-t** endings.
2. The **-st** of the **du-**form ending contracts to **-t** when the verb stem ends in a sibilant (**-s, -ss, -ß, -z,** or **-tz**). Thus, the **du-** and **er/sie-**forms are identical.

verbs with stem-vowel change

Infinitive	geben (e > i)	lesen (e > ie)	fahren (a > ä)
Present	ich gebe	lese	fahre
	du gibst	liest	fährst
	er/sie gibt	liest	fährt
	wir geben	lesen	fahren
	ihr gebt	lest	fahrt
	sie geben	lesen	fahren
	Sie geben	lesen	fahren
Imperatives	gib!	lies!	fahr!
	gebt!	lest!	fahrt!
	geben Sie!	lesen Sie!	fahren Sie!
Conversational past	ich habe gegeben	habe gelesen	bin gefahren

The following verbs used in this text have stem-vowel changes:
e > i: essen, geben, helfen, nehmen, sprechen, vergessen
e > ie: empfehlen, lesen, sehen
a > ä: backen, einladen, fahren, fallen, schlafen, tragen, waschen
au > äu: laufen

irregular verbs

Infinitive	sein	haben	werden	wissen
Present	ich bin	habe	werde	weiß
	du bist	hast	wirst	weißt
	er/sie ist	hat	wird	weiß
	wir sind	haben	werden	wissen
	ihr seid	habt	werdet	wißt
	sie sind	haben	werden	wissen
	Sie sind	haben	werden	wissen
Imperatives	sei!	habe!	werde!	
	seid!	habt!	werdet!	
	seien Sie!	haben Sie!	werden Sie!	
Conversational past	ich bin gewesen	habe gehabt	bin geworden	habe gewußt

present tense of modal auxiliaries

	dürfen	können	müssen	sollen	wollen	mögen	
ich	darf	kann	muß	soll	will	mag	möchte
du	darfst	kannst	mußt	sollst	willst	magst	möchtest
er/sie	darf	kann	muß	soll	will	mag	möchte
wir	dürfen	können	müssen	sollen	wollen	mögen	möchten
ihr	dürft	könnt	müßt	sollt	wollt	mögt	möchtet
sie	dürfen	können	müssen	sollen	wollen	mögen	möchten
Sie	dürfen	können	müssen	sollen	wollen	mögen	möchten

principal parts of irregular weak verbs

INFINITIVE	PAST PARTICIPLE	ENGLISH EQUIVALENT
bringen	gebracht	to bring
denken	gedacht	to think
kennen	gekannt	to know
nennen	genannt	to name
wissen	gewußt	to know

appendix

principal parts of strong verbs used in this text

Compound verbs (like mitgehen) are not included when the basic form of the verb (like gehen) is included, since the principal parts are the same. Stem-vowel changes in the present tense are indicated in parentheses after the infinitive. For additional meanings, see the German-English Vocabulary.

INFINITIVE	PAST PARTICIPLE	ENGLISH EQUIVALENT
ab·biegen	(ist) abgebogen	to turn
an·rufen	angerufen	to telephone
backen (ä)	gebacken	to bake
beginnen	begonnen	to begin
bekommen	bekommen	to get, to obtain
bestehen	bestanden	to pass (a test)
bleiben	(ist) geblieben	to stay
ein·laden (ä)	eingeladen	to invite
empfehlen (ie)	empfohlen	to recommend
essen (i)	gegessen	to eat
fahren (ä)	(ist) gefahren	to drive
fallen (ä)	(ist) gefallen	to fall
finden	gefunden	to find
fliegen	(ist) geflogen	to fly
frieren	gefroren	to freeze
geben (i)	gegeben	to give
gehen	(ist) gegangen	to go
gewinnen	gewonnen	to win
heißen	geheißen	to be called
helfen (i)	geholfen	to help
kommen	(ist) gekommen	to come
laufen (äu)	(ist) gelaufen	to run
lesen (ie)	gelesen	to read
liegen	gelegen	to lie
nehmen (nimmt)	genommen	to take
reiten	(ist) geritten	to ride (horseback)
scheinen	geschienen	to shine
schlafen (ä)	geschlafen	to sleep
schreiben	geschrieben	to write
schwimmen	(ist) geschwommen	to swim
sehen (ie)	gesehen	to see
sein	(ist) gewesen	to be
singen	gesungen	to sing
sprechen (i)	gesprochen	to speak
stehen	gestanden	to stand
tragen (ä)	getragen	to wear; to carry
trinken	getrunken	to drink
tun	getan	to do
vergessen (i)	vergessen	to forget
waschen (ä)	gewaschen	to wash
werden (wird)	(ist) geworden	to become

Supplementary word sets

The following word lists will help you to increase the number of things you can say and write during your study of each chapter. Some of the words may be introduced as active vocabulary later than the chapters for which they are given here.

chapter 1

ADJECTIVES FOR MOOD OR PERSONALITY

ausgezeichnet   excellent
erstklassig   first-rate
furchtbar   horrible
klasse   terrific
miserabel   miserable
schrecklich   dreadful

ADJECTIVES FOR PERSONALITY

clever   clever
doof   idiotic
dumm   stupid
fies   disgusting
klug   smart
lahm   tired
langsam   slow
langweilig   boring
nett   nice
verrückt   crazy

FAREWELLS

auf Wiederhören!   good by *(on the telephone)*
bis bald!   see you soon
bis dann!   see you later
mach's gut!   take it easy
tschau!   so long

chapter 3

MUSICAL INSTRUMENTS

das Akkordeon   accordion
die Blockflöte   recorder
das Cello   cello
das Fagott   bassoon
die Harfe   harp
der Kontrabaß   double bass
die Oboe   oboe
die Orgel   organ
das Saxophon   saxophone
die Posaune (+blasen)   trombone
die Trompete (+blasen)   trumpet
die Tuba (+blasen)   tuba
das Waldhorn (+blasen)   French horn

SPORTS AND GAMES

Billard   billiards
Dame   checkers
Federball   badminton
Golf   golf
Handball (Hallenhandball)   handball
Hockey   hockey
Mühle   Chinese checkers
Schach   chess
Tischtennis   ping pong (table tennis)
Wasserball   water polo

chapter 4

PROFESSIONS

ein Angestellter/eine Angestellte   employee
der Ingenieur/die Ingenieurin   engineer
der Krankenpfleger/die Krankenschwester   nurse
der Mechaniker/die Mechanikerin   mechanic
der Rechtsanwalt/die Rechtsanwältin   lawyer
der Sekretär/die Sekretärin   secretary
der Steward/die Stewardeß   steward(ess)

appendix **361**

FAMILY MEMBERS

die Tante aunt
der Onkel uncle
die Kusine cousin (f.)
der Cousin (der Vetter) cousin (m.)
die Oma grandma
der Opa grandpa
die Großmutter grandmother
der Großvater grandfather
die Stiefmutter stepmother
der Stiefvater stepfather
die Schwiegermutter mother-in-law
die Schwägerin sister-in-law
der Schwager brother-in-law

PHYSICAL DESCRIPTION OF PEOPLE

blond blond
dick fat
dunkel brunette
fett fat
häßlich ugly
hübsch pretty
mager thin
normal normal
schwach weak
stark strong
süß sweet

chapter 5

CLOTHING FOR MEN AND WOMEN

der Anorak jacket with hood
der Hut hat
die Kniestrümpfe (pl.) knee socks
die Latzhose overalls
die Mütze cap
der Parka parka
der Regenmantel raincoat
der Rollkragenpullover turtleneck
die Sandalen (pl.) sandals
der Schlafanzug pajamas
die Shorts shorts
die Strickjacke knitted jacket
das T-Shirt t-shirt
der Trainingsanzug warm-up suit
die Weste vest, cardigan
der Wintermantel winter coat

CLOTHING FOR WOMEN

der Badeanzug bathing suit
das Dirndl(kleid) dirndl
der Hosenanzug pants suit
der Hosenrock culottes
das Kostüm suit
das Trägerkleid jumper

CLOTHING FOR MEN

die Badehose bathing trunks
der Blazer blazer
der Freizeitanzug leisure suit
das Freizeithemd casual shirt
das Polohemd polo shirt

COLORS

orange orange
purpurrot crimson
rosa pink
violett violet
hell(blau) light (blue)
dunkel(blau) dark (blue)

chapter 6

SCHOOL SUBJECTS

Französisch French
Gemeinschaftskunde social studies
Griechisch Greek
Informatik computer science
Italienisch Italian
Religion(skunde) religion
Spanisch Spanish
Werken shop

CLASSROOM OBJECTS

die Federmappe pencil case
der Filzstift felt pen
das Klassenbuch record book
der Klassenschrank cupboard
das Klassenzimmer classroom
die Kreide chalk
der Kurs course
die Landkarte (Wandkarte) map
der Papierkorb wastebasket
das Ringbuch loose leaf binder
der Schwamm sponge
das Sprachlabor language lab
die (Wand)tafel chalkboard

PHYSICAL ATTRIBUTES OF OBJECTS

aus Glas glass
aus Holz wooden
aus Metall metal
aus Papier paper
dunkel dark
hell light
farbig (bunt) colorful
hart hard
weich soft
biegsam pliable
bequem comfortable
gemütlich cozy

chapter 8

STEREO AND AUDIO-VISUAL EQUIPMENT

der Farbfernseher color television
der Kopfhörer headphone
der Lautsprecher loudspeaker
das Mikrophon microphone
der Radiorecorder cassette radio
der Schwarzweißfernseher black-and-white television
das Tonband tape
das Tonbandgerät tape recorder (reel-to-reel)
der Tuner tuner
der Verstärker amplifier

HOBBIES

angeln to fish
Blumen (z.B. Rosen, Dahlien, Lilien) flowers (e.g., roses, dahlias, lilies)
der Garten gardening
malen to paint
schreiben (Gedichte, Geschichten) to write (poems, stories)
zeichnen to draw

COLLECTIBLES

alte Flaschen old bottles
Glas glass
Insekten insects
Münzen coins
Pflanzen (getrocknet) plants (dried)
Puppen dolls
Silber silver
Streichholzschachteln match covers
altes Zinn old pewter

chapter 9

CHORES

(die) Fenster putzen to clean windows
(das) Mittagessen kochen to cook dinner
(das) Abendessen vorbereiten/machen to prepare supper
meinem Vater helfen to help my father
meiner Mutter helfen to help my mother
(die) Wäsche bügeln to iron (clothes)
Wäsche/Kleider flicken to mend clothes
das Haus/den Zaun/das Boot streichen to paint the house/the fence/the boat
(den) Rasen mähen to mow the lawn
(die) Bäume beschneiden/pflanzen/fällen to prune/to plant/to cut trees
die Hecke schneiden to trim the hedge
(das) Unkraut jäten to pull out weeds
(das) Holz sägen/spalten/hacken to saw/to split/to chop wood
(den) Schnee fegen (kehren)/schippen to sweep/to shovel snow

chapter 10

SPORTS

das Ballonfahren ballooning
das Boxen boxing
das Fallschirmspringen parachute jumping
fechten to fence
Freiübungen gymnastics
das Gewichtheben weightlifting
das Jagen hunting
das Kegeln bowling
die Leichtathletik track and field
der Radsport bicycling
das Ringen wrestling
rudern to row
das Schießen shooting
das Segelfliegen glider flying

chapter 11

SMALL SPECIALTY SHOPS

die Apotheke   pharmacy
das Blumengeschäft   florist
die Chemische Reinigung   dry cleaner
die Drogerie   drugstore
das Eisenwarengeschäft   hardware store
das Elektrogeschäft   appliance store
das Feinkostgeschäft   delicatessen
das Fotogeschäft   camera store
der Juwelier   jeweler
der Klempner (Spengler)   plumber
die Konditorei   coffee and pastry shop
das Milchgeschäft   dairy store
der Optiker   optician
das Papiergeschäft   stationery
das Sportgeschäft (Sportausrüstungen)
   sporting goods store (sporting goods)

chapter 12

BREAKFAST FOODS

der Honig   honey
der Joghurt   yogurt
die Margarine   margarine
der Orangensaft   orange juice
der Tomatensaft   tomato juice
das Graubrot   light rye bread
der Pumpernickel   pumpernickel bread
das Schwarzbrot   dark rye bread
das Vollkornbrot   coarse whole grain bread
das Weißbrot   white bread

LUNCH FOODS

die Erbsensuppe   pea soup
die Fruchtsuppe (kalt)   fruit soup (cold)
die Kartoffelsuppe   potato soup
der Bratfisch   fried fish
das Fischfilet   filet of fish
der Kochfisch   boiled fish
der Bohnensalat   bean salad
der gemischte Salat   tossed salad
der grüne Salat   lettuce salad
die Ente   duck
die Gans   goose
die Leber   liver
die Nieren   kidneys
das Reh   venison

die Kasseler Rippchen   smoked pork chops
die Roulade   beef rolls filled with bacon
Königsberger Klopse   meatballs
die Schweinshaxe   pigs feet
die Klöße *(pl.)*/**Knödel** *(pl.)*   dumplings
die Kartoffelknödel *(pl.)*   potato dumplings
die Leberknödel *(pl.)*   liver dumplings
die Dampfnudeln *(pl.)*   steamed dumplings
die Spätzle *(pl.)*   noodles
das Sauerkraut   sauerkraut
die Pilze *(pl.)*   mushrooms
der Rotkohl   red cabbage
der Spargel   asparagus
die Zwiebel   onion

SUPPER FOODS

das Beefsteak Tartar   spiced, raw ground beef
der Räucherfisch   smoked fish
der Speck   bacon
der Quark   cream cheese
der Schnittkäse   sliced cheese
der Streichkäse   spreadable cheese

DESSERTS

das Kompott   stewed fruit
die Melone   melon
die Schokoladencreme   chocolate mousse
der Stachelbeerpudding   gooseberry pudding
die Zitronencreme   lemon mousse

TABLE SETTING

das Besteck   flatware
der Eierbecher   egg cup
der Eßlöffel   tablespoon
das Gedeck   table setting
die Kaffeekanne/die Teekanne   coffee pot/
   teapot
das Milchkännchen   milk pitcher
die Schüssel   bowl
die Serviette   napkin
der Teelöffel   teaspoon
der Teller   plate
die Tortenplatte   cake plate
die Untertasse   saucer
die Zuckerdose   sugarbowl

chapter 13

WEATHER EXPRESSIONS

der Wetterbericht weather report
die Wettervorhersage weather prediction
die Warmfront warm front
die Kaltfront cold front
der Niederschlag precipitation
der Schneefall snowfall
der Hagel hail
der Landregen all-day rain
das Schauer shower
der Nieselregen (Sprühregen) drizzle
der Luftdruck air pressure
das Gewitter thunderstorm
der Blitz/der Donner lightning/thunder
die Windrichtung wind direction
es gießt (in Strömen) it's pouring
es regnet Bindfäden it's raining cats and dogs
es ist naßkalt it's damp and cold
neblig (der Nebel) foggy (fog)
sonnig sunny
schwül humid
eisig icy cold
wolkenlos cloudless
heiter fair
bedeckt overcast

GEOGRAPHICAL TERMS

die Anhöhe (der Hügel) hill
der Atlantik Atlantic
der Bach brook
der Berg mountain
das Bundesland (federal) state
der Bundesstaat (American) state
die Ebbe, die Flut low tide, high tide
der Fluß river
das Gebirge mountain range
der Gipfel peak
der Gletscher glacier
die Hauptstadt capital
die Insel island
der Kanal canal; channel
die Küste coast
das Meer sea
der Pazifik Pacific
der Strand beach
das Tal valley
der Teich pond
das Ufer shore
der Wald woods
die Wiese meadow

chapter 14

MODES OF TRANSPORTATION

der Pferdewagen horse-drawn wagon
die Kutsche carriage
der LKW (= Lastkraftwagen) truck
der PKW (= Personenkraftwagen) passenger car
der Anhänger trailer
die Eisenbahn train, railway
der Güterzug freight train
die Bergbahn mountain railway; cable car
die Fähre ferry
der Schleppkahn barge
das Boot boat
das Ruderboot rowboat
das Segelboot sailboat
das Motorboot motor boat
das Segelschiff sailing ship
der Tanker tanker
das Containerschiff container ship
der Frachter freighter
der Passagierdampfer passenger ship
das Propellerflugzeug propeller plane
der Jet jet
der Hubschrauber helicopter
das Segelflugzeug glider plane

PARTS OF A BICYCLE

die Handbremse hand brake
die Kette chain
die Klingel (Glocke) bell
die Lampe headlight
der Lenker handlebar
die Luftpumpe air pump
das Pedal pedal
das (Vorder-, Hinter-) Rad (front, back) wheel
der Rahmen frame
der Reifen tire
der Sattel seat
das Schloß lock
der Schlüssel key

PARTS OF A CAR

die Batterie   battery
der Blinker   turn signal
die Bremse (das Bremspedal)   brake (pedal)
das Gas (das Gaspedal)   gas (pedal)
die Handbremse   hand brake
der Kofferraum   trunk
der Kotflügel   fender
der Kühler   radiator
die Kupplung (das Kupplungspedal)   clutch (pedal)
das Lenkrad   steering wheel
die Motorhaube   hood
der Rückspiegel   rear-view mirror
der Scheibenwischer   windshield wiper
der Scheinwerfer   headlight
der Sitz   seat
die Stoßstange   bumper
die Wasserpumpe   water pump
die Windschutzscheibe   windshield
die Zündkerze   spark plug

chapter 15

LANDMARKS

die Autobahnauffahrt, die Autobahnausfahrt   expressway on-ramp, off-ramp
die Bahnlinie   railroad (tracks)
der Bauernhof   farm
die Brücke   bridge
die Bundesstraße   federal highway
die Burg   fortress
das Denkmal   monument
das Dorf   village
die Fabrik   factory
der Flugplatz   airport
der Friedhof   cemetery
der Funkturm   radio and TV tower
der Fußweg   footpath
die Kapelle   chapel
das Kloster   monastery
die Mühle   mill
die Ruine   ruin
das Schloß   castle
der Tunnel   tunnel

ASKING DIRECTIONS

Wo ist [der Bahnhof]?   Where is the [train station]?
Wie weit ist es [zum Bahnhof]? nach [Stuttgart]?   How far is it [to the train station]? to [Stuttgart]?
Wie komme ich am schnellsten [zum Bahnhof]?   What is the quickest way [to the train station]?
Wo ist hier in der Nähe [ein Café]?   Is there [a café] around here?
Wissen Sie den Weg nach [Oberndorf]?   Do you know the way to [Oberndorf]?
Wir wollen nach [Stuttgart]. Wie fahren wir am besten?   We're going to [Stuttgart]. What is the best route?
Wo geht's hier [zum Bahnhof]?   How do you get [to the train station] from here?
Wir wollen nach [München]. Müssen/Können wir über [Augsburg] fahren?   We're going to [Munich]. Must/can we go by way of [Augsburg]?
Was ist näher? Ist das näher?   What is closer? Is that closer?

GIVING DIRECTIONS

Sind Sie zu Fuß oder mit dem Auto?   Are you walking or driving?
Da nehmen Sie am besten [ein Taxi, die Bahn].   It's best if you take [a taxi, the streetcar].
Da fahren Sie am besten mit [der U-Bahn].   It's best if you go by [subway].
Nehmen Sie die [Drei].   Take number [three].
[Dort/An der Ecke/An der Kreuzung] ist die Haltestelle.   The stop is [over there/on the corner/at the intersection].
[Zum Bahnhof] sind es [zehn Minuten].   It's [ten minutes] to the [train station].
An der [ersten/zweiten] Kreuzung gehen Sie [rechts].   At the [first/second] intersection turn [right].
Gehen Sie die [erste] Straße [rechts]!   Take the [first] street [to the right].
Gehen Sie [am See/an der Mauer] entlang!   Go along [the lake/the wall].
Fahren Sie um [die Kirche] herum!   Drive around [the church].
Lassen Sie [die Kirche] links liegen!   Keep [the church] on your left.

Supplementary expressions

1. **EXPRESSING SKEPTICISM**

rede keinen Unsinn/Stuß
ist das dein Ernst?
meinst du? wirklich? meinst du das wirklich?
das ist ja komisch/eigenartig
irgendetwas stimmt hier nicht
ist das wahr?
wer sagt das? wer hat das gesagt?
woher weißt du das? wo/von wem hast du das gehört?

2. **EXPRESSING INSECURITY OR DOUBT**

das ist unwahrscheinlich
es ist unwahrscheinlich, daß ... [sie das gesagt hat]
das ist zweifelhaft
ich glaube nicht, daß ... [er das gesagt hat]
ich glaube das nicht
das kann nicht sein

3. **EXPRESSING ANNOYANCE**

Quatsch; Unsinn; Blödsinn
Blödmann; Dussel; Idiot
der hat/du hast wohl nicht alle Tassen im Schrank
bei der/bei dir ist wohl eine Schraube los
hör mal
geh
also, wissen Sie; wirklich; tsk, tsk, tsk
(das ist doch) nicht zu glauben
(das ist) unerhört/unglaublich
(das ist eine) Schweinerei
das tut/sagt man nicht
das kannst du doch nicht machen/sagen

4. **STALLING FOR TIME**

also; na ja; ja nun
hmmmmmm
laß mich mal nachdenken
darüber muß ich (erst mal) nachdenken
das kann ich so (auch) nicht sagen

5. **BEING NONCOMMITTAL**

(das ist ja) interessant
hmmmmmm
wirklich?

6. **EXPRESSING GOOD WISHES**

ich halte (dir/Ihnen) die Daumen
Gesundheit
(ich wünsche) guten Appetit/gesegnete Mahlzeit
Prost; auf Ihr/dein Wohl; zum Wohl
herzlichen Glückwunsch
ich wünsche dir/Ihnen gute Reise
                        gute Besserung
                        viel Glück
                        viel Vergnügen/Spaß
                        alles Gute

7. **COURTESY EXPRESSIONS**

bitte (sehr/schön)
danke (sehr/schön)

8. **SAYING "YOU'RE WELCOME"**

bitte (sehr/schön)
gern geschehen
nichts zu danken

9. **EXPRESSING SURPRISE**

ach nein
(wie) ist das (nur) möglich?
das hätte ich nicht gedacht
das ist ja prima/toll/klasse
ich werd' verrückt
(das ist ja) nicht zu glauben
ich bin von 'n Socken

10. EXPRESSING AGREEMENT (AND DISAGREEMENT)

natürlich (nicht); selbstverständlich (nicht)
warum denn nicht?
das kann (nicht) sein
(das) stimmt (nicht); richtig/falsch
das finde ich auch/nicht
genau; eben

11. RESPONDING TO REQUESTS

bitte; selbstverständlich; natürlich
gern; machen wir; mit Vergnügen
(es tut mir leid, aber) das geht nicht
ich kann (das) nicht . . . [reparieren]
das habe ich nicht
das ist zu schwer/groß/teuer

12. EXPRESSING REGRET

das tut mir leid
es tut mir leid, daß . . . [ich nicht kommen kann]
leider . . . [kann ich morgen nicht]
es geht leider nicht
unglücklicherweise . . . [war ich gestern nicht zu Hause]

13. EXCUSING ONESELF

Entschuldigung; Pardon; Verzeihung; entschuldigen Sie
entschuldigen Sie bitte, daß . . . [ich erst jetzt komme]
hier ist meine Entschuldigung
meine Mutter hat mir eine Entschuldigung geschrieben
das ist keine Entschuldigung

14. EXPRESSING INDIFFERENCE

das ist mir egal
es ist mir egal, ob . . . [er kommt]
das macht mir nichts aus
es macht mir nichts aus, daß . . . [sie mehr verdient]
das ist mir wurscht
das kannst du machen, wie du willst
das kannst du halten wie ein Dachdecker
so kann man das auch machen/sagen
ich habe nichts dagegen

15. EXPRESSING ADMIRATION

ach, wie schön; dufte; klasse
erstklassig; ausgezeichnet
das ist aber nett (von dir, Ihnen, *etc.*)
der/die ist nett
das sind nette Leute

16. EXPRESSING JOY AND PLEASURE

wir freuen uns
wir freuen uns auf ihn/seinen Besuch/die Ferien
wir sind froh
wir sind froh (darüber), daß . . . [er wieder arbeitet]
es freut mich, daß . . . [sie gekommen ist]
das tun/kochen/essen wir gern
das macht mir/uns Spaß
das machen wir zum Vergnügen

17. MAKING REQUESTS

hätten Sie Lust . . . [mitzukommen]?
hätten Sie Zeit, . . . [uns zu besuchen]?
hätten Sie etwas [Zeit] für mich?
ich hätte gern . . . [ein Pfund Äpfel]
könnten Sie . . . [mein Auto reparieren]?
würden Sie bitte . . . [um zehn Uhr hier sein]?
hätten Sie etwas dagegen?
hätten Sie etwas dagegen, wenn . . . [ich mitkomme]?
dürfte ich . . . [ein Stück Kuchen haben]?
macht es Ihnen etwas aus?
macht es Ihnen etwas aus, wenn . . . [mein Bruder mitkommt]?
würden Sie so freundlich sein und . . . [den Brief schreiben]?
ich möchte fragen, ob [ich mitkommen] darf/kann?
könnte ich . . . [um neun Uhr zu Ihnen kommen]?

18. ASKING FOR FAVORS

könntest du mir einen Gefallen tun und . . . [mich mitnehmen]?
ich hätte eine Bitte: könntest/würdest du . . . [mich mitnehmen]?

19. MAKING SURMISES

ich denke ja; ich glaube schon
ich glaube (schon), daß ... [sie das gesagt hat]
das dürfte/könnte wahr/richtig sein
wahrscheinlich; wahrscheinlich [stimmt das]
sicher; ich bin sicher; ich bin ziemlich sicher, daß
    ... [er das gesagt hat]
ich nehme (das) an; ich nehme das (nur) an
ich nehme an, daß ... [das stimmt]
das scheint ... [nicht zu stimmen]

20. EXPRESSING EXPECTATION

hoffentlich; hoffentlich ... [kommt sie]
ich hoffe (es) (sehr)
ich hoffe, daß ... [sie das Paket bekommen hat]
ich freue mich auf ... [die Ferien]

21. EXPRESSING FEARS

ich fürchte, daß ... [sie nicht kommt]
ich habe Angst
ich habe Angst, ... [nach Hause zu gehen]
davor habe ich Angst
ich habe Angst vor ... [dem Hund]
[ich bleibe] lieber [hier]

22. GIVING ADVICE

ich schlage vor, daß ... [wir um acht anfangen]
ich rate dir, ... [zu Hause zu bleiben]
das würde ich dir (nicht) raten
das würde ich machen/sagen
das würde ich anders/so machen
das mußt du so machen
ich zeige dir, ... [wie man das macht]

23. CORRECTING MISUNDERSTANDINGS

das habe ich nicht so gemeint
das habe ich nur aus Spaß gesagt
das war doch nicht so gemeint
das war nicht mein Ernst

German-English vocabulary

The German-English vocabulary contains the basic words and expressions listed in the chapter vocabularies, plus words that occur in headings, captions, cultural notes, and reading material. The symbol ~ signifies the key word (minus the definite article, if any) for that entry. For example, **guten** ~ ! under **Abend** means **guten Abend!** The numbers in italics following the definitions refer to the chapters in which the active words are introduced.

Nouns are listed with their plural forms: **der Abend, -e**. No plural entry is given if the plural is rarely used or non-existent. Both the dative and the plural endings are given for special **der-**nouns: **der Herr, -n, -en**.

Strong and irregular weak verbs are listed with their principal parts. Vowel changes in the present tense are noted in parentheses, followed by the past participle forms. All verbs take **haben** in the past participle unless indicated with **sein**. For example: **fahren (ä; ist gefahren)**. Separable-prefix verbs are indicated with a raised dot: **auf·stehen**.

Adjectives and adverbs that take umlaut in the comparative are noted: **warm (ä)**.

ab·biegen (ist abgebogen)   to make a turn, *15*
der Abend, -e   evening; **guten** ~ !   good evening! *1;* **zu** ~ **essen**   to have supper, *12*
das Abendessen   supper, *12;* **zum** ~   for supper, *12*
abends   evenings, in the evening, *4*
die Abendvorstellung   evening performance
aber   *flavoring word with the meaning of* really, certainly, *2; (coord. conj.)* but; however, *3*
ab·holen   to call for, to pick up, *9*
ab·räumen   to clear, to remove, *9*
ab·stauben   to dust, *9*
das Abteil   (train) compartment
ab·trocknen   to dry up, to wipe dry, *9*
ach   oh, *6;* ~ **so**   oh, I see! *2*
acht   eight, *2*
achtzehn   eighteen, *2*
achtzig   eighty, *4*
adieu   good-by
alle   all, everyone, *9*
allein   alone, *11*
alles   all, everything, *7;* ~ **Gute (zum Geburtstag)**   all the best (on your birthday)
das Alphabet   alphabet
als   than, *9;* as, *12*
also   well, *8*
alt (ä)   old, *2*
am (= an dem)   in the; ~ **Samstag**   on Saturday, *4*

(das) Amerika   America
amerikanisch   American, *13*
die Ampel, -n   traffic signal, *15*
an (+ *acc. or dat.***)**   at, *7;* to
ander   other
ändern   to change
anders   different, *13*
an·machen   to switch on (*the light*), *8*
an·rufen (angerufen)   to call, to telephone, *10*
die Ansichtskarte, -n   picture postcard, *8*
der Anzug, ¨e   man's suit, *5*
der Apfel, ¨   apple, *11;* **der Apfelkuchen**   cake topped with sliced apples
die Apotheke, -n   pharmacy
der Apotheker, -/die Apothekerin, -nen   pharmacist, *4*
der Appetit: guten ~ !   enjoy your meal, *12*
der April   April, *2*
die Arbeit, -en   work, *9*
arbeiten   to work, *4*
der Arbeiter, -/die Arbeiterin, -nen   worker, *4*
der Arzt, ¨e/die Ärztin, -nen   doctor, physician, *4*
der Atlantische Ozean   Atlantic Ocean, *13*
auch   also, too, *1*
auf (+ *acc. or dat.***)**   on; at; ~ **eine Party gehen**   to go to a party, *10*
die Aufgabe, -n   homework, lesson
auf·hängen   to hang up

370   german today, one

auf·machen to open, 8
auf·räumen to put in order, 9
auf·stehen (ist aufgestanden) to get up, 8
das Auge, –n eye
der August August, 2
aus (+*dat.*) out of, from, 15
ausgezeichnet excellent, 12
aus·machen to turn off (*the light*), 8
außer (+ *dat.*) besides, except for, 15
die Aussprache pronunciation
der Ausverkauf clearance sale
ausverkauft sold out, 7
das Auto, –s car, 8
die Autobahn, –en expressway, 14

backen (ä; gebacken) to bake, 9
der Bäcker, –/die Bäckerin, –nen baker, 11
das Badezimmer, – bathroom, 9
die Bahn, –en train, railway, 15
der Bahnhof, ¨e train station, 15
bald soon, 4
der Ball, ¨e ball
die Banane, –n banana, 11
die Band, –s band, 7
die Bank, –en bank, 15
der Basketball, ¨e basketball, 3
basteln to tinker (with), to work at a hobby, 9
die Baustelle construction site
Bayern Bavaria, 15
die Bedienung service
beginnen (begonnen) to start, to begin, 7
bei (+ *dat.*) at, 7; near; with; **beim = bei dem**
beide both, 2
das Beispiel, –e example; **zum ~** (*abbr* **z.B.**) for example
bekommen (bekommen) to get, to receive, 7; **ich bekomme frei** I'll get (the day) off, 7
das Benzin gasoline, 14
bergsteigen gehen to go mountain-climbing, 10
der Bericht, –e report, 13
der Beruf, –e occupation, profession
beschreiben (beschrieben) to describe, 14
besonder special; **besonders** particularly, especially, 13
besser (*comp. of* **gut**) better, 13
bestehen (bestanden): die Prüfung ~ to pass a test, 14
bestellen to order, 12

bestimmt certain(ly)
der Besuch, –e visit, 15; guest, company
besuchen to visit, 11
bewölkt cloudy, overcast, 13
bezahlen to pay, 11
das Bier beer, 12
der Bierdeckel, – coaster (*used under a glass*), 8
billig inexpensive, cheap, 5
die Biologie biology, 6; **die Bio** bio, 6
bis till, until, 4; **~ später** till later, see you later, 1; **~ zu** up to, 15
bitte please; you're welcome, ; **~ schön** please; you're very welcome, 7; **~ sehr** certainly, 12
blau blue, 5
bleiben (ist geblieben) to remain, to stay, 3
der Bleistift, –e (*abbr.* **der Stift**) pencil, 6
der Blick, –e view
die Bluse, –n blouse, 5
der Braten, – roast
brauchen to need, 5
braun brown, 5; **ein Mantel in Braun** a brown coat, 5
die BRD (*abbr. for* **Bundesrepublik Deutschland**) Federal Republic of Germany
der Brei porridge
die Breite width
die Bremse, –n brake, 14
der Brief, –e letter, 4
der Brieffreund, –e/Brieffreundin, –nen pen pal, 4
die Briefmarke, –n postage stamp, 8
bringen (gebracht) to bring, 12
das Brot, –e (loaf of) bread, 11; sandwich
das Brötchen, – hard roll, 12
der Bruder, ¨ brother, 4
der Brunnen, – fountain, well; spring, 15
das Buch, ¨er book, 6
die Buchhandlung, –en bookstore
bummeln (ist gebummelt) to go for a stroll, to take a walk, 15
die Bundesrepublik Deutschland Federal Republic of Germany
der Bus, –se bus, 14
die Butter butter, 11

das Café, –s café, coffee shop, 8
das Camping camping, 10
die Cassette, –n cassette, 8

der Cassetten-Recorder, - cassette recorder, 8
Celsius Celsius
die Chemie chemistry, 6; **die Chemieaufgabe** chemistry homework, 6
der Club, -s club, 15
die (also **das**) **Cola** cola drink, 12

da here, there, 5; then, 13
das Dach, ¨-er roof
die Dame, -n lady, woman, 5
der Dank thanks; **vielen ~ !** many thanks! 12
danke thanks, thank you, 1
dann then, 7
das that, the, 5
daß (sub. conj.) that, 13
der Daumen, - thumb; **halt mir die ~** cross your fingers for me (literally: hold your thumbs for me), 14
die DDR (abbr. for **Deutsche Demokratische Republik**) German Democratic Republic
decken to set (the table), 9
dein your (fam. sg.), 4
denken (gedacht) to think, 13
denn flavoring word often used in questions, 1; (coord. conj.) for, because, 11
der the, 5
(das) Deutsch German (language), 4
deutsch German (adj.)
die Deutsche Demokratische Republik German Democratic Republic
(das) Deutschland Germany
der Dezember December, 2
dich (acc. of **du**) you, 10
dick fat, thick, 6
die the, 5
der Dienstag Tuesday, 6
dieser this, 6
das Ding, -e thing
die Disco, -s disco, discothèque, 8
die Diskussion, -en discussion, debate, 14
doch flavoring word used to persuade or to imply agreement, 8; yes (in response to a negative statement or question), 9
der Donnerstag Thursday, 4
doof goofy, dumb, stupid, 4
dort there, 11
drei three, 2
dreißig thirty, 4
dreizehn thirteen, 2
du you (fam. sg.), 1
dumm(ü) dumb, stupid, 7
dünn thin, 4
durch (+ acc.) through, 11
durch·fallen (ä; ist durchgefallen) to fail, to flunk, 14
dürfen (darf) may, to be permitted to, 7; **was darf es sein?** what would you like?, 11
der Durst thirst, 12; **~ haben** to be thirsty, 12

die Ecke, -n corner, 15
Ehrenwort! honest! on my honor! 9
das Ei, -er egg, 11; **weichgekochtes ~** soft-boiled egg
eifersüchtig jealous, 14
eigentlich really, actually, 8
der Eimer, - pail, 9
ein a, an, 5
einfach simple, simply, 7
ein·fallen (ä; ist eingefallen) to occur to; **da fällt mir gerade ein** it just occurs to me, 15
ein·kaufen to shop, 8; **~ gehen** to go shopping, 8
die Einkaufstasche, -n shopping bag, 11
ein·laden (ä; eingeladen) to invite, 9
einmal once, for once; **noch ~** once again
ein·packen to pack, 11
eins one, 2
der Eintritt admissron
das Eis ice cream; ice, 12
der Elektriker, -/die Elektrikerin, -nen electrician, 4
elf eleven, 2
die Eltern (pl.) parents, 9
empfehlen (ie; empfohlen) to recommend, 12
das Ende end
endlich finally, 13
(das) Englisch English (language), 6
die Ente, -n duck; **eine lahme ~** a dull, boring person, 8
entlang along; **die Straße ~** along (down) the street, 15
die Entschuldigung, -en excuse; **Entschuldigung!** excuse me, sorry, 11
er he, 1
die Erbse, -n pea, 11
die Erdbeere, -n strawberry, 11

hinein in; into
das Hobby, -s hobby, 4
hoch (höher) high, 10; **wie ~ haben sie gewonnen?** by how much did they win? 10
hoffentlich I hope, let's hope, 4
höher (*comp. of* **hoch**) higher, 13
hören to hear, 4
die Hose, -n pants, slacks, 5
hübsch pretty, nice, 5
das Huhn, ⁻er chicken, 12
der Hund, -e dog, 9
hundert hundred, 4
der Hunger hunger, 12; **~ haben** to be hungry, 12

ich I, 1
ihn (*acc. of* **er**) him, 10
ihr you (*fam. pl.*), 2; her, its; their, 4
Ihr your (*formal*), 7
im = in dem in, 2
immer always, 8; **~ geradeaus** straight ahead, 15
in in(to), 3
interessant interesting, 6

ja yes, 1; *flavoring word confirming that what is said is self-evident,* 6; **~, und wie!** sure, I do (I am), 7
die Jacke, -n suit coat, jacket, 5
das Jahr, -e year, 4
die Jahreszeit, -en season, time of year, 13
der Januar January, 2
die Jeans (*pl.*) jeans, 5
jeder each; everyone, 9; *pl.* **alle** all
jemand someone, 15
jetzt now, 3
der Job, -s job
das Jugendzentrum youth center, club, 7
der Juli July, 2
jung (ü) young, 2
der Junge, -n, -n boy, 5
der Juni June, 2

der Kaffee coffee, 9; **~ kochen** to make coffee, 9; **~ trinken** to drink coffee (*with breakfast or with afternoon pastries*), 9; **zum ~ einladen** to invite for coffee and cake, 9
kalt (ä) cold, 13

kaputt broken, out of order, exhausted, 1
die Karotte, -n carrot, 11
die Karte, -n ticket, 7; postcard, menu; (*pl.*) (playing) cards, 4; **~ zu drei Mark** tickets at three marks, 7
die Kartoffel, -n potato, 11
das Kartoffelpüree mashed potatoes, 12
der Käse cheese, 11
die Kasse box office, 7; cashier
die Katze, -n cat, 9
kaufen to buy, 5
kein not a, not any, 5
kennen (gekannt) to know, to be acquainted with, 10
die Keramik ceramics, pottery, 8
das Kilo(gramm) kilogram, 11
der Kilometer, - kilometer, 3
das Kind, -er child, 4
das Kino, -s movie theater, 7
die Kirche, -n church, 15
klar clear; **~!** sure! of course! 6
die Klarinette, -n clarinet, 3
klasse! terrific! 5
die Klasse, -n grade, class, 6
die Klassenarbeit test
die Klassenfahrt, -en class trip, 15
das Klassenzimmer, - classroom, 6
klassisch classical, 4
das Klavier, -e piano, 3
die Klavierstunde piano lesson
das Kleid, -er dress, 5; (*pl.*) clothes
die Kleidung clothing
klein small, short, little, 4
die Kneipe, -n pub, tavern
der Koch, ⁻e/die Köchin, -nen cook
kochen to cook, 4
die Kohle, -n coal
kommen (ist gekommen) to come, 4
kompliziert complicated, 8
die Konfektionsgröße, -n clothing size
können (kann) can, to be able to, 7
das Konzert, -e concert, 7
kosten to cost, 5
krank ill, sick, 1
die Krawatte, -n necktie, 5
kreuzen to cross
die Kreuzung, -en intersection, 15
der Kuchen, - cake, 11
der Kugelschreiber, - (*abbr.* **der Kuli, -s**) ballpoint pen, 6

kühl cool, 13
die Kultur culture
der Kunde, -n, -n/die Kundin, -nen customer, client, 11
die Kunst art, 6
der Kurs, -e course, 14
kurz (ü) short, 6
die Kurzarbeit quiz
die Kürze brevity

lachen to laugh
lahm lame; **eine lahme Ente** a dull, boring person, 9
lang (ä) long, 6
lange (*adv.*) long; **wie ~?** how long? 12
die Langeweile boredom, 8; **ich habe~** I am bored, 8
langsam slow(ly), 14
langweilig boring, 6
(das) Latein Latin (language), 6
laufen (äu; ist gelaufen) to run; to walk, 10
die Lebensmittel (*pl.*) food, groceries, 11
der Lehrer, -/die Lehrerin, -nen teacher, 4
leicht easy, light, 6
leid: das tut mir ~ I'm sorry, 1
leider unfortunately, 5
lernen to learn, to study, 4
lesen (ie; gelesen) to read, 8
das Lesestück, -e reading selection
letzt last, 9
die Leute (*pl.*) people
das Licht, -er light, 8
lieber (*comp.* of **gern**) rather, 13; **~haben** to like better, to prefer, 13; **ich esse ~ ...** I prefer to eat ..., 12
lieber/liebe dear (*opening in letters*), 4
das Lieblingsfach, ̈-er favorite subject, 6
liegen (gelegen) to lie, to be (situated), 13
die Limo(nade) soft drink, 12
links (to the) left, 15
der Liter, - liter, 11; **1 ~ auf 10 Kilometer** 10 kilometers to the liter, 14
die Litfaßsäule, -n poster column
der Löffel, - spoon
das Lokal, -e place to eat, drink, dance; restaurant, 15
los: was ist~? What's the matter? 1; **es ist viel~** there is a lot going on, 15

los·gehen (ist losgegangen) to go, to take off, 10; **wann geht's los?** when does it start? 10
die Lust pleasure, enjoyment; **~haben** to feel like doing something, 7; **er hat zu nichts~** he doesn't feel like doing anything, 8

machen to do, to make, 3; **das macht Spaß** that's fun, 4; **das macht zusammen 10 Mark** that comes to 10 marks, 11
das Mädchen, - girl, 5
der Mai May, 2
das Mal time, occasion, 10; **nächstes~** next time, 10
mal times, 2; *flavoring word that leaves the time indefinite and softens a command,* 7
man (*indef. pronoun*) one, you, they, people, 11
mancher some, several, 12
manchmal sometimes, 12
der Mann, ̈-er man, 5; husband
der Mantel, ̈- coat, 5
die Mappe, -n briefcase, book bag, 6
die Mark basic German monetary unit (**DM = Deutsche Mark = 100 Pfennig**), 5
der Markt, ̈-e market, 11; **auf dem~** at the open-air market, 11
die Marmelade jam, 12
der März March, 2
die Mathematik mathematics, 6; **die Mathe** math, 6
die Maus, ̈-e mouse
mehr more, 7
die Meile, -n mile
mein my, 4
meinen to think; to mean, 5
der Mensch, -en, -en man, human being; **Mensch!** wow! brother! oh, boy! 6
das Messer, - knife
der Meter, - meter, 4
der Metzger, -/die Metzgerin, -nen butcher, 11
mich (*acc. of* **ich**) me, 10
die Milch milk, 11
das Mineralwasser mineral water, 12
die Minute, -n minute, 3
mit (+ *dat.*) with; **~dem Bus fahren** to go by bus, 14
mit·kommen (ist mitgekommen) to come along, 8

mit·nehmen (nimmt mit; mitgenommen) to take along, 13
der Mittag noon, 12; **zu ~ essen** to have lunch, 12
das Mittagessen warm noon meal, lunch, 12; **zum~** for the noon meal, 12
mittags at noon, at lunch time, 12
der Mittwoch Wednesday, 6
die Möbel (*pl.*) furniture, 9
möchte (*form of* **mögen**) would like to, 7
das Mofa, -s moped, motorbike, 14
mögen (mag) to like; **möchte** would like to, 7
der Moment moment; **einen~** just a moment, 11; **~mal** just a moment, 15
der Monat, -e month, 2
der Montag Monday, 4
der Morgen, - morning; **guten~!** good morning! 1
morgen tomorrow, 7; **~abend** tomorrow evening, 7; **~früh** tomorrow morning
morgens in the morning
das Motorrad, ̈er motorcycle, 14
müde tired, 1
der Müll garbage, 9
der Mülleimer garbage pail, 9
das Museum (*pl.* **Museen**) museum, 15
die Musik music, 4
musikalisch musical, 4
die Musikbox juke box
das Musikinstrument, -e musical instrument, 3
müssen (muß) to have to, must, 7
die Mutter, ̈ mother, 4

na well, 10; **~und?** so what?, 10
nach (+ *dat.*) after; to (*with cities or countries*), 15; **~Hause** home (*direction*), 3
der Nachmittag, -e afternoon; **am~** in the afternoon, 6
nachmittags in the afternoon, 12
nächst next, 10; **nächstes Mal** next time, 10
die Nacht, ̈e night; **gute~!** good night! 1
der Nachtisch dessert, 12
der Name, -n (*acc. and dat.***-n**) name, 4
nämlich namely, you know, 11
naß wet, 13
natürlich naturally, of course, 2
nehmen (nimmt, genommen) to take, 7
nein no, 1

nennen (genannt) to name, to call, 9
nett nice, 11
neu new, 5
neun nine, 9
neunzehn nineteen, 2
neunzig ninety, 4
nicht not, 1; **nicht?=nicht wahr?** isn't that so! isn't that right? 2; **~nur... sondern auch** not only... but also, 12
nichts nothing, 7; **~mehr** nothing left, 7
niemand no one, 14
noch still, yet, 4; **~nicht** not yet, 7
der Norden north, 13
nördlich (von) northern, north (of), 13
der November November, 2
null zero, 2
nun now, 8
nur only, just, 1

ob (*sub, conj.*) if, whether, 13
der Ober, - waiter, 12
das Obst fruit, 11
oder (*coord, conj.*) or, 2
oft (ö) often, 3
ohne (+ *acc.*) without, 11
der Oktober October, 2
die Orange, -n orange, 11
der Osten east, 13
(das) Österreich Austria
östlich (von) eastern, east (of)

paar: ein~ a few, some, 7
packen to pack, 11
das Papier, -e paper, 6; (*pl.*) papers, documents
der Park, -s park, 15
die Party, -s party, 10
passen to fit; to match, 5
die Pause, -n break; intermission, 6
Pech: so ein~ what bad luck, how unfortunate, 15
der Pfannkuchen pancake
der Pfennig, -e (*abbr.* **Pf**) German monetary unit: **1 Pf = 1/100 Mark**, 11
das Pfund (*abbr.* **Pfd.**) pound (**1 Pfd. = 500 g**), 11
die Physik physics, 6
das Picknick, -s picnic, 10
die Pille, -n pill

die Pinte, -n   pub
der Plan, ⸚e   plan; schedule, 6
die Platte, -n   record, 8
der Plattenspieler, -   record player, turntable, 8
der Platz, ⸚e   square, 15; seat
die Pommes frites (*pl.*)   French fries, 12
die Post   post office, mail, 15
das (*also* der) Poster, -   poster, 8
praktisch   practical, 14
preiswert   worth the money, reasonably priced, 5
prima   excellent, fine, great, 1
pro   per, 14
das Problem, -e   problem
die Prüfung, -en   exam, test, 14
der Pudding   pudding, 12
der Pulli, -s   pullover, 5
der Pullover   pullover
putzen   to clean, 9

Quatsch!   nonsense! rubbish! 10
das Quiz   quiz

das Rad, ⸚er   wheel; bicycle (*short for* das Fahrrad), 14
der Radfahrer   bicyclist
der Radiergummi, -s (*abbr.* der Gummi)   eraser, 6
das Radio, -s   radio, 8
der Radioamateur, -e   "ham" radio operator, 8
der Rappen   Swiss monetary unit (1/100 Franken)
das Rathaus, ⸚er   town hall, 15
raus·tragen (ä; rausgetragen)   to carry out, 9
recht: ~haben   to be right, 13
rechts   (to the) right, 15
das Reden   speaking
das Reformhaus   health food store
der Regen   rain, 13
der Regenmantel   raincoat
der Regenschirm, -e   umbrella, 13
regnen   to rain, 13
reiten (ist geritten)   to ride (horseback), 10
reparieren   to repair, 8
das Restaurant, -s   restaurant, 13
richtig   correct, right, 2
der Rindsbraten   roast beef, pot roast, 12
der Rock   rock (music), 4

der Rock, ⸚e   skirt, 5
rodeln (ist gerodelt)   to toboggan; to go sledding, 13
rot   red, 5
das Rührei   scrambled egg

die Sache, -n   thing; (*pl.*) clothes, 5
der Saft, ⸚e   juice, 11
sagen   to say, to tell, 8
der Salat, -e   (head of) lettuce, salad, 12
Salut   hello
die Sammelfreude, -n   joy of collecting
sammeln   to collect, 8
der Samstag   Saturday, 4; am~   on Saturday, 4
sarkastisch   sarcastic, 9
sauer   cross, annoyed; sour, 1
schade   too bad, 5
die Schallplatte, -n   record, 8
schauen   to look, 15
scheinen (geschienen)   to shine, 13; to seem 15; so scheint's   so it seems, 15
der Scherz   joke
der Schi, -er (*also* Ski)   ski, 10
das Schikjöring   Norwegian sport in which skier is pulled by horses or motorcycles
Schi laufen (äu)   to ski, 10
schick   chic, stylish, 5
das Schiff, -e   ship, 14
das Schild, -er   sign, 15
der Schilling   basic Austrian monetary unit
der Schinken   ham, 11
das Schinkenbrot, -e   ham sandwich, 12
schlafen (ä; geschlafen)   to sleep, 9
das Schlagzeug, -e   drums, 3
schlank   slender, slim, 4
schlecht   bad, 1
schließlich   after all
schlimm   bad, 6
der Schlittschuh, -e   ice skate, 10
Schlittschuh laufen (äu)   to ice-skate, 10
schmecken   to taste (good), 9
der Schnee   snow, 13
der Schneemann   snow man
schneien   to snow, 13
schnell   fast, 14
die Schokolade, -n   chocolate, hot chocolate; bar of chocolate, 12
schon   already, 2; das ~   that's true, 7
schön   beautiful, 5; nice, 4

schreiben (geschrieben) to write, 4
der Schuh, -e shoe, 5
die Schuhgröße shoe size
die Schule, -n school, 6
der Schüler, -/die Schülerin, -nen student (*in high school*), 4
schwarz (ä) black, 5
das Schweigen silence
das Schwein pig; ~ **haben** to be lucky, 14
das Schweinskotelett, -s pork chop, 11
die Schweiz Switzerland
schwer difficult, heavy, 6
die Schwester, -n sister, 4
schwimmen (ist geschwommen) to swim, 3
(das) Schwyzerdütsch Swiss German (language)
sechs six, 2
sechzehn sixteen, 2
sechzig sixty, 4
der See, -n lake, 14; **an den ~** to the lake, 14
segeln to sail, 10
sehen (ie; gesehen) to see, to watch, to look, 8
sehr very, 1
sein his, its, 4
sein (ist) to be, 1
seit (+ *dat.*) since, for, 15
selbst oneself, myself, *etc.*, 11
der Senf mustard
der September September, 2
Servus! hello (*in Austria*)
sicher sure, certain(ly), 7
sie she, 1; they, 2
Sie you (*formal*), 7
sieben seven, 2
siebzehn seventeen, 2
siebzig seventy, 4
das Silber silver
singen (gesungen) to sing, 4
der Sinn, -e sense; mind
so so, 1; ~ **... wie** as ... as, 11
die Socke, -n sock, 5
solcher such, 12
sollen (soll) should, to be supposed to, 7
der Sommer summer, 10
der Sommerschlußverkauf summer clearance sale
das Sonderangebot special offer
sondern (*coord. conj.*) but (on the contrary), 12
die Sonne sun, 13

der Sonnenschirm sunshade, parasol
der Sonntag Sunday, 4
sonst (noch) in addition; **was sonst?** what else? 3; ~ **noch was?** anything else? 11
Spaß: das macht ~ ! that's fun! 4
spät late; **zu ~** too late, tardy, 4; **wie ~ ist es?** what time is it? 6; **bis später** till later, see you later, 1
der Spatz, -en sparrow
spazieren to walk, to stroll, to go for a walk, 3
der Spaziergang, ¨e walk, stroll; **einen ~ machen** to go for a walk, 9
die Speisekarte, -n menu, 12
das Spiegelei fried egg
das Spiel, -e game, 10
der Spielautomat slot machine, pinball machine
spielen to play, 3
die Spielsache, -n toy, plaything
der Spinat spinach, 11
spinnen to spin; **du spinnst** you're crazy, 13
der Sport sport, 6; ~ **treiben** to be active in sports, 4
der Sportfreund sports fan
der Sportverein sports club
spottbillig dirt-cheap, 5
sprechen (i; gesprochen) to speak, 13
spülen to wash dishes, 9; to rinse
die Stadt, ¨e city, 8
der Stadtplan, ¨e city map, 15
der Stau, -s traffic jam
der Staub dust, 9; ~ **saugen** to vacuum, 9
stehen (gestanden) to stand, 15
die Stereoanlage, -n stereo system, 8
der Stiefel, - boot, 15
still still, quiet; calm
stimmen to be true, correct, 13; **das stimmt** that's right, 8
der Strandkorb, ¨e (canopied) beach chair
die Straße, -n street, 3
die Straßenbahn, -en streetcar, 14
stricken to knit
das Stück, -e piece, 11
der Student, -en, -en/die Studentin, -nen student (*at a university*), 15
die Stunde, -n hour; class, 6
der Stundenplan, ¨e class schedule, 6
suchen to look for, 15
der Süden south, 13
südlich (von) southern, south (of), 13

der Supermarkt, ⸚e supermarket, *11*
die Suppe, -n soup, *12*

der Tag, -e day; ~ ! hi, *1*; **guten ~!** hello! *1*
täglich daily
die Tankstelle, -n service station, gas station, *15*
tanzen to dance, *4*
die Tasche, -n bag; pocket
das Taschengeld pocket money, allowance
die Tasse, -n cup, *12*
die Taube, -n dove; pigeon
tausend thousand, *4*
der Tee tea, *12*
der Teig dough; batter
die Temperatur, -en temperature, *13*
das Tennis tennis, *3*
teuer expensive, *5*
das Theater, - theater, *7*
die Theaterkarte theater ticket
theoretisch theoretical
das Thermometer, - thermometer, *13*
tief deep
der Tisch, -e table, *9*
toll great, fantastic, *1*; crazy
die Tomate, -n tomato, *11*
das Tor, -e gate, *15*
die Torte, -n layer cake, *9*
die Tour, -en tour, trip, *14*
tragen (ä; getragen) to wear, *5*; to carry
der Traum, ⸚e dream, *14*
treiben: treibst du Sport? are you active in sports? *4*
der Trimm-dich-Pfad marked path for jogging and exercising
trinken (getrunken) to drink, *9*
trocken dry, *13*
tschüß! so long! (*informal*), *1*
tun (getan) to do, *7*
die Tür, -en door, *8*
die Tüte, -n bag, sack, *11*

die U-Bahn, -en subway, *14*
über (+ *acc. or dat.*) about, above, over, *13*
überall everywhere
übermorgen the day after tomorrow, *7*
die Übersicht summary

die Übung, -en exercise
die Uhr, -en clock, watch, *6*; **um wieviel ~ ?** at what time? *6*; **wieviel ~ ist es?** what time is it? *6*
um (+ *acc.*) at, around, *6*; ~ **ein Uhr** at one o'clock, *6*
unabhängig independent, *14*
und (*coord. conj.*) and, *1*
unentschieden undetermined; tied (*in scoring*), *10*
ungewöhnlich unusual
unglücklich unhappy, *1*
uns (*acc. of* **wir**) us, *10*
unser our, *4*
unsicher dangerous; unsure, insecure, *14*
Unsinn! nonsense! *1*
unter (+ *acc. or dat.*) under
der Unterricht lesson, instruction, *14*

der Vater, ⸚ father, *4*
das Verbot prohibition, ban
verderben (i; verdorben) to spoil
verdienen to earn
vergessen (i; vergessen) to forget, *15*
der Verkäufer, -/die Verkäuferin, -nen salesperson, *4*
das Verkehrszeichen, - traffic sign
verlieren (verloren) to lose, *10*
verstehen (verstanden) to understand, *8*
versuchen to try, *7*
viel (mehr) much, many, a lot, *3*; **vielen Dank!** thank you very much, *12*
vielleicht maybe, perhaps, *7*
vier four, *2*
das Viertel, - quarter, *6*
vierzehn fourteen, *2*
vierzig forty, *4*
die Vokabel, -n (vocabulary) word; (*pl.*) vocabulary
der Volleyball, ⸚e volleyball, *3*
von (+ *dat.*) from, *3*
vor (+ *acc. or dat.*) before, *6*; in front of
vor·haben to plan, *8*
die Vorstellung, -en performance, *7*
der VW (= Volkswagen) *14*

wahrscheinlich probably, *13*

wandern (ist gewandert) to hike, to go hiking, 3
das Wanderwetter hiking weather
wann when, 2
war (*past tense of* **sein**) was, 11
das Warenhaus, ¨er department store, 15
warm (ä) warm, 5
warum why, 1
was what, 1; ~ **ist (denn) los?** (well,) what's the matter?, 1; ~ **sonst?** what else? 3; ~ **für (ein)** what kind of (a), 14
die Wäsche laundry, 9
waschen (ä; gewaschen) to wash, 9
das Wasser water, 10
weil (*sub. conj.*) because, 15
der Wein, -e wine, 12
weiß white, 5
weit far (away), 3
weiter further, 13
welcher which, 5
die Welt world
wem (*dat. of* **wer**) (to) whom, 14
wen (*acc. of* **wer**) whom, 10
weniger minus, less, 2
wenigstens at least, 9
wenn if, when, 13
wer who, 2
werden (wird; ist geworden) to become, 13
wertvoll valuable, 8
der Westen west, 13
westlich (von) western, west (of)
das Wetter weather, 13
wie how, 1; as, 9; ~ **geht's?** how are you (doing)? 1; ~ **alt bist du?** how old are you? 2; ~ **(immer)** as (always), 9
wieder again, 1
die Wiederholung, -en review
Wiederhören: auf ~ good-by (*on the telephone*)
Wiederschauen: auf ~ good-by, 11
Wiedersehen: auf ~ good-by, 1
wieviel how much, 2; ~ **Uhr ist es?** what time is it? 6
der Wind wind, 13
windig windy, 13
die Windjacke windbreaker
windsurfen to go wind surfing, 10
der Winter winter, 10
der Winterschlußverkauf winter clearance sale

das Wintersportzentrum center for winter sports
wir we, 2
wirklich really, 1
wissen (weiß; gewußt) to know, 8
wo where, 3
die Woche, -n week, 11
das Wochenende, -n weekend, 4
wohin where (to), 8
wohl indeed, probably, 11
wohnen to live, 3
die Wolle wool
wollen (will) to want, to intend to, to wish, 7
das Wort, ¨er word
das Wörterbuch dictionary
der Wunsch, ¨e wish, desire, 11
die Wurst, ¨e sausage, cold cuts, 11
das Würstchen, - frankfurter, 11
die Würze spice; flavor

die Zahl, -en number, 2
zahlen to pay, 12
zart tender, delicate, 12
zehn ten, 2
die Zeit, -en time, 7
zelten to camp, to pitch a tent, 10
das Zentimetermaß measuring tape
der Zentimeter, - centimeter, 4
das Zeugnis, -se report card; grades
ziemlich quite, 3
das Zimmer, - room, 9
zu (+ *dat.*) to; too, 3; shut, closed, 15; ~ **Hause** (at) home, 3; ~ **Abend essen** to have supper, 12; ~ **Mittag essen** to have lunch, 12; ~ **Fuß** on foot, 15
zufrieden content, satisfied, 1
der Zug, ¨e train, 14
zuletzt last
zum (= **zu dem**); ~ **Abendessen** for supper, 12; ~ **Frühstück** for breakfast, 12; ~ **Kaffee einladen** to invite for coffee and cake, 9
zu·machen to shut, 8
zurück back, 11
zusammen together, 11; **das macht** ~ **10 Mark** that comes to 10 marks, 11
zwanzig twenty, 4
zwei two, 2
zwischen (+ *acc. or dat.*) between, 14
zwölf twelve, 2

English-German vocabulary

The symbol ~ signifies the repetition of the key word in that entry.

a/an ein, eine
able: to be ~ to können
about über
above über
acquainted: to be ~ with kennen
addition: in ~ sonst
after nach
afternoon der Nachmittag, –e; **this ~** heute nachmittag; **in the ~** am Nachmittag, nachmittags
again wieder
against gegen
ahead: straight ~ immer geradeaus
airplane das Flugzeug, –e
all alle, alles; **~ the best** alles Gute
almost fast
alone allein
along entlang; **~ the street** die Straße entlang; **to come ~** mit·kommen
already schon
also auch
always immer; **as ~** wie immer
am: I ~ ich bin
American (adj.) amerikanisch
and und (coord. conj.)
apple der Apfel, ¨
are: you ~ du bist, ihr seid, Sie sind; **they ~** sie sind; **we ~** wir sind
around um
art die Kunst
as als; wie; **~ ... ~** so ... wie
ask fragen
at an; auf; bei; um; **~ one o'clock** um ein Uhr
autumn der Herbst

back zurück
bad schlecht; schlimm; **too ~** schade
bag die Tüte, –n; **shopping ~** die Einkaufstasche, –n
bake backen
baker der Bäcker, –/die Bäckerin, –nen
banana die Banane, –n
band die Band, –s
bank die Bank, –en
basketball der Basketball, ¨e
bathroom das Badezimmer
be sein
beautiful schön
because denn (coord. conj.); weil (sub. conj.)
become werden
beer das Bier
before vor
begin beginnen
believe glauben
belt der Gürtel, –
besides außer
better besser
between zwischen
beverage das Getränk, –e
bicycle das Fahrrad, ¨er; das Rad
big groß
biology die Biologie
birthday der Geburtstag, –e; **it's my ~** ich habe Geburtstag; **happy ~!** herzlichen Glückwunsch zum Geburtstag!
black schwarz
blouse die Bluse, –n
blue blau
book das Buch, ¨er; **~ bag** die Mappe, –n
bored: I am ~ ich habe Langeweile
boredom die Langeweile

boring langweilig; **a ~ person** eine lahme Ente
both beide
bottle die Flasche, –n
box office die Kasse
boy der Junge, –n, –n; **oh, ~!** Mensch!
brake die Bremse, –n
bread das Brot, –e
break die Pause, –n
breakfast das Frühstück; **for ~** zum Frühstück; **to have ~** frühstücken
briefcase die Mappe, –n
bring bringen
broken kaputt
brother der Bruder, ¨; **~!** Mensch!
brown braun; **a ~ coat** ein Mantel in Braun
bus der Bus, –se
businessman der Geschäftsmann, ¨er (also pl. Geschäftsleute)
businesswoman die Geschäftsfrau, –en
but aber; sondern; **not only ... ~ also** nicht nur ... sondern auch
butcher der Metzger, –/die Metzgerin, –nen
butter die Butter
buy kaufen
by bei; **to go ~ bus** mit dem Bus fahren

café das Café, –s
cake der Kuchen, –; **layer ~** die Torte, –n
call an·rufen; nennen
camping das Camping; **to go ~** zelten
can können

382   german today, one

capital die Hauptstadt, ⸚e
car das Auto, –s; der Wagen, –
card die Karte, –n, **to play ~s** Karten spielen
carrot die Karotte, –n
carry tragen; **to ~ out** raus·tragen
cassette die Cassette, –n; **~ recorder** der Cassetten-Recorder, –
cat die Katze, –n
centimeter der Zentimeter, –
ceramics die Keramik
certain(ly) bestimmt; sicher; bitte sehr
cheap billig; **dirt-~** spottbillig
cheese der Käse
chemistry die Chemie; **~ homework** die Chemieaufgabe
chic schick
chicken das Huhn, ⸚er
child das Kind, –er
chocolate die Schokolade, –n
church die Kirche, –n
city die Stadt, ⸚e; **~ map** der Stadtplan, ⸚e
clarinet die Klarinette, –n
class die Klasse, –n; **~ trip** die Klassenfahrt, –en; **~room** das Klassenzimmer, –
classical klassisch
clean putzen, auf·räumen
clear ab·räumen
clock die Uhr, –en
close zu·machen; **~d** zu
clothes die Sachen (pl.), die Kleider (pl.)
cloudy bewölkt
club der Club, –s
coaster der Bierdeckel, –
coat der Mantel, ⸚
coffee der Kaffee; **~ shop** das Café, –s; **to make ~** Kaffee kochen; **to invite**

for ~ and cake zum Kaffee einladen; **to have ~** Kaffee trinken
cola drink die (also das) Cola
cold kalt
collect sammeln
color die Farbe, –n; **what ~ is ...** welche Farbe hat ...
come kommen; **to ~ along** mit·kommen; **that comes to 10 marks** das macht zusammen 10 Mark
complete(ly) ganz
complicated kompliziert
concert das Konzert, –e
content zufrieden
cook kochen
cool kühl
corner die Ecke, –n
correct richtig; **to be ~** stimmen
cost kosten
course der Kurs, –e; **of ~!** klar! natürlich!
crazy: you're ~! du spinnst!
cross sauer
cup die Tasse, –n
customer der Kunde, –n, –n/die Kundin, –nen

dance tanzen
dangerous unsicher
day der Tag, –e
dear (in letters) lieber/liebe
degree der Grad
department store das Warenhaus, ⸚er
describe beschreiben
dessert der Nachtisch
different anders
difficult schwer
diligent fleißig
dirt: ~-cheap spottbillig
disco die Disco
discussion die Diskussion, –en
dishes (pl.) das Geschirr; **to**

wash ~ (Geschirr) spülen
do machen, tun; **that won't ~** das geht nicht
doctor der Arzt, ⸚e/die Ärztin, –nen
dog der Hund, –e
door die Tür, –en
dream der Traum, ⸚e
dress das Kleid, –er
drink trinken
drive fahren
driving: ~ instructor der Fahrlehrer, –/die Fahrlehrerin, –nen; **~ school** die Fahrschule; –n; **~ lesson** die Fahrstunde, –n
drums das Schlagzeug, –e
dry trocken; **to ~** ab·trocknen
dumb doof, dumm
dust der Staub; **to ~** ab·stauben

each jeder
early früh
east der Osten; **~ (of)** östlich (von)
eastern östlich
easy leicht
eat essen
egg das Ei, –er
electrician der Elektriker, –/die Elektrikerin, nen
else: what ~? was sonst?; **anything ~?** sonst noch was?
eraser der Radiergummi, –s
especially besonders
evening der Abend, –e; **good ~!** guten Abend!; **in the ~** abends; **this ~** heute abend
everyone alle, jeder
everything alles
exactly gerade
exam die Prüfung, –en
excellent ausgezeichnet, prima
except außer

excuse: ~ me Entschuldigung!
exhausted kaputt
expensive teuer
expressway die Autobahn, –en

fail durch·fallen
fall fallen
family die Familie, –n
fantastic toll
far weit
fast schnell
fat dick
father der Vater, ¨
favorite: ~ subject das Lieblingsfach, ¨er
feed füttern
feel: to ~ like doing something Lust haben; **he doesn't ~ like doing anything** er hat zu nichts Lust
few: a ~ ein paar
finally endlich
find finden
finished fertig
first erst
fish der Fisch, –e
fit passen
flute die Flöte, –n
fly fliegen
foot der Fuß, ¨e; **on ~** zu Fuß
for für; seit; denn
forget vergessen
fountain der Brunnen, –
frankfurter das Würstchen, –
free frei
freeze frieren
French fries die Pommes frites (pl.)
fresh frisch
Friday der Freitag
friend der Freund, –e/die Freundin, –nen
from aus; von
fruit das Obst

fun: that's ~ das macht Spaß
furniture die Möbel (pl.)
further weiter

game das Spiel, –e
garage die Garage, –n
garbage der Müll; **~ pail** der Mülleimer
gardening die Gartenarbeit
gas station die Tankstelle, –n
gasoline das Benzin
gate das Tor, –e
gentleman der Herr, –n, –en
geography die Erdkunde, die Geographie
get bekommen; **I'll ~ the day off** ich bekomme frei; **to ~ up** auf·stehen
girl das Mädchen, –
give geben
glad froh
gladly gern
glass das Glas, ¨er
glove der Handschuh, –e
go gehen; fahren
good gut; **~ night** gute Nacht; **~ evening** guten Abend; **~ morning** guten Morgen; **~-by** auf Wiedersehen, tschüß
gram das Gramm
grandparents die Großeltern (pl.)
gray grau
great prima, toll
green grün
groceries die Lebensmittel (pl.)
group die Gruppe, –n
guitar die Gitarre, –n

hairdresser der Friseur, –e/die Friseuse, –n
half halb; **at ~ past eight** um halb neun

ham der Schinken; **~ sandwich** das Schinkenbrot
happy glücklich, froh
have haben; **to ~ to** müssen
he er
healthy gesund
hear hören
heavy schwer
hello guten Tag; Grüß Gott
help helfen
her ihr (adj.); sie (pron.)
here da; hier
hi! Tag!
high hoch; **~er** höher
hike wandern
him ihn
his sein
history die Geschichte
hobby das Hobby, –s
home: (at) ~ zu Hause; **~ (direction)** nach Hause
homework die Hausaufgaben (pl.)
honest! Ehrenwort!
hope: I ~, let's ~ hoffentlich
hot heiß
hour die Stunde, –n
house das Haus, ¨er
how wie; **~ are you?** wie geht's?; **~ old are you?** wie alt bist du?
however aber
hunger der Hunger
hungry: to be ~ Hunger haben
husband der Mann, ¨er

I ich
ice cream das Eis
ice skate der Schlittschuh, –e; **to ~** Schlittschuh laufen
if ob (sub. conj.); wenn
in(to) in
indeed wohl
independent unabhängig
instruction der Unterricht

intend to wollen
interesting interessant
intersection die Kreuzung, –en
invite ein·laden
is: he/she is er/sie ist
it es
its ihr, sein

jacket die Jacke, –n
jam die Marmelade
jealous eifersüchtig
jeans die Jeans (*pl.*)
juice der Saft, ⸚e
just gerade, nur

kilogram das Kilo(gramm)
kilometer der Kilometer, –
know kennen; wissen

lady die Dame, –n
lake der See, –n; **to the ~** an den See
last letzt
late spät; **too ~** zu spät
later später; **see you ~** bis später
laundry die Wäsche; **to do the ~** (die) Wäsche waschen
lazy faul
learn lernen
least: at ~ wenigstens
left links; **to the ~** links
leisure time die Freizeit
less weniger
lesson die Aufgabe, –n
letter der Brief, –e
lettuce der Salat, –e
license: driver's ~ der Führerschein
light leicht; das Licht, –er
like gern haben, mögen; **how do you ~ ...?** wie findest du ...?; **what would you ~?** was darf es sein?; **I would ~ ...** ich hätte gern ...; **he would ~ (to)** er möchte ...
liter der Liter, –; **10 kilometers to the ~** 1 Liter auf 10 Kilometer
live wohnen
long lang; **how ~?** wie lange?; **so ~!** tschüß!
look schauen, sehen; **to ~ for** suchen
lose verlieren
lot viel; **there's a ~ going on** es ist viel los
luck: what bad ~ so ein Pech
lucky: to be ~ Schwein haben
lunch das Mittagessen; **to have ~** zu Mittag essen; **for ~** zum Mittagessen; **at ~ time** mittags

make machen
man der Mann, ⸚er
many viele; **how ~** wieviele
market der Markt, ⸚e; **at the ~** auf dem Markt
match passen
mathematics die Mathematik; **math** die Mathe
matter: what's the ~? was ist los?
may dürfen
maybe vielleicht
me mich
meal das Essen
mean meinen; **what do you ~?** was heißt das?
meat das Fleisch
menu die Speisekarte, –n
meter der Meter, –
milk die Milch
mineral water das Mineralwasser
minus weniger
minute die Minute, –n
Miss Fräulein
model airplane das Flugzeugmodell, –e
moment: just a ~ Moment mal, einen Moment
Monday der Montag
money das Geld
month der Monat, –e
moped das Mofa, –s
more mehr
morning der Morgen, –; **good ~!** guten Morgen!; **this ~** heute morgen; **in the ~** morgens
mother die Mutter, ⸚
motorcycle das Motorrad, ⸚er
movie theater das Kino, –s
mountain-climbing: to go ~ bergsteigen gehen
Mr. Herr
Mrs. (or Ms.) Frau
much viel; **thank you very ~** vielen Dank; **how ~** wieviel
museum das Museum (*pl.* Museen)
music die Musik
musical musikalisch; **~ instrument** das Musikinstrument
must müssen
my mein

name der Name (*acc. & dat.* –n), –n; **my ~ is ...** ich heiße ...; **what's your ~?** wie heißt du?; **to ~** nennen
named: to be ~ heißen
namely nämlich
naturally natürlich
near bei
necktie die Krawatte, –n
need brauchen
new neu
next nächst; **~ time** nächstes Mal
nice nett, schön

night die Nacht, ⸚e; **good ~!** gute Nacht!
no nein; **~ one** niemand
nonsense! Quatsch!, Unsinn!
noon der Mittag; **at ~** mittags
north der Norden; **~ (of)** nördlich (von)
northern nördlich
not nicht; **~ at all** gar nicht; **~ a, ~ any** kein
notebook das Heft, –e
nothing nichts; **~ left** nichts mehr
now jetzt, nun
number die Zahl, –en

occur: it just occurs to me da fällt mir gerade ein
o'clock: it's (one) ~ es ist (ein) Uhr
often oft
oh ach; **~, I see!** ach so!
OK ganz gut; es geht
old alt
on auf; an; **~ Saturday** am Samstag
one eins; man (*indef. pron.*)
oneself selbst
only nur; erst
open auf·machen
or oder (*coord. conj.*)
orange die Orange, –n
order bestellen
our unser
out: ~ of aus

pack ein·packen, packen
pail der Eimer, –
pants die Hose, –n
paper das Papier, –e
parents die Eltern (*pl.*)
park der Park, –s
party die Party, –s; **to go to a ~** auf eine Party gehen
pass: to ~ a test die Prüfung bestehen
pay bezahlen, zahlen

pea die Erbse, –n
pedestrian zone die Fußgängerzone, –n
pen: ballpoint ~ der Kugelschreiber, –; der Kuli, –s; **~ pal** der Brieffreund, –e/die Brieffreundin, –nen
pencil der Bleistift, –e
per pro
performance die Vorstellung, –en
permitted: to be ~ dürfen
pharmacist der Apotheker, –/die Apothekerin, –nen
photograph fotografieren
physics die Physik
piano das Klavier, –e
pick up ab·holen
picnic das Picknick, –s
piece das Stück, –e
plan der Plan, ⸚e; **to ~** vor·haben
play spielen
please bitte, bitte schön
pork chop das Schweinskotelett, –s
post office die Post
postcard: picture ~ die Ansichtskarte, –n
poster das (*also* der) Poster, –
potato die Kartoffel, –n; **mashed potatoes** das Kartoffelpüree
pound das Pfund
practical praktisch
prefer lieber haben; **I ~ to eat . . .** ich esse lieber . . .
present das Geschenk, –e; **birthday ~** das Geburtstagsgeschenk
pretty hübsch
probably wahrscheinlich; wohl
pudding der Pudding
pullover der Pulli, –s

quarter das Viertel; **~ to five** Viertel vor fünf

question die Frage, –n
quite ziemlich

radio das Radio, –s; **"ham" ~ operator** der Radioamateur, –e
railway die Bahn, –en
rain der Regen; **to ~** regnen
read lesen
ready fertig
really eigentlich; wirklich
reasonably: ~ priced preiswert
recommend empfehlen
record die Schallplatte, –n, die Platte, –n; **~ player** der Plattenspieler, –
red rot
repair reparieren
report der Bericht, –e
restaurant das Restaurant, –s; das Lokal, –e
ride fahren; **to ~ horseback** reiten
right richtig; rechts; **to the ~** rechts; **to be ~** Recht haben; **that's ~** das stimmt
roast: ~ beef, pot ~ der Rindsbraten
rock (music) (der) Rock
roll das Brötchen, –
room das Zimmer, –
run laufen

sail segeln
salad der Salat, –e
salesperson der Verkäufer, –/die Verkäuferin, –nen
sarcastic sarkastisch
satisfied zufrieden
Saturday der Samstag; **on ~** am Samstag
sausage die Wurst, ⸚e
say sagen
schedule der Stundenplan, ⸚e; der Plan, ⸚e

school die Schule, –n
season die Jahreszeit, –en
see sehen
seem scheinen; **so it seems** so scheint's
serious: you can't be ~! das ist doch nicht dein Ernst!
set: to ~ the table den Tisch decken
she sie
shine scheinen
ship das Schiff, –e
shirt das Hemd, –en
shoe der Schuh, –e
shop das Geschäft, –e; **to ~** ein·kaufen
shopping: ~ bag die Einkaufstasche; **to go ~** einkaufen gehen
short klein; kurz
should sollen
sick krank
sign das Schild, –er
signal: traffic ~ die Ampel, –n
simple einfach
simply einfach
since seit
sincerely herzliche Grüße
sing singen
sister die Schwester, –n
situated: to be ~ liegen
size die Größe, n
ski der Schi, –er (also Ski); **to ~** Schi laufen
skirt der Rock, –̈e
sleep schlafen
slim schlank
slippery glatt
slow(ly) langsam
small klein
snow der Schnee; **to ~** schneien
so so; **~ what?** na und?; **isn't that ~?** nicht? nicht wahr?
soccer der Fußball; **~ game** das Fußballspiel, –e
sock die Socke, –n

soft drink die Limo(nade)
sold: ~ out ausverkauft
some mancher; ein paar
someone jemand
something etwas
sometimes manchmal
soon bald
sorry: I'm ~ es tut mir leid; Entschuldigung!
soup die Suppe, –n
sour sauer
south der Süden; **~ (of)** südlich (von)
southern südlich
speak sprechen
spinach der Spinat
sports der Sport; **to be active in ~** Sport treiben
spring der Frühling
square der Platz, –̈e
stamp die Briefmarke, –n
stand stehen
start beginnen; los·gehen; **when does it ~?** wann geht's los?
stay bleiben
stereo system die Stereoanlage, –n
still noch
store das Geschäft, –e; **department ~** das Warenhaus, –̈er
story die Geschichte, –n
strawberry die Erdbeere, –n
street die Straße, –n; **~ car** die Straßenbahn, –en
stroll der Spaziergang, –̈e; **to ~** bummeln, spazieren
student der Schüler, –/die Schülerin, –nen (in school); der Student, –en/die Studentin, –nen (in university)
study lernen
stupid doof, dumm
subject das Fach, –̈er
subway die U-Bahn, –en
such solcher
suit der Anzug, –̈e (for men); das Kostüm, –e (for women)

summer der Sommer
sun die Sonne
Sunday der Sonntag
supermarket der Supermarkt, –̈e
supper das Abendessen; **to have ~** zu Abend essen
supposed: to be ~ to sollen
sure sicher; **~!** klar!; **~, I do!** ja, und wie!
swim schwimmen
switch on an·machen

table der Tisch, –e
take nehmen; **to ~ along** mit·nehmen
take off los·gehen
tall groß
taste (good) schmecken
tea der Tee
teacher der Lehrer, –/die Lehrerin, –nen
telephone an·rufen
television der Fernseher, –; **to watch ~** fern·sehen
tell erzählen; sagen
temperature die Temperatur, –en
tender zart
tennis das Tennis
terrible, terribly furchtbar
terrific! klasse!
than als
thanks danke; **many ~** vielen Dank!
that das; daß (sub. conj.)
the der, das, die
theater das Theater, –; **movie ~** das Kino, –s
their ihr
them sie
then da, dann
there da, dort; **~ is, ~ are** es gibt
thermometer das Thermometer, –
they sie
thick dick

thing die Sache, –n
think denken, meinen
thin dünn, schlank
thirst der Durst
thirsty: to be ~ Durst haben
this dieser
through durch
Thursday der Donnerstag
ticket die Karte, –n
tied unentschieden
time das Mal; die Zeit, –en; **next** ~ nächstes Mal; **what** ~ **is it?** wie spät ist es? wieviel Uhr ist es?; **at what** ~? um wieviel Uhr?
times mal
tinker basteln
tired müde
to an; auf; nach; zu
toboggan rodeln
today heute
together zusammen
tomato die Tomate, –n
tomorrow morgen; ~ **evening** morgen abend; **the day after** ~ übermorgen
tonight heute abend
too auch; zu
tour die Tour, –en
town die Stadt, ̈e; ~ **hall** das Rathaus, ̈er
train der Zug, ̈e; ~ **station** der Bahnhof, ̈e
true richtig; **that's** ~ das schon
try versuchen
Tuesday der Dienstag
turn ab·biegen; **to** ~ **off** aus·machen
turntable der Plattenspieler, –

ugly häßlich
umbrella der Regenschirm, –e
understand verstehen
unfortunately leider
unhappy unglücklich
until bis
up auf; ~ **to** bis zu
us uns
usually gewöhnlich

vacuum Staub saugen
valuable wertvoll
vegetable das Gemüse, –
very sehr
violin die Geige, –n
visit der Besuch, –e; **to** ~ besuchen
volleyball der Volleyball, ̈e

waiter der Ober, –
walk der Spaziergang, ̈e; **to** ~ spazieren, laufen, gehen; **to go for a** ~ spazieren, einen Spaziergang machen, bummeln
want wollen
warm warm
was war (*past tense of sein*)
wash waschen; **to** ~ **dishes** (Geschirr) spülen
watch die Uhr, –en; **to** ~ sehen; **to** ~ **TV** fern·sehen
water das Wasser
we wir
wear tragen
weather das Wetter
Wednesday der Mittwoch
week die Woche, –n; ~ **end** das Wochenende, –n
welcome: you're ~ bitte, bitte schön
well (*interj.*) also, na; (*adj.*) gut; gesund; **pretty** ~ ganz gut
west der Westen; ~ **(of)** westlich (von)
western westlich
wet naß
what was; ~ **kind of (a)** was für (ein); ~**'s the matter?** was ist los?
when wann, wenn
where wo; ~ **(to)** wohin
whether ob (*sub. conj.*)
which welcher
white weiß
who wer
whom wen, wem
why warum
wife die Frau, –en
win gewinnen; **by how much did they** ~? wie hoch haben sie gewonnen?
wind der Wind; **to go** ~ **surfing** windsurfen
window das Fenster, –
windy windig
wine der Wein
winter der Winter
wish der Wunsch, ̈e; **to** ~ wollen
with mit; bei
without ohne
woman die Frau, –en; **young** ~ das Fräulein
work die Arbeit, –en; **to** ~ arbeiten; **to** ~ **at a hobby** basteln
worker der Arbeiter, –/die Arbeiterin, –nen
wow! Mensch!
write schreiben
wrong falsch

year das Jahr, –e; **time of** ~ die Jahreszeit, –en
yellow gelb
yes ja, doch
yesterday gestern
yet noch, **not** ~ noch nicht
you du; ihr; Sie
young jung
your dein; euer; Ihr
youth center das Jugendzentrum

Index

aber (flavoring word) 24
accusative case
   definite article 114
   dieser-words 260–262
   direct object 114
   ein and **ein-**words 114, 116
   indefinite articles 114
   personal pronouns 209–210
   possessive adjectives 116, 136
   prepositions with 243
   special **der-**nouns 242
   time expressions 262
   wer 209
adjectives
   comparison of equality 282–283
   comparison of inequality 282–283
   descriptive 13, 110
   possessive
      accusative 116, 136
      dative 305
      nominative 61–63, 136
adverbs
   comparison of equality 282–283
   comparison of inequality 282–283
alphabet 110
apostrophe to indicate omission of **e** 19
arithmetic problems 26
articles
   definite, accusative 114
   definite, dative 303–304
   definite, nominative 87, 89
   indefinite, accusative 114
   indefinite, dative 305
   indefinite, lack of plural 92
   indefinite, nominative 92
   indefinite, omission with nouns of profession 55
audio-visual equipment 160

capitalization
   Du and **Ihr** in letters 66
   nouns 19
chores 184
classroom objects 109
clauses
   dependent 285–286
   independent 268
clock time 112–113
clothing 81–82
   sizes 84
cognates viii
colors 85
comparison of adjectives and adverbs
   irregular 283
   of equality 282–283
   of inequality 282–283
conjunctions
   coordinating (**aber, denn, sondern, oder, und**) 264–265
   subordinating (**daß, ob**) 285, 287
contractions
   accusative prepositional 245
   dative prepositional 331
conversational past
   dependent clause 286
   inseparable prefixes 213
   past participle of strong verbs 189–190
   past participle of weak verbs 187
   separable-prefix verbs 191
   werden 284
   with auxiliary **haben** 187
   with auxiliary **sein** 239
currencies 102–103

dative case
   definite article 303–304
   dieser-words 304
   ein and **ein-**words 305
   plural nouns 304
   prepositions with 310, 326–330
   special **der-**nouns 306
   wer 307
days of the week 106
definite article
   accusative 114
   dative 303–304
   nominative plural 89
   nominative singular 87
demonstrative pronouns
   accusative 117
   nominative 117
dependent clauses 285–286
dieser 260
dieser-words
   accusative 260–262
   dative 304
   nominative 260–262
direct object 114
directed questions 158
directed statements 203
doch
   as positive response 183
   contrasted with **ja** 183
   flavoring word 161
dürfen 140

ein
   accusative 114
   dative 305
   lack of plural 92
   nominative 92
   omission with nouns of profession 55
ein-words
   accusative 116
   dative 305
   nominative 61–62
ess-tset 19

farewells 12
flavoring words
   aber 24
   denn 10
   doch 161

ja 109
   mal in commands 133, 161
   mal in statements 161
food 236, 254, 257
future time 44

geography
   Austria 24
   BRD 9, 294
   DDR 9
   Switzerland 37
gern
   with **haben** 45
   with verbs 45
glottal stop 42
greetings and farewells 12

haben
   as auxiliary 187, 286
   present tense 31, 33
   with **gern** 45
handshaking 10
height 57
hiking 39

imperatives 165–166
   du-forms 161, 165
   ihr-forms 166
   sein 167
   Sie-forms 166
   separable-prefix verbs 169
   verbs with stem-change **e** to **i**, **e** to **ie** 165
indefinite article
   accusative 114
   dative 305
   lack of plural 92
   nominative 92
   omission with nouns of profession 55
indirect questions 287
indirect statements 285
infinitive
   concept of 47
   ending in **-eln** 172
   omission of, with modals 141
   with modals 137

inseparable prefix verbs 213
inverted word order for statements 60

ja
   contrasted with **doch** 183
   flavoring word 109
jeder 261, 267

kein
   accusative 114
   dative 305
   nominative 93
   vs. **nicht** 98
kennen vs. **wissen** 208
können 137

mancher 262
maps
   Austria xv
   Federal Republic of Germany xiv
   German Democratic Republic xiv
   German-speaking countries in Europe xiii
   Munich 319
   Switzerland xv
measurement 237
metric system
   Celsius 279
   Gramm 237
   Kilometer 301
   Liter 237
   Meter 57
möchte 141, 147
modal auxiliaries 137–141, 286, 290
   omission of infinitive 141
mögen 147
months of year 27
musical instruments 40
müssen 139, 147
   negative 147

nach Hause, zu Hause 46

names
   list of names 347
   possession with proper names 61
narrative past of **sein** 241
nicht 17
   vs. **kein** 98
nominative case
   definite article 87, 89
   dieser-words 260–262
   ein-words 93, 98
   indefinite article 92
   kein 93
   possessive adjectives 61–63, 136
   subject pronouns 16, 29, 30, 135
noun compounds 132
noun-pronoun relationship 90–91
nouns
   accusative 114
   capitalization 19
   dative 304
   nominative 94
   plural nouns 89, 95–96, 304
   special **der-**nouns 242, 306
   with suffixes **-er** and **-erin** 205
numbers
   1–19 26
   20–1000 56

past participles
   inseparable-prefix verbs 213
   separable-prefix verbs 191
   strong verbs 189–190
   weak verbs 187
possession with proper names 61
possessive adjectives
   accusative 116, 136
   dative 305
   nominative 61–63, 136
prepositional contractions
   accusative 245
   dative 331
prepositions
   contractions 245, 331

with accusative 243
with dative 310, 326–330
present tense
   duration of time 263
   future meaning 44
   haben 31
   infinitive ending in **-eln** 172
   meanings of 44
   modal auxiliaries 137–141
   regular verbs 42–43
   separable-prefix verbs 168
   stem-changing verbs 87, 137, 163, 208
   stem ending in **-d** or **-t** 59, 165
   stem ending in a sibilant 59
   werden 284
professions 55
pronouns
   demonstrative, accusative 117
   demonstrative, nominative 117
   personal, accusative 209–210
   personal, nominative 16, 29, 30, 135
pronunciation
   [a], [A] 134
   [ai], [ɔi], [ao] 162
   [ə] 259
   [e], [ɛ] 28
   [i], [I] 15
   [o], [ɔ] 111
   [ø], [oe] 58
   [u], [U] 86
   [y], [Y] 41
   [ç] 302
   [x] 281
   [k] 281
   [l] 325
   [ŋ] 325
   [r], [R] 207, 238
   [ʌ] 238
   [ts], [z], [s] 186
   glottal stop 42
punctuation
   apostrophe for omission of **e** 19
   commas before subordinate clauses 290

exclamation marks with imperative 170

quantity expressions in singular 237
questions
   directed 158
   general 32, 287
   indirect 287, 291
   specific 31, 287

school subjects 106
seasons 204, 277
sein
   as auxiliary 239, 286
   imperative forms 167
   narrative past 241
   present tense 16, 29
separable-prefix verbs
   conversational past 191
   imperative 169
   present tense 168, 285
   used with modal auxiliaries 168
solcher 262
sollen 139
special **der-**nouns 242
sports 38, 39, 204
statements
   directed 203
   indirect 285
   verb second 60
stem-changing verbs
   a > ä 87
   a > äu 208
   e > i 137, 165
   e > ie 163, 165
strong verbs 189
   past participles 189–191
subordinating conjunctions **daß** and **ob** 285, 287
suffixes
   -er and **-erin** 205

temperature 279
time expressions
   clock time 112–113

duration of time 263
in the accusative 262
town buildings 322
transportation 300

verbs
   imperative forms 165–166
   infinitives ending in **-eln** 172
   inseparable-prefix verbs 213
   regular verbs 42–43
   separable-prefix verbs 168–169, 285
   stem-changing verbs 87, 137, 163, 208
   with stem ending in **-d** or **-t** 59, 165
   with stem ending in a sibilant 59

weak verbs 187, 193
   past participles 187, 193
weather 276, 278
   weather expressions 277, 279, 280
welcher 261
wer
   accusative 209
   dative 307
werden
   conversational past 284
   present 284
wissen 164
   vs. **kennen** 208
wo vs. **wohin** 163
wollen 140
word order
   in dependent clauses 285–286, 287
   in directed statements 203
   in independent clauses 264
   in questions 31–32, 287
   infinitive in final position 137
   position of past participle 187
   verb in second position 60
written German, notes on 19, 66

zu Hause, nach Hause 46

Art credits

Illustrations

Anne Burgess: pp. i, xii, 11, 12, 13, 20, 26, 30, 38, 40, 44, 55, 57, 67, 69, 71, 88, 91, 92, 99, 100, 109, 110, 112, 113, 116, 120, 122, 138, 150, 160, 164, 182, 184, 194, 204, 218, 222, 223, 236, 237, 249, 256, 257, 277, 279, 280, 300, 313, 320, 322, 340, 341, 342.

Chris Demarest: pp. viii, ix, x, xi, 15, 28, 41, 58, 86, 111, 134, 162, 186, 207, 238, 259, 281, 302, 325.

Larry Johnson: pp. 52, 200, 296.

James Loates: pp. xiii, xiv, xv, 319.

Color Photographs

Cover: Owen Franken/Stock, Boston

Stage 1: Ich und du

P. 1, Carol Palmer/Andrew Brilliant; p. 2, Owen Franken/Stock, Boston; p. 3, (top) Peter Menzel, (middle and bottom) Owen Franken/Stock, Boston; p. 4, Owen Franken/Stock, Boston; p. 5, Carol Palmer/Andrew Brilliant; p. 6, Carol Palmer/Andrew Brilliant; p. 7, (background) Dave Bartruff, (insets) Carol Palmer/Andrew Brilliant; p. 8, Carol Palmer/Andrew Brilliant.

Stage 2: So leben wir
P. 73, Carol Palmer/Andrew Brilliant; p. 74, (top) Milt and Joan Mann, (bottom) Ralph Gates; p. 74–75, (background) Gunter Brinkmann/Peter Arnold, Inc.; p. 75, (left inset) Owen Franken/Stock, Boston, (right inset) World Film Enterprises/Black Star; p. 76, (background) Carol Palmer/Andrew Brilliant, (inset) Uta Hoffmann; p. 77, (top) David Moore/Black Star, (bottom) Carl Purcell; p. 78, (top) Vic Cox/Peter Arnold, Inc.; p. 78–79, (bottom) Cary Wolinsky/Stock, Boston; p. 79, Carol Palmer/Andrew Brilliant; p. 80, Carol Palmer/Andrew Brilliant.

Stage 3: Zum Städtele hinaus
P. 225, Carol Palmer/Andrew Brilliant; p. 226, (background) Jackie Foryst/Bruce Coleman, Inc., (left inset) Carl Purcell, (right inset) Owen Franken/Stock, Boston; p. 227, (top) Cary Wolinsky/Stock, Boston, (bottom) Dave Bartruff; p. 228, (top left) Carol Palmer/Andrew Brilliant, (top center) Dave Bartruff, (top right) Eric Lessing/Magnum; p. 228–229, (bottom) Vic Cox/Peter Arnold, Inc.; p. 229, (top left) Sabine Weiss/Photo Researchers, (right) Ralph Gates; p. 230, (background) Ralph Gates, (inset) Carol Palmer/Andrew Brilliant; p. 231, (top left) Owen Franken/Stock, Boston, (top right) Vic Cox/Peter Arnold, Inc., (bottom left) Carol Palmer/Andrew Brilliant, (bottom right) Owen Franken/Stock, Boston; p. 232, Carol Palmer/Andrew Brilliant.

Black and White Photographs

All black and white photographs by Carol Palmer/Andrew Brilliant except:
P. x, Anne Converse/The Picture Cube; p. 52, (background) Owen Franken/Stock, Boston; p. 81, Fredrick D. Bodin; p. 82, Fredrick D. Bodin; p. 142, (top and bottom) Tom Bross/Studio 20; p. 148, Museum of Modern Art/Film Stills Archive; p. 173, (middle) Edith Reichmann/Monkmeyer Press Photo Service, (bottom) Peter Arnold, Inc.; p. 200, (inset) Peter Southwick/Stock, Boston; p. 216, (top right) Sven Simon/Katherine Young, (bottom left and right) German Information Center; p. 219, Sven Simon/Katherine Young; p. 235, Tom Bross/Studio 20; p. 239, Werner H. Müller/Peter Arnold, Inc.; p. 241, Tom Bross/Studio 20; p. 242, Tom Bross/Studio 20; p. 245, Tom Bross/Studio 20; p. 266, (bottom) Tom Bross/Studio 20; p. 275, Andy Bernhaut/Photo Researchers; p. 285, Poly-Press/Katherine Young; p. 286, German Information Center; p. 288, Werner H. Müller/Peter Arnold, Inc.; p. 294, (middle) Hinz/Black Star; (right) Tim Gidal/Monkmeyer Press Photo Service; p. 296, (background) Belzeaux/Kay Reese and Associates; p. 298, Verkehrs-Verlag Crusius; p. 299, Eckhard Supp/Kay Reese and Associates; p. 309, (inset) Edith Reichmann/Monkmeyer Press Photo Service; p. 314, German Federal Railroad; p. 324, (bottom left) Katherine Young, (bottom right) Phelps/Kay Reese and Associates; p. 332, Verkehrsverein Heidelberg; p. 335, German Information Center; p. 338, Farrell Grehan/Photo Researchers; p. 343, Susan McCartney/Photo Researchers.